EFFECTIVE SOCIAL WORK WITH
CHILDREN AND FAMILIES

SAGE has been part of the global academic community since 1965, supporting high quality research and learning that transforms society and our understanding of individuals, groups and cultures. SAGE is the independent, innovative, natural home for authors, editors and societies who share our commitment and passion for the social sciences.

Find out more at: **www.sagepublications.com**

EFFECTIVE SOCIAL WORK WITH CHILDREN AND FAMILIES

A Skills Handbook

Peter Unwin and Rachel Hogg

Los Angeles | London | New Delhi
Singapore | Washington DC

First published 2012

SAGE Publications Ltd
1 Oliver's Yard
55 City Road
London EC1Y 1SP

SAGE Publications Inc.
2455 Teller Road
Thousand Oaks, California 91320

SAGE Publications India Pvt Ltd
B 1/I 1 Mohan Cooperative Industrial Area
Mathura Road
New Delhi 110 044

SAGE Publications Asia-Pacific Pte Ltd
3 Church Street
#10-04 Samsung Hub
Singapore 049483

Library of Congress Control Number: 2011932846

British Library Cataloguing in Publication data

A catalogue record for this book is available from the British Library

ISBN 978-0-85702-729-0
ISBN 978-0-85702-730-6 (pbk)

Typeset by C&M Digitals (P) Ltd, Chennai, India
Printed and bound by CPI Group (UK) Ltd, Croydon, CR0 4YY
Printed on paper from sustainable resources

CONTENTS

INTRODUCTION

Who would want to be a social worker these days, especially with children and young people? Well, we hope you will and that is why you are reading this book. The media and most people you meet will all have their own opinions about social work, many of which may be negative as they only hear about the failures and tragedies. This is because of confidentiality issues, which means that most social work success stories stay in the private domain.

This book is intended for students on social work courses and for newly qualified staff; it may also be useful for professionals across other disciplines whose everyday work brings them into contact with social workers.

We have written this book with the intention of playing a part towards changing the image of social work to that of an exciting, dynamic and ever-changing profession which deals with issues that are far more challenging than are found in the commercial and business worlds. We have tried to keep the book as jargon free as possible and have included a glossary which gives an explanation for the words and topics that appear in the text in **bold**.

The book is designed to help social workers become more effective in the very complex, messy environment in which they work. We did not want it to be a 'How to Survive Social Work' type book, but rather one aimed more at 'How to Thrive in Social Work' by sharing practice wisdom, skills and information intended to help you thrive and flourish in what should be an exciting, political and socially valued role.

We believe that an effective social worker with children and families is a person who is:

- Aware of self and how they present to others
- Aware of their strengths and weaknesses
- Clear about their motivation for being in social work
- Willing to invest in children and families whom others may have given up on
- Empathic but wary of superficial explanations
- Knowledgeable, open to new learning and able to learn from and work with others
- Able to form meaningful, if often brief, relationships with children and families
- Politically aware and committed to social justice and equality of opportunity
- Child-centred in their work
- Organised and efficient with paper and IT systems
- Able to recognise that personal and organisational resources are finite
- Innovative and creative
- Able to find the requisite balance between home life and work life.

Social work practice never stands still, and English social work has a long history, which can be traced back to the nineteenth century. However, the actual title of social worker has only been protected by law since 2005, when social workers were first required to register in order to practise. This initiative was written into the Care Standards Act 2001 (Section 61) and finally operationalised after the **General Social Care Council** (GSCC) was set up under the same legislation. With the establishment of the social work degree as the new qualifying award after 2002 and its increased emphasis on practical skills, this recent period can be seen as one of immense change and opportunity for the social work profession following the challenges and recriminations arising from the **Victoria Climbié** tragedy (Laming, 2003).

Something of a new wind is blowing as we write this book, the **Social Work Reform Board** (2010) and *The Munro Review of Child Protection. Final Report* (Department for Education (DfE), 2011b) both having extensively reviewed the state of social work in England and both having come up with very positive recommendations for the best ways forward, including the encouragement of a learning culture, better induction and support for social workers. Whether these recommendations bear fruit however, is partly down to government and partly down to you. Will you be a social worker who keeps on top of research and practice development, who develops the interpersonal skills to be appropriately both empathic and at times authoritative, who has the **resilience** to achieve a **work–life balance**, and who is able to perform the necessary administrative duties that effective social work demands while remaining all the time focused on the needs, rights and protection of children? We sincerely hope that you will, and that this book will spur you to a long-lived career, characterised by continual improvement so that each year your effectiveness increases; and that your practice will become inspirational to others, colleagues, the children and their families.

Our combined career experiences, which include those of social worker, foster carer, team manager, senior manager, trustee, inspector, nurse, midwife, academic, board member, service user and entrepreneur have all informed our input into this book. We do not claim to 'know it all', however, and are constantly learning new things about ourselves and our practice. We learn much on a day-to-day basis from our colleagues in social work in Coventry and beyond, and from staff and students at the University of Worcester – where thanks go out especially to Lisa Hughes, Linda Merris and Philip Hoare for their help and guidance in the compilation of this book.

STRUCTURE OF THE BOOK

This book is designed as a skills handbook that can be either read from start to finish or dipped into for the content, reflective exercises and case studies contained within the chapters. The relevance of each chapter to the *Proposed Professional Capabilities Framework for Social Workers* (Social Work Reform Board, 2010) and the *Draft Standards of Proficiency for Social Workers in England* (Health Professions Council, 2011) is laid out at the beginning of all chapters to help you reflect on your developing career and on the areas against which your professional registration will be measured. The contents of the book pertain primarily to the situation within social work in England, although the models of social work and the skills discussed have a far wider resonance across social work in general. References are made throughout the book to the findings from recent enquiries and **serious case reviews,** which hold much valuable information that we all need to read first hand to improve the accuracy of our knowledge base and to reflect on and improve our own practice.

Chapter 1 looks at what it is that social workers actually do with children and families and explores the volatile context of social work practice. Chapter 2 considers the wide range of theories, methods and values that characterise contemporary social work practice. Chapter 3 covers that vitally important arena of legislation and policy, highlighting key areas of knowledge that you must have at your fingertips and giving tips on how best to make that knowledge work for the benefit of children and families. Chapter 4 looks at child development, with a critical skill for you being that you have a sound grasp of the spectrum of children's developmental stages and associated behaviours against which you will be making judgements. Chapter 5 explores the communication skills that are so necessary to be effective with children and families across the diversity of our communities. The skills of assessment are covered in Chapter 6, which then leads into Chapter 7 on **safeguarding** and **child protection.** Chapter 8 is concerned with that critical skill of analysis, so often lacking in practice, as recent enquiries and serious case reviews demonstrate all too clearly. Chapter 9 explores issues of effectiveness in planning your work, and leads into Chapter 10 on recording, where the need for accountability and transparency is highlighted. Chapter 11 reflects on what it is like to work in and around a social work organisation and does not pull any punches about the day-to-day tensions that exist in such complex and contested environments. Looking after yourself and achieving an appropriate work–life balance should not be a cliché but an everyday reality and Chapter 12 looks at how you might achieve such balance, drawing on the views of children and families in terms of what they expect from an effective social worker. Finally, we bring together the messages within the book in a cautiously optimistic conclusion, hopeful that the unprecedented recent focus of the media and the government-commissioned reviews will indeed create a working environment in which those of you with the skills and outlooks that we have promoted in this book will be able to effectively promote the welfare and safeguard the lives of the children and families with whom you work.

Each chapter concludes with suggestions for further specialised reading and resources, with new websites and training materials appearing all the time as the contested areas of children and families social work continue to attract emotional, moral, political and practice attention. Hopefully, you will keep up your knowledge base and always be open to new learning and insight, starting perhaps with this book. Effectiveness and meaningful social work with children and families is more than league tables and completing reports and meeting deadlines. The effectiveness of your social work skills is likely be measured by some of the children and families with whom you work in less tangible ways and we also know that for other children and their families the difference between effective social work and ineffective social work can be one of life and death.

Reflective point

Would the following five considerations represent the way in which you would want to practise? What else might you add?

- Do I have sound knowledge about human development/law/policy/procedures?
- Do I work from a clear ethical base?
- Do I treat people as individuals without prejudice?
- Do I put the people with whom I work at the centre of my considerations/decisions?
- Do I work in an efficient, safe and healthy manner?

1 WHAT DO SOCIAL WORKERS DO?

Key Points of Chapter

- You can thrive rather than just survive as a social worker
- Social work is kinetic and volatile – it will never stand still
- Social work is a contested moral and political activity
- Social work is not a 'win–win' occupation
- Social workers need a strong knowledge base
- Social work offers a range of opportunities and different ways of working
- Social workers need a work–life balance

Proposed Professional Capabilities Framework areas covered in this chapter

- Professionalism
- Values and Ethics
- Critical Reflection and Analysis
- Contexts and Organisations

(Social Work Reform Board, 2010 – see Appendix 1)

Draft Standards of Proficiency for Social Workers in England covered in this chapter

2 Be able to practise within the legal and ethical boundaries of their profession
3 Be able to maintain fitness to practise
10 Be able to maintain records appropriately
11 Be able to reflect on and review practice

(Health Professions Council, 2011 – see Appendix 2)

INTRODUCTION

Most people 'know' what social workers with children and families do. They 'know' because they read the papers and watch television, where hardly a week passes without another 'failing' of social workers being lambasted or without some ineffectual soap opera caricature being on screen, usually in the role of child snatcher. A little knowledge is dangerous, however, and we want the social workers of the future to have a lot of knowledge, to be proud to be social workers and to be effective because they have finely honed skills. Headlines such as 'Youngster turns life around after trust built up with social worker' or 'Abused mother thanks social worker for protecting her children' are unlikely, partly because they do not fit with the media's expectation of a social work story and partly because the vast majority of social work is a private affair wherein ethical considerations, such as respect for confidentiality, rule out the broadcasting of its many success stories.

Those of you considering entering the social work profession or already in the profession have not chosen an easy career and you are unlikely to be the type of person seeking accolades and personal glory. However, we all like some positive strokes for the work we do and there is no doubt that the current environment in which social work with children and families takes place is heated and volatile and rather lacking in such positive strokes. This is all the more reason for you to seek out the positives in your work, to be effective in your practice and as sure of your ground as you can be in a profession that is neither an exact science nor a business, but a contested moral and political undertaking. Social work has increasingly acquired the attributes of traditional professions, such as regulation and protected title, but has some strong distinguishing factors such as its political essence, its 'use of self' and its commitment to social justice.

One way of looking at the complexity of the social work world is using the model that we call the **Kinetic** Pie (Figure 1.1).

Social work is critically influenced by global and UK social and economic policy and social attitudes, and the amount of money available for the government to allocate to social work largely determines the size of the pie, a pie that is increasingly regulated by laws, policies, and procedures. Let's look at a slice of this pie and see what ingredients lie within (Figure 1.2).

In the real world of social work, the various ingredients of this pie are volatile and ever moving, in other words, kinetic, and despite the sayings you may often hear in your

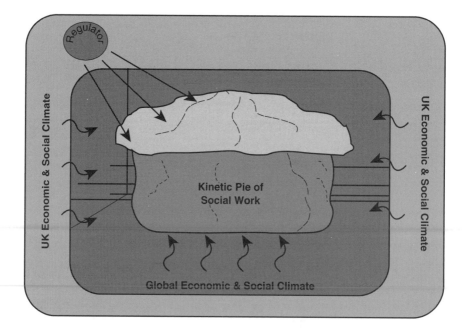

Figure 1.1   The kinetic pie of social work

Unwin, 2011a

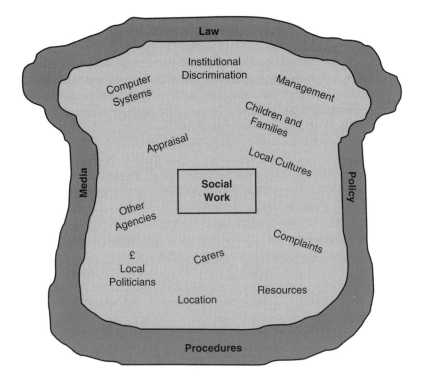

Figure 1.2   A slice of the kinetic pie

Unwin, 2011b

work settings – such as 'When things settle down'; 'When we are fully staffed'; 'After the reorganisation' – the reality is that if you want a career that is settled, routinised and clearly respected and understood by others, then social work is not for you. Social work will never 'settle down' – it is a contested activity, whose modes of delivery and priorities change as society changes. Social work today is very different from social work even 20 years ago although the personal and relationship needs of families and communities for help and support have in many ways stayed the same – it is the social work responses to those needs that have changed beyond all recognition, as this book will explore.

Reflective point

What other 'ingredients' might go to make up the kinetic pie from your experience/view of social work with children and families?

Although we have stated above that in many ways the needs of families and communities have stayed largely the same over the past 20 years, in what ways have changes in society developed that constitute greater risks to children and families?

A QUESTION OF BALANCE

Trying to get a balance between the rights of parents, children, your profession, your organisation and your responsibilities towards the wider community, while at the same time being aware of the regulatory and press scrutiny of your work makes for a very demanding job. Make sure that you find support by joining professional organisations such as the **College of Social Work** and that you receive sufficient personal support from friends and colleagues. New ways of working may mean that you find yourself in a workplace that does not have a traditional office space and does not therefore offer the team support that social workers would have historically been afforded on a day-to-day basis. Such support is critical, particularly in your developing years as a social worker, and you will need to find ways of obtaining it, should this be the type of working environment in which you find yourself.

The media have been a significant influence on public perception of social work in recent years, and partly in an attempt to reverse the almost universal negative images of failing social workers and children being let down by the system, the **Social Work Task Force** (2009) invited the agony aunt from *The Sun*, Deirdre, to join the task force as a member. There were a range of differing reactions to this very unusual step but in many ways it can be seen as an innovative attempt to try to get a more balanced view from the tabloid press about the complexities of the work carried out by contemporary social work teams. The ingredients of the kinetic pie (Figure 1.2) are indeed complex and it is difficult to relay these complexities to other professionals or to family and friends.

Some student social workers and **newly qualified social workers** (NQSWs) sometimes find it difficult to talk about their work role in social situations and we would strongly encourage you to try to be honest about the work that you do and not try to fudge the question when asked about social work. Some workers have reported just saying that they work for 'local government' whereas others have fabricated their occupations rather than face a barrage of enquiry and criticism about the alleged shortcomings of social work. Far better would be to spend some time preparing how you would present your job to people in social situations. Also, try to engage people in a balanced discussion rather than stay quiet and thereby perhaps colluding with the negative stereotypes and images of the social work profession that do not accurately reflect the everyday realities of social work achievements.

THE SOCIAL WORK REFORM BOARD (2010) AND THE *MUNRO REPORT* (DfE, 2011b)

The Social Work Task Force was instigated by the New Labour government in 2009 as a result of a series of enquiries into the failings of social work across both adults and children and families services. Its brief was to produce new systems, models and training provision for social work in England that would produce a better quality social worker, better working conditions and therefore hopefully lead to a culture wherein social work is valued and appreciated for the good work it does. The recommendations of the task force, as adopted by the Social Work Reform Board (2010: 25), are as follows.

1 **Calibre of entrants**: that criteria governing the calibre of entrants to social work education and training be strengthened.

2 **Curriculum and delivery**: an overhaul of the content and delivery of social work degree courses.

3 **Practice placements**: that new arrangements be put in place to provide sufficient high quality practice placements, which are properly supervised and assessed, for all social work students.

4 **Assessed Year in Employment (AYSE)**: the creation of an **assessed and supported year in employment** as the final stage in becoming a social worker.

5 **Regulation of social work education**: more transparent and effective regulation of social work education to give greater assurance of consistency and quality.

6 **Standard for employers:** the development of a clear national standard for the support social workers should expect from their employers in order to do their jobs effectively.

7 **Supervision**: the new standard for employers should be supported by clear national requirements for the **supervision** of social workers.

8 **Frontline management:** the creation of dedicated programmes of training and support for frontline social work managers.

9 **Continuing professional development:** the creation of a more coherent and effective national framework for the continuing professional development of social workers, along with mechanisms to encourage a shift in culture which raises expectations of an entitlement to ongoing learning and development.

10 **National career structure**: the creation of a single, nationally recognised career structure for social work.

11 **National College of Social Work**: the creation of an independent national college of social work, developed and led by social workers.

12 **Public understanding**: a new programme of action on public understanding of social work.

13 **Licence to practise:** the development of a licence to practise system for social workers.

14 **Social worker supply**: a new system for forecasting levels of supply and demand for social workers.

15 **National reform programme**: the creation of a single national reform programme for social work.

The current NQSW role is likely to become a mandatory AYSE as social work follows the route of other professions such as teaching and nursing in the creation of an assessed first year in practice, which all NQSWs will have to successfully complete in order to work as social workers. This year should be characterised by a protected caseload, which will demand an increase in resources at a time of severe financial constraints. In addition, the Social Work Reform Board has developed an overarching standards framework called the **Proposed Professional Capabilities Framework for Social Workers in England (Social Work Reform Board**, 2010), which is referred to at the beginning of each chapter in this book (see Appendix 1 for full details of these capabilities). This framework is designed to support and inform the national career structure and is relevant to all levels of staff within the new structure. The term 'capabilities' has been used to confirm that learning and development is a continuous process throughout the whole career of a social worker. As indicated in Figure 1.3, each of the nine dimensions is relevant for all levels and demonstrates a development of capability over time and through progression, rather than being a 'one-off' achievement.

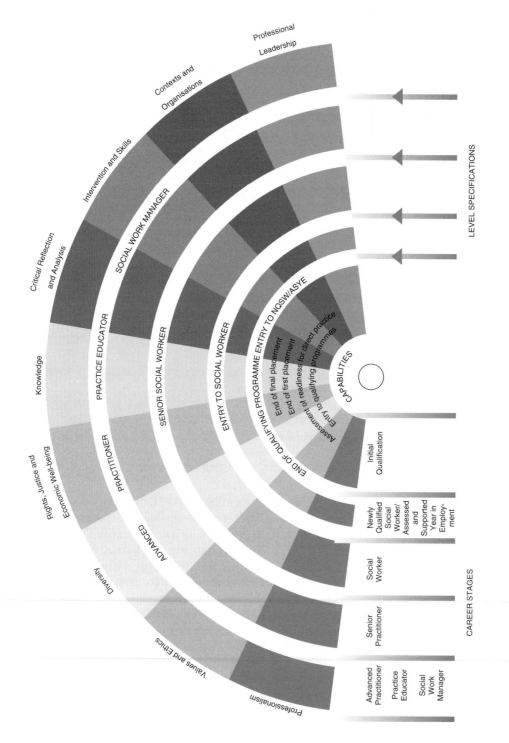

Figure 1.3 The proposed professional capabilities framework (Social Work Reform Board, 2010)

The *Munro Report* (DfE, 2011b), which looked specifically at child protection systems in England, made the following key recommendations:

- The Government should remove the specific statutory requirement on **local authorities** for completing assessments within often artificial set timescales, so that professionals can give equal weight to helping children, young people and families, as well as assessing their problems.
- Local services that work with children and families should be freed from unhelpful government targets, national IT systems and nationally prescribed ways of working. They should be free to re-design services that are informed by research and feedback from children and families, and that pay more attention to the impact on children's safety and welfare.
- A change of approach to Serious Case Reviews (SCRs), learning from the approach taken in sectors such as aviation and health care. There should be a stronger focus on understanding the underlying issues that made professionals behave the way they did and what prevented them from being able properly to help and protect children. The current system is too focused on what happened, not why.
- The introduction of a duty on all local services to coordinate an early offer of help to families who do not meet the criteria for social care services, to address problems before they escalate to child protection issues.
- **Ofsted** inspections of **children's services** should add more weight to feedback from children and families, directly observe social workers' interaction with children and families, as they do when inspecting schools, and pay more attention to whether children have benefited from the help given.
- Experienced social workers should be kept on the frontline even when they become managers so that their experience and skills are not lost. The expertise and status of the social work profession should be improved with continual professional development that focuses on the skills that are needed in child protection.
- Each local authority should designate a Principal Child and Family Social Worker to report the views and experiences of the frontline to all levels of management. At national level, a Chief Social Worker would be established to advise the Government on social work practice. (DfE, 2011b).

Taken together, these two reports set the scene for what should be a very exciting time for social work, with more opportunity for time spent with children and families, less bureaucracy and a new Ofsted inspection regime that is more focused on outcomes and unannounced visits.

RECRUITMENT AND RETENTION

The Social Work Task Force was also charged with looking at issues of recruitment and retention in social work. Curtis et al. (2010) report that, at eight years, the expected working life of a social worker is considerably shorter than that of other human services professionals. Netten and Knight (1999) estimate that a doctor's average working life is 25 years whereas Curtis et al. state that 15 years is the average career span for a nurse. Clearly, this is not a situation that should prevail when we are looking to establish social work teams that have experience, knowledge, wisdom and the resilience to offer long-term and consistent relationships to the children and families in the communities where they work. Young people in particular comment that what they really want in a social worker is consistency, someone who sticks around for a significant part of their life, rather than an unfamiliar person who flits in and out of their life (McLeod, 2010).

'Damned if you do, damned if you don't' tends to be a phrase that reflects the public image of social work; social workers either intervene too late and do not prevent a child's death (Laming, 2009) or alternatively they intervene apparently unnecessarily in private family business and remove children on occasions when this should never have happened (Beckett et al., 2007). Most people coming into the social work profession are motivated by humanistic reasons and want to carry out a meaningful role in society, while hopefully enjoying the benefits that come with a professional job:

> Most of my mates said I was mad and that if I was smart I would follow them into accountancy or banking. I really wanted to make a difference in people's lives though and to get a job with a human touch. (Barry, 21 years, BA Social Work Student)

> I know that it is not going to be an easy job as a social worker – that's not why I am going into it. I did not have the best childhood myself and would like to think that I could play a part in helping ensure that others do not have to go through what my mum and me went through. (Sobia, 32 years, MA Social Work Student)

Many social workers have a personal drive or motivation, rooted in their own life experiences and many have a political perspective on the world and are committed to the principles of social justice. **Statutory social work**, in other words, work carried out in **children's social care** teams in local authority settings, where much of the work is regulated by law and a range of guidance and regulations, requires a worker who is comfortable with the use of authority and who is able to recognise that many of the decisions with which they will be involved will not lead to happy **outcomes** for all concerned.

Reflective point

How comfortable are you with 'authority'?

Reflect back on instances in your work, family or community life when you have experienced authority being used in both positive and oppressive ways.

How do you think these experiences have shaped your likely approach to authority in a social work role?

ENFORCER OR CHAMPION OF THE OPPRESSED?

Much of statutory social work is not a 'win-win' situation and in the traumatic, dysfunctional and often tragic lives that characterise many of the families who come to the attention of statutory children's social care services, there are often no ideal solutions. Although one hopes that all decisions that are made are genuinely child-centred, the kinetic pie's ingredients (see Figure 1.2 above) also include those of resource limitations, different **thresholds of eligibility**, different interpretations among different agencies about levels of need and risk and it is often difficult to realise some of the aspirations for quality outcomes that social workers may wish to effect in the lives of the families with whom they work. Professional social work in statutory settings is about balancing the role of enforcer of **legislation** and policy with being a champion of the oppressed. There is also scope for therapeutic interventions with children and families even within statutory services, although much of this intervention may be brief in nature. It is important to remember, however, that even the briefest of relationships can be significant in a young person's life, and in many of our own lives we may have been profoundly influenced by a person, for example, a teacher, relative or other professional, who we felt was authentic and who made a difference to the way we perceive and run our lives.

Reflective point

Can you think of a person who had a significant effect (positive or negative) on your view of life, even if you perhaps only knew that person for a short or brief period?

- What do you think it was about that person that led to this effect?
- What skills/attributes might you have that has an effect on others?
- Are these all positive effects? If not, are there aspects of your presentation of self that you will want to work on in order to become an effective social worker?

THE DIVERSE SETTINGS AND ROLES WITHIN SOCIAL WORK

Social work in the voluntary or **independent sector** can offer different types of opportunities and challenges to a professional social worker and it may be that during your course of study or in the early years of your career you choose to experience a number of different settings, some of which will afford a greater opportunity to engage in **relationship-based practice** (Ruch, 2010). Effective social work takes place in diverse work settings and across a diversity of communities, the social work profession having a strong commitment to equality of opportunity and to inclusive social policy. In order to be effective, social workers need to win community support and this will often mean taking the time to ask about and read about the cultures and mores in the communities where you work. Fear of the '**race card**' being played or some misunderstandings around **political correctness** mean that certain issues that are pertinent to effective social work are not often discussed in teams and communities. This 'don't go there' culture needs to change if we are all to develop better mutual understandings about the role and jurisdiction of social work within our diverse communities.

BUREAUCRACY – MAKING IT WORK FOR YOU

Some newly qualifying social workers find themselves overwhelmed by the amount of paperwork, IT and bureaucracy that surrounds their jobs, particularly in statutory positions. However, with self-awareness, experience and support, it should be possible to get your working life in perspective and to find the right job that fits your own value base and motivation. This will include finding a job that provides an appropriate balance between administrative work and direct work with children and families. Such balance may be more likely to become reality if some of the recommendations of the *Munro Report* (DfE, 2011b) and the Social Work Reform Board (2010) come to fruition. Despite the welcome focus in such reports on the need to free social work of the shackles and strictures of systems and bureaucracy, work such as the preparation of court reports and involvement in the reviews of **looked after** children should not be seen merely as paperwork, but as administrative duties that advocate for and protect children. Sometimes the systems that overlay social work are unduly cumbersome, however, and these should be challenged whenever a fresh face on to the job perceives them to be unhelpful in making professional decisions around their work.

Some commentators estimate that children's social workers in statutory teams spend approximately 80 per cent of their time or four days per week behind a computer or carrying out other functions in meetings (Social Work Task Force, 2010). This is not a situation that should be allowed to continue and the Social Work Reform Board (2010) is charged with reducing the 'red tape' that has come to so dominate much of contemporary statutory social work (DfE, 2011b; Social Work Reform Board, 2010).

Reflective point

It may well be that in your new settings you can identify paperwork and procedures that could be simplified, without presenting any risk to children or to the accountability of your organisation or profession.

How might you present any such suggestions to management?

It is interesting to note that some team members with whom you will work seem to spend far more time than others in the office rather than out visiting. Management has a responsibility here and effective management would ensure that there was some parity between workers and their ability to complete administrative tasks while at the same time spending the requisite amount of time with their children and families. Student social workers have reported being under such pressure in some teams that they have been asked to write reports on children and families whom they feel that they do not even know as individuals. This is clearly a dangerous and unacceptable state of affairs and any such requests should be challenged at the earliest possible opportunity. Social workers are required (see Health Professions Council (HPC), 2011) to be IT and systems competent rather than rely on the tradition of administrative support to carry out a range of supporting technical duties. There has been no systematic evaluation of these new ways of working to date (see Coleman and Harris, 2008) and the effect of such systems in terms of support for social workers and accessibility for children and families can only be estimated. The removal of local office presence and the removal of collegiate, office-based support can be viewed purely as a business strategy, designed to save money rather than improve the social work service.

The current reality is that many social workers use systems of **mobile and flexible working** that rely on hand-held computers/mobile phones in their daily work and hence it is imperative that these systems are mastered. However, our advice is that they are not mastered in such a way that social workers become enslaved to such systems but in a way that administrative tasks can be dealt with efficiently, communication be swift and effective, and staff (in theory at least) freed up to spend time carrying out their social work roles within their communities.

WORKING IN VOLUNTARY OR PRIVATE SECTOR SETTINGS

One of the great advantages of social work is that there are many different contexts in which your work could be carried out, ranging across work in **children's centres**, **adoption** and **fostering** teams, youth justice teams, outreach work and work in **interdisciplinary** community-based settings such as medical centres. Many of these settings are to be found in the independent sector, where charities and private-for-profit businesses all work towards meeting the legislative and social care needs of children and their families. Your choice of social work job will be governed by a range of factors such as the prevailing job market, your **value base**, the potential to carry out therapeutic work with children and families, your preference for statutory work and your wish to be part of a team that is traditionally, or is not, office based.

The underpinning factor will probably be your value base in terms of a preference to work in state, voluntary or private organisations. Some smaller voluntary and private organisations (e.g. independent fostering agencies) do offer benefits of shorter lines of communication and often are more specialised in focused roles. You should be aware that there are business/moral tensions within all these organisations, particularly in for-profit organisations, which may not sit comfortably with your value base. This is not to say that all private sector care is inherently bad, more that the overriding value base in the private sector to be profitable can compromise ethical decisions regarding children and families. Equally, one cannot state that all local authority or statutory care exemplifies good, ethical child-centred decisions and much of the dissatisfaction within statutory social work teams (e.g. Collins, 2008) stems from what is often seen as an overly bureaucratic and delaying process, particularly where decisions seem to be made at various levels above the social worker's head.

Doing away with unnecessary delays in making decisions about children's lives was a core principle of the 1989 Children Act. Unfortunately, this is one core principle that has not been delivered, delays within the legal system in particular making it difficult to expedite certain decisions in children's lives. An increasing tendency of social workers to have to refer every decision back to '**management**' is not helpful for the child or colleagues such as foster carers. An effective social worker should know the extent/limits of their autonomy in decision making, whether this be about budgets or risk. Being unable to make decisions about routine matters on the spot is ineffective social work and the nebulous layers of management/administration that still seem to exist in many social work settings must be challenged if your working day is to be effective and only contain the stresses that come from the nature of your work, not the systems that surround it.

USE OF SELF

Reconciling the limitations of any social work job call for a balanced and mature perspective that starts from knowing your own strengths and values. Knowing who you are and where you are coming from is a core quality that will have been explored on your social work course, social work being the profession more than any other where use of self is uppermost. Even professions such as counselling and medicine can often practise in ways in which the use of self is a marginalised or denied role and the message that comes over to children and families can be that you are dealing with a professional who is unlikely to share any particular humanity or life experiences with you. Appropriate use of self/self-disclosure and boundary negotiation are essential to effective social work (see Appendix 2 draft standard 2 – HPC, 2011).

Reflective point

- How aware were you of your 'use of self' prior to considering a social work career?
- How well do you 'know yourself'?
- Do you 'see yourself as others see you'?
- How might you find out more about 'use of self'?

Areas for your development such as use of self will be constantly reflected on during your social work career and the aspiration is that year on year you will become a better social worker and that your confidence, your use of self, your personal and professional development, your knowledge of legislation, procedures, managerial systems and the needs and strengths within the families and communities with whom you work will be enhanced. There are still many people in social work with over 30 years' experience and it is to be hoped that those of you reading this book will be social workers who will commit similar lengths of your life to social work and that you will be part of reversing the current reality wherein the average social work professional life is a mere eight years (Curtis et al., 2010).

CHAPTER SUMMARY

Social work with children and families is a complex and demanding job that is kinetic, ever-changing, at times volatile and dangerous and at times satisfying and fulfilling. An effective social worker needs a sound knowledge base, personal coping systems and to be aware of the standards against which their everyday work should be constructed.

Social work, despite attempts to bring in models from business, is not a 'win-win' undertaking. As you begin to experience a range of settings, you will be able to decide where you can be most effective and what roles are most likely to bring you that necessary work–life balance.

FURTHER RESOURCES AND READING

Barefoot Social Worker website – This is a radical and passionate take on the problems facing social work (www.radical.org.uk/barefoot/).

Barnardo's website – This is a well-respected children's charity, which has carried out much innovative work with children, families and communities (www.barnardos.org.uk/).

Children's Voice website – Consistently missing from the myriad of serious case reviews and enquiries is the voice of the child. This excellent website goes some way to rectifying this failing in social work (https://sharestreet.cwdcouncil.org.uk/ChildrensVoice.aspx).

Community Care Inform website – This is a very helpful and authoritative web-based resource which consists of contemporary information from academics and practitioners across a range of children and family issues (www.ccinform.co.uk/home/default.aspx).

Department for Education (2011b) *The Munro Review of Child Protection. Final Report. A Child Centred System.* London: HMSO. This recommends proposals for reform in order to meet the needs of children and families and support social workers to provide a good service (www.education.gov.uk/publications/.../Cm%208062.pdf).

Health Professions Council (2011) Standards of Proficiency for Social Workers (England) Professional Liaison Group (PLG) (www.hpc-uk.org/assets/documents/10003381Item05-enc3-draftstandardsofproficiency2-SOPs.pdf).

Social Work Reform Board website – A useful website that contains all the details of the workings of this government commissioned body set up in 2010 to reform social work in England. The Board has strong links to the *Munro Report* (www.education.gov.uk/swrb).

2

SOCIAL WORK THEORIES, VALUES AND METHODS: WHERE DOES YOUR PRACTICE FIT?

Key Points of Chapter

- You must have a 'grand theory' of the world to help you understand your actions and the lives of the children and families with whom you work
- You must have sufficient understanding of the theories relating to child development if you are to make informed judgements and be able to discuss issues knowledgably with professionals from other disciplines
- Theory is not just for the classroom – theory is necessary to support effective social work
- Rigid adherence to only one theory does not do justice to the complexity of social work with children and families
- Merely saying that you are eclectic in your approach to theory may be a mask for your not knowing very much about any one theory of child development
- Social work with children and families offers a range of opportunities (case work/group work/outreach work) that you should try to fit with your strengths/value base

Proposed Professional Capabilities Framework areas covered in this chapter

- Professionalism
- Values and Ethics
- Rights, Justice and Poverty
- Knowledge
- Critical Reflection and Analysis
- Contexts and Organisations

(Social Work Reform Board, 2010 – see Appendix 1)

Draft Standards of Proficiency for Social Workers in England covered in this chapter

4 Be able to practise as an autonomous professional, exercising their own professional judgement
11 Be able to reflect on and review practice
13 Understand the key concepts of the bodies of knowledge which are relevant to their profession
14 Be able to draw on appropriate knowledge and skills to inform practice

(Health Professions Council, 2011 – see Appendix 2)

INTRODUCTION

As an NQSW, you are likely to have been introduced to the many different theories surrounding social work during your qualifying course and you may find yourself in work settings where colleagues and managers have no time for theory – seeing theory as something of academic interest only, interesting to debate but of no applicability or relevance to the hard pressed world of referrals, targets and deadline dates for reports that can be the overwhelming reality of everyday practice. Such a view should be challenged because all professional practice should flow from a theoretical base and, if you have a sound grasp of key theory, perhaps you can introduce this perspective into your work in a way that indeed brings a greater depth and understanding and may lead to a re-thinking of an agency's perspective on a child, family or community.

Much has changed in social work theory since the dominance of psychosocial theories in the 1950s and 1960s, and the more politically aware world of practice that includes user perspectives and an increased awareness of structural oppressors such as poverty and racism is now reflected in the array of intervention theories and evidence-informed perspectives (see Howe, 2009; Payne, 2005). This broad range of theories reflects the complex, messy world of social work with children and families, and enables us to work in ways which are sensitive to the diverse needs, circumstances and strengths of the communities with which we work.

We also experience demographic change which requires social workers to adjust their thinking. People are living longer, babies are surviving with needs that may require lifelong support, and geographical mobility for employment has impacted on family life. The global growth of materialism and the consumer culture impacts on how we feel about ourselves and our capacity to parent as do the pressures to 'get on' in our society and the sense for many that they are not keeping up, that they are failing. The contemporary world is very different from the post-war beginnings of the welfare state in the UK which saw the development, expansion and professionalisation of the social work workforce. Never has theory been more essential both in terms of how we see the world and how we engage with children and families.

Only when we have a clear theoretical understanding of children, their families, their communities and the environments around them can we make sense of our interventions. While this book is primarily a practical guide to carrying out social work, this chapter will give an overview of the key social work theories, the values that stem from those theories and the methods that flow from these considerations.

Reflective point

A social work student placed in a long-term children and families team was asked to complete a core assessment regarding a two-year-old boy, considered to be a 'child in need' under Section 17 of the Children Act 1989. In her assessment of the family and environmental factors

(Continued)

(Continued)

that had an impact upon the mother's capacity to care for him, the student reflected upon how structural oppression in the form of unchallenged, white British middle-class values among professionals might detract from them taking a strengths perspective on the alternative values and models of raising children found among the settled traveller families to which mother and child belonged. The student social worker was asked by the team manager to remove this reference to anti-oppressive practice and theory with the explanation that 'we don't talk about values' and 'parents don't understand'. On further reading of assessments by other members of the team, the student found that a collective attitude of non-engagement with values did indeed prevail, in sharp contrast to the families she was working with who, far from being ignorant of values, would articulate and uphold their understanding about parenting.

If you found yourself in a similar situation to that above, what would be your response/strategy?

John, 44 years, a student on the second year of a master's in social work course reflected as follows on one of his positive experiences in using a strengths-based approach:

Working with the family was an encouraging experience for me. I have (occasionally) observed colleagues recounting cases where they felt helpless, because they cannot identify any positive prospects with particular families. The outcomes in this instance were excellent, and especially so because it became apparent that the family already held the answers to their problems. They simply needed support from someone who could help them to recognise and believe in their own abilities.

DEFINITIONS OF THEORY

There are many different theories surrounding social work, and since the purpose of this book is to consider effectiveness, this chapter is concerned with exploring theory in regard to how a grasp of key theories can inform effective practice.

Coulshed and Orme give a basic definition of theory as:

the basis for planning what needs to be done to maintain, improve or bring about change in the client, the environment or both. (2006: 24)

Beckett develops such a definition in the following way, viewing theory as:

a set of ideas or principles used to guide practice, which are sufficiently coherent that they could if necessary be made explicit in a form which was open to challenge. (2007: 33)

This above definition embraces both formal and informal theory and suggests that social work practice might always be open to challenge, particularly given the evolving nature of social work alongside changes in society's mores and expectations. Beckett (2007) goes on to distinguish explanatory theories (which are needed at assessment stages of social work with children and families) and interventions theory (regarding the changes needed to bring about a change in a situation being assessed). Explanatory theories might take more from generally accepted bodies of wisdom about attachment and risk (e.g. Bowlby, 1980; Cairns, 2002) whereas theories regarding the most appropriate interventions in a family might give more weight to social workers' local experience and be shaped by the thresholds and indeed the resources available to bring about change in a particular locality. Social workers need to reflect on their own theories about why they do what they do, the values on which they base their decisions and why they adopt the methods they do in their interventions with children and families. Such reflection is likely to be more effective if it is developed against the backdrop of core knowledge including established theories of families and children.

VALUE-BASED APPROACHES

Approaches to or perspectives on social work are seen as the ways, or frameworks, in which we order our values or views of the world.

Payne (2005, Chapter 1) outlines three main approaches to social work:

- reflexive–therapeutic views
- socialist–collectivist views
- individualistic–reformist views.

Reflexive–therapeutic adherents are those who view social work as promoting the well-being of individuals, their groups and communities via relationship-based 'therapeutic' interventions that are dynamic and reflexive. Increased awareness of strengths within a person or a community leads to insight and helps realise potentials that bring about transformation in circumstances.

The Socialist–collective approach sees social work as essentially **emancipatory**, constituting a structural challenge to the social orders that are viewed as having brought about the underlying disadvantage or **oppression** in individuals and their communities. Individuals and communities are encouraged to seek empowerment to change and transform, rather than fit in with the prevailing social order.

Individualistic–reformist views about social work would seek to bring about individual/group levels of change, rather than challenge the wider social order. Social work is seen as being primarily concerned with maintenance and helping people fit into wider society in ways that are constructed as being mutually beneficial.

These above three approaches to social work endure in their applicability to social work and indicate what a complex occupation it is, social workers needing to take a view of the fit between their values and preferred approach when deciding which sector/model of social work they are best suited to work in. These approaches represent ideal types, and Payne suggests that while social workers may have a preference they may usefully position themselves to embrace all three dimensions.

> ### Reflective point
>
> Which one of Payne's (2005) approaches to social work is the one that you feel most fits with your preferred sets of theories, values and methods?
>   What do you think were the drivers that have led you to taking your preferred approach?

MAKING SENSE OF THE COMPLEXITY WITHIN SOCIAL WORK

Healy (2005) states that the tasks within social work are extremely varied and lists a range of tasks, acknowledging that a primary task is often assigned by the institutional context. She lists the tasks as being those of:

> risk management; implementation of statutory law; support and advocacy; therapeutic intervention; community education; community capacity building; research; policy development, implementation, and evaluation; **social services** administration. (2005: 3 (emphasis added))

Within these tasks can be seen the need for approaches that might need to embrace emancipatory models such as autonomy, choice and empowerment while at the same time calling for skills in rationing, risk assessment and enforcement. Jordan (2004), looking back over the past 25 years, believes that it is the latter type of tasks that have increasingly come to predominate within contemporary British social work. Dominelli (2004) also highlighted an increasing tendency towards **technicist ways of working** at the expense of complex relational ways of working.

These above debates about theories, values and methods all present considerable challenges to social workers across all sectors, depending on the particular pressures within settings and the balance between resources, rationing and opportunities for creativity, innovation and discretion. Given the far-reaching consequences and complexities of many social work decisions, it might be reasonably expected that social workers have some core 'thought through' theory on which to base their personal actions and interventions. Many of the theories used by social workers are not exclusive to the social work profession and borrow from philosophy, medicine and organisational theory. What is perhaps unique about social workers' use of theory is the attempt to adapt theory to the many individualistic problems that the social work profession is tasked with trying to improve. Other professions, such as medicine and education, are often faced with more technical/rational problems and hence their adherence to specific theories may be more evident.

Social work is a contested, complex and messy arena, not because social workers are muddled (though they can be), but because the children and families with whom they work experience the mess and distress of **transition**, chaos, crisis, violence and oppression. Theory helps social workers make sense of all this. In practice, you may be working with those who dismiss theory and that may also be your preference, to see theory as a classroom activity of dubious value in the real world. We strongly contest this position.

We all, including the disparagers and the eclecticists, develop and use practice theory built up on and from our day-to-day practice in order to make sense of and see patterns in how people act and what we do. We think this is very important and develop this below. Nevertheless, we also argue that practice experience which ignores theory and systematic evidence can be grounded in cynicism and even prejudice, and certainly undermines the potential for social workers to be effective agents for change.

Reflective point

- Do you think that social work should be mainly about practical problem solving?
- Do you think that social workers should be more autonomous and less accountable to management?
- What is your personal theory regarding the role of social work in the UK?

VALUES AND CODES OF PRACTICE

Part of the distinctive nature of social work is its claim to a value base that treats people as individuals; being non-judgemental, valuing diversity and having a commitment to social justice (see Banks, 2006). Many codes of practice list 'integrity' as a core value of social work, integrity being associated with qualities such as honesty, trustworthiness, reliability and impartiality. Authenticity, being genuine, is another key value that all social workers should role model, but all such value positions need to be supplemented by some of the values flowing from recent enquiries such as the value of practising authoritatively (DfE, 2011b) and holding a position of respectful uncertainty (Laming, 2003) when assessing the risk factors in a family.

Theories, as well as developing out of evidence, are also influenced by our values. Again, as is the case with theory, there are core established social work values and there are values that you may hold as an individual as a result of your life experiences or your professional experiences. Jones (2006) states that the value of social work that makes it special is its distinctive cluster of values, competences and roles. He lists these as (2006: 33):

- Having a concern for social justice
- Confronting discrimination
- Valuing people not rejecting

- Realism as well as idealism
- Seeing people in context
- Recognising and developing people's strengths and skills
- Problem-solving in partnership
- Enabling and facilitating
- A focus on relationships
- Providing structure and space within chaotic experiences
- Being an ally in promoting independence and choice
- Harnessing resources
- Taking actions to protect and control where necessary.

Reflective point

- To what extent does your organisation subscribe to the above 13 values?
- To what extent does your organisation deliver on the above 13 values?
- What influence might you be able to have on helping your organisation to deliver its values?

As regards models of working within social work, the model adopted will depend primarily on the practice context. Interventions in social work tend to be individual, family, group or community. If you are primarily working in a counselling setting you are likely to be working with individuals, whereas if you are working in a community outreach project you will probably be working primarily with groups. Much traditional social work was carried out with individuals; indeed psychosocial casework (see Hollis, 1964) was the bedrock of social work during its emergence in the 1950s and 1960s. The theory behind casework was essentially that if a therapeutic relationship could be established with an individual via a constructive helper, whether or not that helper took on a psychodynamic or a person-centred approach, 'healing' would flow. Such an individualistic approach to social work has its benefits but in the contemporary world of social work with children and families, such relationships have to be balanced against the need to effect change within families and communities.

When children themselves are asked about what they want from social workers they place great store upon consistency, length of time spent working with that child and friendliness. Such attributes might be found in a social worker who operates under a personal and professional code of practice. Codes of practice and codes of ethics are to be found in most professions as frameworks that guide, rather than prescribe, practice and represent commonly held values across a profession. A good example of how values might translate into practice can be seen in the British Association of Social Work's code of ethics, whose key principles for practice are (BASW, 2011):

HUMAN DIGNITY AND WORTH

- Respect for human dignity, and for individual and cultural diversity
- Value for every human being, their beliefs, goals, preferences and needs
- Respect for human rights and self determination
- Partnership and empowerment with users of services and with carers
- Ensuring protection for vulnerable people.

Social justice

- Promoting fair access to resources
- Equal treatment without prejudice or discrimination
- Reducing disadvantage and exclusion
- Challenging the abuse of power.

Service

- Helping with personal and social needs
- Enabling people to develop their potential
- Contributing to creating a fairer society.

Integrity

- Honesty, reliability and confidentiality.

Competence

- Maintaining and expanding competence to provide a quality service.

Interestingly, you will see in the above code a professional body's attempt to make values 'real' in terms of the political and the pragmatic, maintaining competence and challenging the abuse of power being very practical ways in which social workers can empower people. Values into action should be the way that social workers go about their daily business and codes such as this are a good framework to use for reflection about your practice.

EVIDENCE-BASED PRACTICE

Since the publication of the White Paper *The New NHS* (Department of Health (DH), 1997), contemporary public services have placed great emphasis on **evidence-based practice** with the New Labour government becoming increasingly concerned both with value for money and seeking best evidence for what works. At the same time, the **Social Care Institute for Excellence** (SCIE) was created to disseminate and promote best evidence-based practice across the social care sector. The applicability of evidence-based practice to social work, however, has been challenged by commentators such as Beresford (2007) who argues the need for an emphasis on knowledge-based practice that recognises that the lived experiences of people using services and the **practice wisdom** of practitioners are just as valid as any systematic evidence-based research.

Theory might therefore be expected to be created and adapted in the light of developing bodies of evidence. For example, if you were a social worker in an adoption team, you would be expected to have read all the relevant research documents on issues such as contact and cross-cultural **matching** and you would then be aware of a theory that led to the development of your team's practice. You will develop your own theory, based on intuition and personal experience, but you will always have an eye to the core theory that surrounds the area of your professional expertise. Whatever team you are working in you should be up to date with key research and have theory at your finger tips in order that you can explain your particular perspective on a child or family or justify a decision you might be challenged on.

FAMILY AND GROUP WORK

Family work has been increasingly recognised as critical for effective social work. **Systems theory** would suggest that it is of limited value if change can be brought about in a child but then that child is returned to a family whose standards and approaches to that child are damaging. Foster care might be a good example of this whereby a child may be temporarily removed to a foster home in which the approach might be a respectful one that gives the child individuality and appropriate boundaries. If such a child were to be returned to a family where no change had been effected in terms of issues such as attitude and boundaries, then any change is going to be very short lived.

Group work is promoted by those who believe that the particular type of support that is available from groups, particularly peer groups, is of a qualitatively different nature than that which can be realised by individual work only. In essence, the theory is that people who have shared similar experiences, for example, of abuse or dependency, are best placed to offer support and coping mechanisms to people currently in that type of situation. Group work has its disadvantages, however, and the games that people play in groups have been the subject of much academic debate. 'Difficulties in groups and teams are amplified by the complex dynamics involved, and their semi-public nature' (Doel, 2006: 114).

Some individuals, practitioners and children, are not comfortable working in groups. A good social worker will not present their way of working as the only way of working, a more individualistic approach being one that would consider one-to-one work, group work, and work within the wider community such as within a school setting where problems may be experienced.

MULTIDISCIPLINARY/COMMUNITY-BASED WORKING

Tragedies in childcare have often led to new initiatives and new ways of working, the emphasis on the centrality of **multidisciplinary** working having begun as early as the 1980s after the death of Maria Colwell, and subsequent child tragedies such as those of **Victoria Climbié** (Laming, 2003) and **Peter Connelly** (DfE, 2010) have further emphasised the need for agencies to work together. The evidence base for best ways of multidisciplinary working is not a well proven one, yet we know in children's services that not working together with other professionals can produce poor practice and even tragedy (see Herefordshire Safeguarding Children Board, 2009b). There is clearly much to be gained from listening to and learning from other professionals' points of view, although much multidisciplinary working remains ineffective and blighted by different professional cultures, status and interpretations (see Laming, 2003). Barlow and Scott (2010) have suggested that a **transdisciplinary** model is the most appropriate one for effective social work with children and families, such a model meaning that teams are made up of professionals across traditional boundaries rather than being just different sets or compartments of teams that work together, largely in informal settings.

As a social worker in multidisciplinary/transdisciplinary settings it always remains your professional duty to ensure that the child is kept at the centre of all deliberations. Some other professionals may want to focus on one aspect of a child, for example, their offending or their attachment behaviour, whereas the social work imperative is to ensure that such focused interests are always considered as part of the child's holistic, family and community make-up.

Community work is at the heart of several recent social policy initiatives, for example, **Sure Start** (Department for Education and Skills (DfES), 2003) and is an approach to children and families which believes that only when communities themselves are healthy in terms of their environment, their schools, their crime rate and their job opportunities, can children be brought up in ways that will ensure their own resilience and success. Some of the families with whom you work will be families who have experienced generations of dysfunction and possibly abuse, hence it is likely that even if the area in which they live is well provided for in terms of community initiatives such as Sure Start and other outreach services, that they will still need individualistic or possibly group work intervention. The problem with community-based initiatives is that they take some time to bear any fruit and in an age where politicians want instant results, certain schemes, despite their massive potential for good, can fall prey to government whim and economic considerations. The coalition government of 2010 has expressed its concerns about the massive investment by the previous New Labour government in initiatives such as Sure Start and indeed has even criticised the policy *Every Child Matters* (DfES, 2003) for not having produced some of the tangible results, for example, improvement in parents finding employment and the increased rates of breastfeeding. There are clearly larger economic and national and cultural factors that impact on targets that are set around such issues and it is difficult to argue for services that do not demonstrate immediate impact. It is to be hoped, however, that much of the grounds set for children's services through initiatives such as *Every Child Matters* will continue to provide a backdrop within which statutory social work with children can best operate.

The whole safeguarding mission around social work has tried to bring about cultural change whereby interventions into the lives of children and families with complex difficulties are not just seen as being the social worker's job. The most effective social workers will be those who are able to explore the potential within the family, community and other agencies in helping to share their workload and interventions.

RELATIONSHIP-BASED PRACTICE

As you will have noted by now, there are many different views about the role of contemporary social work (see Harris and White, 2009) and there is ongoing debate about whether established social work values such as those of emancipation and empowerment (Payne, 2005) and relationship-based practice (Ruch, 2010) hold any sway in an increasingly managed, prescriptive and resource-constrained world of practice. Recent influential reports such as that of the Social Work Reform Board (2010) and the *Munro Report* (DfE, 2011b) suggest that these core values may, indeed, be coming back into the ascendant.

It is our view that even the briefest of social work contacts need some kind of relationship base to them if they are to be effective and insightful rather than merely superficial and procedural. Ruch (2010) is clear that the contemporary context for relationship-based practice draws on psychoanalytical and psychosocial theory regarding the ways in which past experiences can subconsciously affect current attitudes and behaviours. A relationship-based approach can enable practitioners to work at depth and move away from any reductionist view of children and families. Understanding that every interaction between social worker and children and families is unique, and being able to explore issues in depth from a relationship-based platform can produce insights that effectively help challenge power imbalances and structural oppression.

CHAPTER SUMMARY

Social work with children and families is a complex moral undertaking, subject to political direction and scrutiny, and one which does not enjoy high social status and confidence. You have a chance to play your part in changing this picture and if you are clear about your values, your theoretical base and able to work in a setting that meets your preferred working style, you will find the ingredients for success are present. Knowledge will bring you the confidence to deal with complex family situations and to perform effectively in the multidisciplinary environments that characterise contemporary practice.

Making Foster Placement Decisions

Twin white British boys aged eight years, live with their single mother who also cares for two younger children. She has some mental health problems and has been finding it increasingly difficult to cope with the children's needs, which include a diagnosis of attention-deficit hyperactivity disorder (ADHD). The twins are very boisterous and have been missing school a lot. When they do attend they are inappropriately dressed, disruptive in lessons and always hungry. A voluntary arrangement had been made where their mother had requested that the local council place the children into foster care until such time that she could meet their needs.

You are the social worker in your local authority team who supports foster carers. The current vacancies (all approved for up to three foster children aged between four and 18 years) you have are as follows:

1 Mary O'Brien, a single carer, with a long history of fostering children of all ages. She currently has a long-term placement, a 15-year-old girl who is a wheelchair user. Mary is an in-house local authority carer and lives 20 miles away from the boys' current address.

2 Mr and Mrs Carruthers, who are in their early 30s, have a four-year-old daughter of their own. They have no other children currently placed and have had a wide variety of successful placements in the two years that they have fostered. Mr and Mrs Carruthers foster for a private sector agency. They live two miles away from the boys' current address.

3 John Smith and Paul Taylor, a homosexual couple, in their mid-30s who have been fostering for two years, specialising in fostering teenage boys. John and Paul are in-house local authority carers and live 15 miles away from the boys' current address.

4 Mr and Mrs Choudhury are a Hindu couple who were born in India. Their own children have left home. They are aged 45 and 46, respectively, and live a very active lifestyle, both being very keen on sport. Their own children have left home and their only fostering experience since approval two months ago has been two brief respite periods for a 14-year-old girl. The Choudhurys are in-house local authority carers and live five miles away from the boys' current address.

Given the options above, what considerations would you take into account when deciding the best foster placement for the twins?

What are the value bases of those considerations?

What are the theoretical bases for your decision?

Discuss this with colleagues and see if you are persuaded by their viewpoints.

Comment

Your preferred placement choice should be driven by your knowledge of the research base, particularly regarding what that research base says about what works in foster care from a child-centred perspective and what issues are involved in making same-race placements. The views of the twins should be core to your decision making and the potential to make a traumatic experience less distressful may depend on their ability to keep 'anchor' points with schools and familiar surroundings. A policy preference of local solutions for children's placement needs is important but any resourcing implications should come down the priority list, although the fee for a private sector placement might be three times more than an *in-house* placement. The practice wisdom of your team in knowing the strengths and track records of the foster carers being considered is important and you must reflect on your own value base about whether you believe that twin boys would best be fostered by a couple or a single carer.

FURTHER RESOURCES AND READING

Branfield, F. and Beresford, P. (2006) *Making User Involvement Work: Supporting Service User Networking and Knowledge*. Joseph Rowntree Foundation (www.jrf.org.uk/publications/making-user-involvement-work-supporting-service-user-networking-and-knowledge).

Department for Education (2009) *Early Identification, Assessment of Needs and Intervention – The Common Assessment Framework for Children and Young People: A Guide for Practitioners*. Leeds: Children's Workforce Development Council (www.education.gov.uk/publications/eOrderingDownload/CAF-Practitioner-Guide.pdf) (www.everychildmatters.gov.uk/caf or search www.teachernet.gov.uk/publications using the ref: 0337-2006BKT-EN).

Doel, M. (2006) *Using Group Work (The Social Work Skills Series)*. London: Routledge Taylor & Francis Group.

Every Child Matters website – This Department of Education resource explains the children and families policies that underpinned the Children Act, 2004 (www.education.gov.uk/childrenandyoungpeople/sen/earlysupport/esinpractice/a0067409/every-child-matters).

Glasby, J. and Dickinson, H. (2008) *Why Partnership Working Needs Interprofessional Training. Training Together to Work Together*. This article explores the need for training for successful partnership working (www.communitycare.co.uk/Articles/2008/07/14/108849/Interprofessional-education-and-training.htm).

Herefordshire Safeguarding Children Board (2009) *Serious Case Review Relating to HB A Child Who Died Age 7 Years*. Herefordshire Safeguarding Children Board. This is an example of some of the things that can go wrong in multidisciplinary working and you should read as many similar cases as you can, particularly local ones (www.herefordshire.gov.uk/hscb/docs/hb_-_executive_summary.pdf).

Joseph Rowntree Foundation (2000) *Working with Families Where there is Domestic Abuse* (www.jrf.org.uk/publications/working-with-families-where-there-domestic-violence) – This article focuses on domestic violence research involving women, children and men.

The Meriden Family Programme. This NHS programme supports families with sensitive issues and works with organisations to promote a high standard of mental health services by offering valuable research, publications and resources (www.meridenfamilyprogramme.com/resources.php).

3 LEGISLATION AND POLICY: WHAT YOU NEED TO HAVE AT YOUR FINGERTIPS TO BE EFFECTIVE

Key Points of Chapter

- You must have a critical appreciation of how laws and policies interact
- Social workers need to know the detail of key legislation
- Most of your work will be in the area of public law
- The Children Act 1989 remains the key piece of legislation pertinent to your practice
- Much of the law is contested and effective decisions by social workers have a key role in ensuring child-centred outcomes
- The welfare of the child must be paramount in all legal considerations

Proposed Professional Capabilities Framework areas covered in this chapter

- Professionalism
- Values and Ethics
- Rights, Justice and Poverty
- Critical Reflection and Analysis
- Interventions and Skills
- Contexts and Organisations

(Social Work Reform Board, 2010 – see Appendix 1)

Draft Standards of Proficiency for Social Workers in England covered in this chapter

2 Be able to practise within the legal and ethical boundaries of their profession
8 Be able to communicate effectively
9 Be able to work appropriately with others
10 Be able to maintain records appropriately
11 Be able to reflect on and review practice
13 Understand the key concepts of the bodies of knowledge which are relevant to their profession
14 Be able to draw on appropriate knowledge and skills to inform practice

(Health Professions Council, 2011 – see Appendix 2)

INTRODUCTION

As a social worker your career is set within a statutory framework and you need to have knowledge of what this means for you and for the families with whom you will be working. If you do not understand the law and are therefore not able to act within the law children will be seriously let down or harmed. Your experienced colleagues and managers can offer you guidance regarding working within the legal system and the protocols of court work. Working in the legal arena can be quite daunting and much time is unfortunately spent waiting around in courts for legal arguments to play out. Your local authority or independent agency will have their own legal advisers who will guide you through the law, including how to present reports and evidence. The more efficient you are at preparing reports that are succinct (see Chapter 10) and the better you are able to advocate in court for the child in question, the more likely it is that the Section 1(6) 'no delay' principle of the Children Act 1989 will become a reality. Unfortunately, many children still suffer unacceptable delays within the 'system' with regard to settling their welfare – a recent estimate (Barnardo's, 2010) is that the average length of time for care proceedings to be completed is over 12 months.

Timescales are very important, especially where young lives are concerned, and many of the procedural changes brought about in recent years have set strict deadlines for the completion of assessments and reports. Such procedural and managerial strictures have come under increasing criticism (e.g. DfE, 2011b) and there is growing pressure to re-emphasise that professional judgement should be the key determinant of outcomes for children and families, not proceduralism. Again, here is an example of some of the tension that characterises social work with children and families.

Social workers make up a very small part of the social care workforce and initiatives such as the **Common Assessment Framework** (CAF) (DfES, 2004) and the many preventative initiatives brought about under *Every Child Matters* (DfES, 2003) are to be applauded for spreading the message that the promotion of child welfare and the safeguarding of children is everybody's business (see Chapters 7 and 11). Once certain thresholds are crossed, however, and a child's welfare becomes a matter for legal concern, social workers are the key non-legal practitioners who carry the responsibility of working with children's legislation. In legal terms, a child refers to a person under the age of 13 and also to any person aged up to 20 who has been **in care** (since the age of 16) or has a learning disability.

The core piece of legislation central to your practice is the Children Act 1989 which will be considered in detail below, the rights base of this act being underpinned by generic legislation and policies such as the following.

Human Rights Act 1989 – this is fundamental to the rights and freedom of every citizen in the UK, and as such, it is essential to have a good understanding of this Act, which is also often referred to as the European Convention on Human Rights. This Act 'provides social work with an opportunity to promote culture of rights for service users'. More importantly, this Act is the foundation for many other Acts that help the practice of social work protect and support children and families.

UN Convention on the Rights of the Child 1989 – this international policy spells out the basic human rights to which children everywhere are entitled. There is, however, a difference between 'entitlement' and 'provision' – the UK's commitment to the Rights of a Child was challenged in a memorandum submitted to Parliament by The Children's Society (House of Commons, 2009) wherein concerns about issues such as the age of criminal responsibility (10 years in England) and the use of custodial options for young people were highlighted.

Children Act 1989 – this Act introduced key changes in the legislation in England and Wales and changed the focus of public and private law regarding children. The Act:

- Legislated to protect children who may be suffering or are likely to suffer **significant harm**
- Stated that the welfare of children must be the paramount consideration when legal decisions need to be made
- Emphasised the concept of parental responsibility, replacing the concept of parental rights
- Gave children the ability to be parties to legal proceedings; separate from their parents
- Laid duties on local authorities to identify children in need and to safeguard and promote their welfare
- Conferred certain duties and powers on local authorities to provide services for children and families
- Stipulated a welfare checklist of factors that must be considered by the courts before reaching decisions
- Introduced the 'no order' principle, whereby orders under this Act should not be made unless it can be shown that such a course would be better for the child than not making an order
- Introduced the 'no delay' principle stressing the importance of making swift decisions because delaying decisions regarding children is likely to prejudice their welfare.

We will now examine the sections of the Children Act 1989 that you will use most often, roles and responsibilities, the range of orders available, what you need to be effective in court settings, other key legislation that you need to be aware of and more recent recommendations made by Lord Laming in relation to the enquiries in respect of Victoria Climbié (Laming, 2003) and Peter Connelly (Haringey Local Safeguarding Children Board (LSCB), 2009).

As far back as 1998 a Social Services Inspectorate report in England and Wales, *Someone Else's Children* (DH, 1998), described 'a catalogue of concerns about how important decisions are made and the arrangements to ensure that children are safe' (Paragraph 1.3). These concerns came about because of a failure to understand and to act within the legal framework and it remains of great concern that more recent reports (e.g. Haringey LSCB, 2009) continue to draw attention to unacceptable practice regarding the appropriate, authoritative and timely use of legal systems. Social workers who know the law, its interpretation and ways to utilise the law in the best interests of children are the social workers who will be effective. We want you to be one of those social workers, professionals who read case law, who attend training and conferences and who continually update and question their own knowledge.

THE WELFARE OF THE CHILD IS PARAMOUNT

The most important section of the Children Act 1989 for social workers working with children is:

When a court determines any question with respect to –

the upbringing of a child; or

the administration of a child's property or the application of any income arising from it, the child's welfare shall be the court's paramount consideration. Section 1(1)

The child's welfare must always be uppermost in a social worker's thoughts throughout any piece of work with any family and this is what should focus all of the interventions you will make. It is also vital that the child's wishes and feelings are ascertained as a primary consideration; this should be considered separately from the wishes and feelings of parents. As the Cleveland inquiry into the removal of large numbers of children into care in the 1980s in the North East of England stated – 'the child is a person not an object of concern' (Butler-Sloss, 1988: 245). The Welfare Checklist first appeared in Section 1(3) of the Children Act and states that the court must have regard in particular to:

1 the ascertainable wishes and feelings of the child concerned (considered in the light of his age and understanding)
2 his physical, emotional and educational needs
3 the likely effect of any change in his circumstances
4 his age, sex, background and any characteristics of his which the court considers relevant
5 any harm which he has suffered or is at risk of suffering
6 how capable each of his parents, and any other person in relation to whom the court considers the question to be relevant, is of meeting his needs
7 the range of powers available to the court under this Act in the proceedings in question.

This core checklist has since been customised by the Adoption and Children Act 2002 in respect of looked after children going for adoption and by the Welfare Checklist (Public Law Outline) 2008, which was introduced to encourage children needing to be accommodated to be placed with relatives where possible. The principles of such checklists are that they help ensure that social workers do indeed look at the whole child, their family and wider environment.

CHILDREN IN NEED

The Children Act 1989 is a very influential piece of legislation with a philosophy that states most children should be brought up within their own families and that the local authority should provide support which will enable this to happen.

Section 17 of the Children Act sets out the duties of the local authority in respect of children in need in their area:

1 It shall be the general duty of every local authority (in addition to the other duties imposed on them by this Part) –

   (a) to safeguard and promote the welfare of children within their area who are in need; and

   (b) so far as it is consistent with that duty, to promote the upbringing of such children by their families by providing a range and level of services appropriate to those children's needs.

The majority of children you will work with are likely to come under Section 17 of the Children Act. The work is expected to be of a preventative nature and the definition is broad with three main elements:

(a) standard of health or development; reasonable
(b) significant impairment of health or development;
(c) disability.

'Development' means physical, intellectual, emotional, social or behavioural and 'health' means physical or mental health. It is expected that the local authority will consider services for those children who fall into any of these categories.

It is these children who will also possibly need to have an initial assessment (see Chapter 3 in *Framework for the Assessment of Children and their Families* (DH, 2000b) followed by provision of preventative services directly to the child or to the wider family in order to support them to safeguard the child's welfare. With such support it would be anticipated that the welfare of the child would be enhanced and that the child could be successfully cared for within the family.

This kind of low-level intervention with families is what would generally be tried first, providing there are no immediate safeguarding concerns, and will be done with a view to preventing any more intrusive, and possibly compulsory, interventions.

THE CONCEPT OF SIGNIFICANT HARM

Section 47 (1) of the Children Act sets out the statutory duty of local authorities to investigate where it is suspected that a child is suffering, or is likely to suffer significant harm:

Where a local authority:

(a) are informed that a child who lives, or is found, in their area –

   (i) is the subject of an emergency protection order; or
   (ii) is in police protection; or

(iii) has contravened a ban imposed by a curfew notice within the meaning of Chapter 1 or Part 1 of the Crime and Disorder Act 1998;

or

(b) have reasonable cause to suspect that a child who lives, or is found, in their area is suffering or is likely to suffer significant harm, the authority shall make, or cause to be made, such enquiries as they consider to be necessary to enable them to decide whether they should take any action to safeguard or protect the child's welfare.

The child protection process will be considered in detail in Chapter 7, the essence of child protection being that as soon as a local authority has 'reasonable cause to suspect' the possibility of significant harm, it has an overall duty to investigate, alongside other agencies, and to make a decision as to whether action needs to be taken to safeguard the child's welfare.

Section 20 of the Children Act sets out the power of a local authority to provide accommodation for a child if it believes that this would promote the child's welfare, this is, however, subject to parental consent and at any time a parent, or someone with parental responsibility, may remove the child from this accommodation:

(1) Every local authority shall provide accommodation for any child in need within their area who appears to them to require accommodation as a result of:

(a) there being no person who has parental responsibility for him;
(b) his being lost or having been abandoned;

or

(c) the person who has been caring for him being prevented (whether or not permanently, and for whatever reason) from providing him with suitable accommodation or care.

Section 20 (7) states:

A local authority may not provide accommodation under this section for any child if any person who:

(a) has parental responsibility for him;
(b) is willing and able to:

(i) provide accommodation for him; or
(ii) arrange for accommodation to be provided for him, objects.

Section 20 (8) Any person who has parental responsibility for a child may at any time remove the child from accommodation provided by or on behalf of the local authority under this section.

It therefore follows that if a child is accommodated under Section 20 and the person with parental responsibility withdraws their consent and you are seeking to safeguard that child, you will need to look at other means of achieving this.

Reflective point

The 'no delay' principle of the Children Act 1989 has much to commend it as legal proceedings can be very divisive, drawn out and costly. Most of all, this delay can be very confusing to the child and create attachment disorder.

How might you, as a child's social worker, involve the child's foster carers in helping build up a strong case that further delays are against the best interests of the welfare of the child?

Comment

Foster carers and their crucial role in a child's progress are often overlooked, despite that they often have the best insights into the effect that drawn out proceedings can have on a child. You could ask foster carers to keep a detailed record for possible presentation to the court about the behaviours experienced, say, due to protracted contact with birth parent/s. You could also encourage the foster carers to attend a training course on attachment and how best to cope with such difficult situations as a child moving on to adoption or back to their birth family. You could encourage the *guardian ad litem* to spend more time than usual with the foster carers. You should always be open and honest about the reality of delay and make sure that none of this delay is down to you not having met deadlines/arranged specialist assessments.

RANGE OF ORDERS AVAILABLE

A range of orders are available for the protection of children and should be considered when all preventative alternatives have been exhausted. There is a duty on local authorities to begin care proceedings if this is the most appropriate way of safeguarding the child and ensuring the child's well-being. Social workers must be clear about this and not see care proceedings as something to be avoided at all costs. Situations calling for care proceedings may arise as an emergency or more measured business. For example, it may be that an emergency situation has arisen such as when a parent has withdrawn consent for Section 20 accommodation and the child is placed in danger, necessitating a decision to be made about what course of action to take.

A Police Protection Order gives the police power, under Section 46 of the Children Act, to remove a child and keep the child in a safe place for 72 hours without any court order. This is more usually used in 'out of hours' situations, as during office hours local authorities should be being proactive in acting to safeguard any children known to them. The police must inform the local authority if it has taken this action and it must also inform the child's parents, although the police do not require parental consent. The local authority is obliged to convene a strategy meeting with a view to commencing a Section 47 enquiry (see Chapter 6).

The local authority can apply to the court for an Emergency Protection Order (EPO) under Section 44 of the Children Act. This is an order that allows the local authority to remove a child on a short-term basis, to accommodate a child in a place of safety or enforce the removal of an alleged abuser from the child's home (this requires the consent of the child's carer). The grounds for an EPO are easier to prove but it is short term and its powers are limited and so the social worker must expect to be back in court very soon with a lot more evidence to put before the court.

In all but real emergencies it can be difficult to persuade a court to hear evidence for an EPO as it is sometimes not possible for all parties to get representation at such short notice; also clear power differentials arise where some parties are represented and others are not. It is sometimes also the case that the local authority has not acted immediately to safeguard a child, often with a valid reason such as not having all of the available information or background about a family, in which case it will then be very difficult for the authority to make any emergency application to the court.

Whatever type of order is being applied, it cannot be overstated that the decision to remove a child from his or her family is massive as the consequences of this action will be lifelong for that child and also for his or her parents. The responsibility on the social worker is great and they will need to focus, during all interventions, on what is in the best interests of the child and to remain self-aware so that they do not succumb to any notion of being a 'knight on a white charger'.

The local authority can apply to the court for an Interim Care Order (ICO) under Section 38 of the Children Act. The initial interim order cannot last more than eight weeks and subsequent interim orders cannot last longer than four weeks. A full Care Order is a long-term order which commits a child to the care of the local authority. The grounds for applying for a care order are known as 'threshold criteria' and these are the minimum criteria needed for the court to consider what compulsory interventions are required in family life.

Section 31 (2) states that a court may only make a care order or supervision order if it is satisfied:

(a) that the child concerned is suffering, or is likely to suffer, significant harm; and
(b) that the harm, or likelihood of harm, is attributable to:

  (i) the care given to the child, or likely to be given to him if the order were not made, not being what it would be reasonable to expect a parent to give to him; or
  (ii) the child's being beyond parental control.

The court, therefore, needs to be satisfied that the child is suffering significant harm and that the criteria are met and only then will it go on to consider the welfare of the child and whether the granting of an order is needed. The child's voice will be heard in the court via the guardian ad litem, who is appointed by the court as an independent representative of the child.

Care and supervision orders require the same grounds to be met but a Care Order is more intrusive and gives the local authority shared parental responsibility for the child; it may or may not mean removing the child from the family home. A Supervision Order puts the child under the supervision of either a social worker or a probation officer. The local authority will make its application for what order it believes is needed and the court will decide on the most proportionate response.

OTHER RELEVANT LEGISLATION

Specific legislation that is relevant to social work practice with families and children that has complemented (note: not replaced), the Children Act 1989 includes:

Adoption and Children Act 2002 – this replaced the Adoption Act 1976 and modernised the legal framework for domestic and inter-country adoption. The aim was to ensure the following:

- Needs of the child are at the centre of the adoption process
- Birth parents understand the impact of consenting to adoption
- Disputes are resolved early.

Children Act 2004 had the intentions to encourage integrated planning, commissioning and delivery of services as well as to improve multidisciplinary working, increase accountability and improve joint inspections in local authorities. As will be discussed later on in the book, the complex systems brought about by the good intentions of this Act have come in for considerable criticism (e.g. *Munro Report*, DfE, 2011b).

PUBLIC LAW OUTLINE

In April 2008 the Public Law Outline (PLO) was introduced by the Ministry of Justice with a view to reducing timescales for care proceedings, encouraging a more equitable approach between parties and ensuring that preparation for proceedings is thorough, with less need for 'expert assessments' throughout the court process. The PLO introduced a significant cultural change for social workers applying to the courts for orders.

The range of orders remains the same as described above but it is expected that there will have been an initial assessment, strategy meeting, Section 47 enquiry, child protection conference and subsequent child protection plan. A thorough core assessment should have been completed by the social worker as well as any specialist assessments which are required, such as a community-based assessment in respect of parenting. The social worker should have assessed what the capacity is of the wider family to care for the child and support the parents, and a family group conference, encouraging the family to find their own solutions, should have been considered. There must be openness with families and any care plan which is put before the court should demonstrate that consideration has been given to the possible solution within friends and family.

This pre-proceedings phase ensures that preparation is thorough with less chance of delays in decision making for the child; it also means that families are totally aware of what is happening and what is being proposed and so they too have more time to prepare for what is, almost always, a very difficult and distressing time for them. It must be emphasised that where there are any communication issues, for instance use of different languages or deafness, an independent interpreter should be used from the beginning. If there are issues around understanding, such as a parent with learning difficulties or someone from a country with totally different systems, every effort, perhaps with the help of an advocate, must be made to assist them to understand what is happening.

A standard 'letter before proceedings' will be sent to parents, which will be a trigger for them to seek their own legal advice. There will also be a pre-proceedings meeting, which parents will attend, to agree a plan to safeguard the child and to agree on timescales. Although it may seem to be a little harsh, it is important that parents are made aware of all of the possible outcomes of the court process and that parallel planning will be undertaken, so that they understand from the outset that adoption is a real possibility. Families will be much better prepared and will have more faith in the process if social workers are honest and open with them. Another recent initiative is the Issues Resolution Hearing, which is designed to identify, discuss and resolve key remaining issues.

The preparation of court papers, chronology, statement and care plan, will continue as usual but the social worker will have much more information already gathered, meaning that the quality of assessments and information being put forward should be much improved.

PRIVATE LAW

As a social worker you will usually be working in the area of public law that deals with cases brought by public authorities, such as care proceedings. However, you should also be aware of private law, which deals with cases brought forward by private individuals. The most common reason for social workers being involved in private law cases is in relation to contact with children for parents who have separated or divorced. If the child or children are known to the local authority, the social worker may be directed by the court to write a Section 7 report or a Section 37 report.

Under Section 37, the court will expect the local authority to investigate and to consider if it wishes to apply for a Care Order or a Supervision Order or to offer support to the family or take some other action in relation to the child. In effect this is a Section 47 enquiry. A Section 7 report is more akin to a Section 17 child in need report, where the social worker is expected to give a view about contact arrangements.

A Residence Order is made by the courts to settle whom a child should live with, and parental responsibility is given to the person who has the Residence Order. The court will generally presume that residence with a biological parent is the preferred option unless there is evidence to the contrary. A Special Guardianship Order is designed to give a child a legally secure family placement when they are not able to live with either birth parent and adoption is not considered to be an option. The local authority must investigate and prepare a report for the court in these matters.

WORKING WITH YOUR LEGAL DEPARTMENT

Whenever you want any legal advice as a social worker you will be speaking to your legal department. This can be about any matter that you are unsure about regarding the law, and is always the case when you are considering initiating care proceedings.

You might invite a legal representative to a child protection conference and have a closed access session where you take some advice. What you need to be very clear about is that this is advice rather than a decision. It will be you, as the social worker, alongside your manager, who will be making the necessary decisions in respect of families you are working with. Your legal representative will be able to clarify for you if thresholds for care proceedings have been met. In addition, the independent reviewing officer, along with conference members, may offer recommendations and these should be seen as your decision-making mechanism. It would be ill-advised to discount what others are saying and decisions regarding legal proceedings should be made in a multiagency context. It is vitally important to understand where responsibilities lie across the complexities of the legal system.

CHAPTER SUMMARY

This chapter has provided a 'lightning tour' of the legislation that all social workers who work with children and their families need to be aware of in order to work effectively. The key piece of legislation pertinent to your practice remains the Children Act 1989.

You do not need to know the details of every legal paragraph in any piece of legislation, but you do need to understand the key applications of law in regard to working with children and families. You should also keep abreast of case law and reports of key enquiries/serious case reviews and there are several children's websites that are particularly helpful in this regard (see Further resources and reading below). The next chapter will discuss child development and the importance of being able to form judgements for arenas such as the courts that are based on a sound understanding of children's developmental expectations.

CASE STUDY 3.1

Carmen

Carmen's mother, Joanne, was 19 years old when she was born and had learning disabilities. During the pregnancy, anonymous phone calls to the local authority said that Joanne's flat was regularly used as a crack house by local youths.

A home visit was made by you, accompanied by a senior practitioner. You were concerned at the state of the housing association flat (piles of left-over fast food and unwashed clothing scattered around) and that Joanne did not seem able to understand the nature of your visit; she wanted to chat about music and whether you liked her favourite songs. You asked about how the pregnancy was going (although you said you had come in response to an anonymous call, Joanne thought you were from the doctor's) and Joanne said she was fine. She was unable to name the father and seemed very sketchy about how she even became pregnant, seeming to be a very vulnerable young woman. Joanne was unable to say what antenatal care she had received and thought the baby was due 'in the hot weather'. Her elder sister lives locally and apparently visits 'quite a lot to keep an eye on her'. Joanne's last words to you as you left were that she was going to look after a friend's big dog for him as he had to go away for a period of time.

What are the legal considerations in this case?

What avenues might be pursued most usefully?

CASE STUDY 3.2

Angel

Angel is three years old and was found wandering alone on a busy road quite near her home. She was unable to say where she lived, so was taken to the local police station. The police officers were able to find her address but when police officers went to the house, the parents were both intoxicated and there were lots of people in the house apparently having a party. It was not possible to identify any adult who could care safely for Angel, and her parents seemed to be oblivious to what was happening. There had been a few previous contacts with this family but never any ongoing children's social care intervention.

What legal steps might need to be taken immediately?

What might determine whether Angel is a child in need or a child at risk of significant harm?

Which principles of children's legislation might drive the social work practice in this case?

FURTHER RESOURCES AND READING

Brammer, A. (2010) *Social Work Law*, 3rd edn. Harlow: Pearson Education Limited.

Children Act 2004. London: The Stationery Office.

Data Protection Act 1998 (www.opsi.gov.uk/acts/acts1998/ukpga_19980029_en_1).

Department for Education and Skills (2003) *Every Child Matters*. Cm 5860. London: HMSO.

Department of Health (1999) *Working Together to Safeguard Children: A Guide to Inter-Agency Working to Safeguard and Promote the Welfare of Children*. (www.dh.gov.uk/en/Publicationsandstatistics/Publications/PublicationsPolicyAndGuidance/DH_4007781).

Department of Health (2000) *Framework for the Assessment of Children in Need and their Families*. London: HMSO. (www.dh.gov.uk/en/Publicationsandstatistics/Publications/PublicationsPolicyAndGuidance/DH_4003256).

Family Law Week website. This is a very good source of up to date legal argument, case decisions and analysis (www.familylawweek.co.uk/site.aspx?i=fo13).

House of Commons (2009) *Memorandum submitted by The Children's Society, Select Committee on Home Affairs* (www.publications.parliament.uk/pa/cm200405/cmselect/cmhaff/80ii/80we11.htm).

Human Rights Act 1998 (www.opsi.gov.uk/ACTS/acts1998/ukpga_19980042_en_1).

The Children's Centre. This centre offers legal representation and advice for children and 'looked after' young people. The website also provides factsheets, publications and videos covering a wide range of legal issues specifically aimed towards children and young people (www.childrenslegalcentre.com/Legal+Advice/Child+law).

4 CHILD DEVELOPMENT: THE IMPORTANCE OF HAVING A SOUND UNDERSTANDING ABOUT LIFE STAGES IN CHILDREN

Key Points of Chapter

- You must have sufficient understanding of child development if you are to make informed judgements and be able to discuss issues knowledgably with professionals from other disciplines
- Much mainstream child development literature is based on children who enjoyed safe and secure early backgrounds. Many of the children with whom you work will not have had such early experiences and hence their development will often be significantly impaired or delayed
- Rigid adherence to only one theory or model of child development does not do justice to the complexity of social work with children and families
- Merely saying that you are eclectic in your approach to theory may be a mask for your not knowing very much about the theories and models of child development

Proposed Professional Capabilities Framework areas covered in this chapter

- Professionalism
- Values and Ethics
- Interventions and Skills
- Critical Reflection and Analysis
- Contexts and Organisations

(Social Work Reform Board, 2010 – see Appendix 1)

Draft Standards of Proficiency for Social Workers in England covered in this chapter

4 Be able to practise as an autonomous professional, exercising their own professional judgement
6 Be able to practice in a non-discriminatory manner
8 Be able to communicate effectively
9 Be able to work appropriately with others
11 Be able to reflect on and review practice
13 Understand the key concepts of the bodies of knowledge which are relevant to their profession
14 Be able to draw on appropriate knowledge and skills to inform practice

(Health Professions Council, 2011 – see Appendix 2)

INTRODUCTION

Before social workers can make any judgements about the children and families with whom they are working, they have to have a sufficient understanding of the key developmental stages that children will usually experience. Normative studies of child development (e.g. Sheridan et al., 2007) are useful as guides, but remember that many of the children and families with whom you will come in contact as a social worker will not be children and families who necessarily have been adequately nurtured and supported. Hence, although you need to be aware of normative development and milestones, it is essential that you take into consideration cultural and other influences. This may mean that some of the families and children with whom you work do not develop and thrive in the same way that others may do. This chapter describes a model of child development called the 'dry stone wall model' (Figure 4.1). Just as the stones in a dry stone wall are of different shapes and sizes that do not fit together symmetrically, so children do not pass from stage to stage in a precise manner, especially if they have health or environmental problems.

The capacity of a child's carers to provide parenting is often a core focus for social work concern, whether that concern is about how best to support, say, a lone parent with physical disability, or about how best to protect a child whose parents were both heroin users. The **toxic trio (Cleaver et al., 1999)** of domestic violence, mental illness and substance abuse has serious implications for children's development (see Merthyr Tydfil LSCB, 2010).

A recent initiative aimed at making the care proceedings route swifter and more child-centred in cases involving substance abuse is the Family Drug and Alcohol Court (FDAC) project (Harwin et al., 2011). Prior to care proceedings, the parents/carers are given the opportunity to commit to radically changing their lifestyle in order to enable children to return to live with them. A contract is signed agreeing to rehabilitation, two-weekly appearances before the same judge, and to undertake therapy on an intensive basis. Such a system gives a real chance to both parents and children, and actively involves parents in a way that the relative passivity of care proceedings does not. Success rates so far are positive and even where parents have relapsed, there has been feedback that they are now more accepting of the reasons why their child cannot return and are possibly in a stronger position to cope with any children who may be born in the future.

In situations of domestic violence, women are the predominant victims and survivors, often suffering physical, sexual and psychological abuse. Women's capacity to nurture their children's development is clearly compromised in home environments where there is constant fear of threats and violence. Many women trapped in such situations will not seek help, especially not from social workers, whose media image of child snatcher (Neate and Philpot, 1997) acts as a deterrent from seeking help and support.

IMPACT ON PARENTING

Some forms of mental illness can mean that adults are wrapped up in their own world. This must be due to a depressive state in which the adult cannot look after

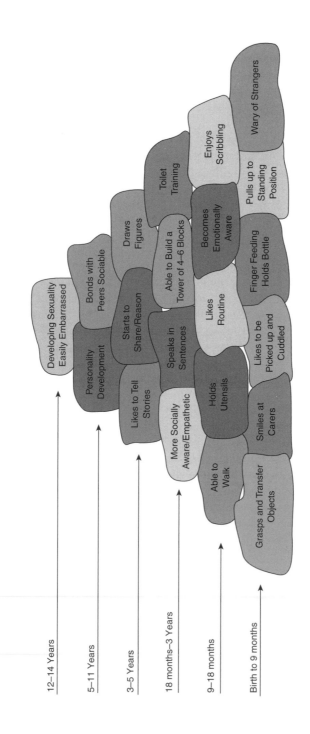

12–14 Years

5–11 Years

3–5 Years

18 months–3 Years

9–18 months

Birth to 9 months

Figure 4.1   The dry stone wall of child development

themselves, let alone the needs of their children or due to a delusional state whereby an adult might occasion actual harm to a child or act in such a manner that the child's own mental health suffers. Many parents of children take drugs or drink heavily, but the vast majority do not find their children on a social worker's caseload. Each situation is unique and social workers must be vigilant in assessing risks where they relate to the child's developmental levels and resilience. Levels of supervision are especially important and the careless management of prescribed drugs such as methadone can also have lethal consequences for young children (see Birmingham SCB, 2009). Green and Willis (2011) suggest the following questions should be borne in mind when assessing risk to a child who might suffer harm due to a substance-abusing environment:

- How vulnerable is the child?
- What is the extent of the problem/concerns and just how long standing or repeated an issue is this?
- How do you think this is impacting on the child?
- What will happen if no action is taken?
- Has the law been broken?
- What protective factors are in place that mitigate the risks?

Reflective point

What might be the effect on the development of children across the age ranges where their carers' lives are very chaotic and dominated by hard drugs?

Comment

- Where carers do not use substances responsibly, children's physical safety and emotional well-being is put at risk, especially younger children.
- Attachment disorders may present if carers are overly dismissive or critical.
- Children may be removed from the home to kin or foster care and returned when the problems ameliorate. If this happens more than once, then young children in particular are likely to suffer developmentally.
- Older children might be influenced by their carers' role modelling.
- Older children may blame themselves, become the carer and pass up on their own life's potential.
- Money spent on drugs may mean money not being spent on essentials for the children.

CHILDREN IN NEED OR AT RISK

Much statutory work in children's social work teams is concerned with establishing whether a child is a child 'in need' or 'at risk'. The legal system suggests that decisions about the normal health and development of a child should be made against the criteria within the Children Act 1989 which defines a child in need as (Section 17 (10)):

he is unlikely to achieve or maintain, or have the opportunity of achieving or maintaining, a reasonable standard of health or development without appropriate provision for him of services by a local authority under this Part;

His health or development is likely to be significantly impaired, without the provision for him or her of services by a local authority under this Part;

He is disabled.

The Children Act 2004, which placed new duties on local authorities in terms of improving the health and well-being of children and young people was underpinned by the *Every Child Matters* Green Paper (DfES, 2003), which identified five outcomes that provided the foundation for promoting the health and welfare of children and young people. The five outcomes were arrived at after consultation with children, young people and families, and reflected their greatest concerns, namely (Section 10 (2)):

1   Being healthy: enjoying good physical and mental health and living a healthy lifestyle
2   Staying safe: being protected from harm and neglect
3   Enjoying and achieving: getting the most out of life and developing the skills for adulthood
4   Making a positive contribution: being involved with the community and society and not engaging in anti-social or offending behaviour
5   Economic well-being: not being prevented by economic disadvantage from achieving their full potential in life.

Some children grow up in families where lives are characterised by domestic violence, substance misuse, poverty, dislocation, prejudice and oppression. Social workers may take a different view from their colleagues about a child's developmental needs/progress and one of social work's claims to excellence should be that it does indeed take a holistic view of a child and their family and the support systems and wider environment. The DH's (2000b) *Framework for the Assessment of Children in Need and their Families* (Figure 4.2) explores the key domains of a child's life and this is a very useful tool by which to start to make judgements about the needs of a child and whether those needs are such that they present a risk of significant harm and indicate that protective measures should be initiated.

This model, referred to in practice as the *Assessment Framework*, was introduced to bring about a holistic approach in a system and culture that seemed to only be concerned with risk and risk incidents, rather than seeing such incidents within a wider context of potential support. This *Assessment Framework* has stood the test of time and should also be familiar to professionals across other disciplines such as health and education. It is an evidence-based model with the child at its centre, which should be embedded in all aspects of practice. Thus the key to effective use of this model is to keep the child firmly as the focus of your assessment and analysis and not become obsessed with completing the accompanying paperwork/systems. Munro's (DfE, 2011b) review of social work

Figure 4.2   The framework for assessment of children in need and their families (DH, 2000b)

practice in this area was critical both of the amount of bureaucracy surrounding such a model and the rigid deadlines which can detract from safe and effective practice.

LESSONS FROM ENQUIRIES REGARDING CHILD DEVELOPMENT

We will now look at some of the developmental stages associated with healthy child development and refer to cases wherein social workers seemed to have failed because they did not equate a child's behaviour or development with any cause for concern. In the case of Peter Connelly (Haringey LSCB, 2009) there was considerable criticism of both social work involvement and that of various medical staff for not having picked up that Peter's developmental behaviours, especially his lack of mobility and engagement, masked serious neglect and risk.

This serious case review made several references to behavioural issues demonstrated by Peter, some of which included self-harming. It was also reported that he had recurrent bruising, infections and considerable weight loss, despite being reported as having a healthy appetite. Shortly before his death, Peter was seen in his buggy with chocolate smeared over his face to hide his bruises. Peter's short life was in fact characterised by chronic neglect and with its associated detrimental effects on a child's health, development and well-being. Had the visiting social worker perhaps taken more notice of the way in which Peter was very quiet and sitting very still during her last visit to the family home prior to his death, it may be that subsequent intervention would have been of a different nature and may have led to the prevention of his murder. Criticism was also made in this serious case review of the collusive nature of the professionals' relationships with Peter's mother, failing to challenge her explanations.

EXPECTATIONS OF SOCIAL WORKERS' KNOWLEDGE

Many NQSWs will not have children of their own and may not even be part of families that have young children. This does not mean that they are any less of a social worker although they are likely to have to defend their lack of actual parenting experience in some families. Social workers do not need to be parents to be effective – their insight, enthusiasm and communication skills should outweigh their actual lack of parenting experience. It is not necessary to have been a parent to be able to know when a child is in need or a child is at risk just as it is not necessary to have been mentally ill to know when a person with whom you are working is suffering significant mental health problems.

However, in order to be effective as a social worker you do need to have a good grasp of child development. The advice you give to families and the critical decisions that you will be involved in should be based on a clear knowledge of child development, its various stages and any aspects of a child's development that may mean that they are a child in need or perhaps a child at risk of significant harm. This obligation is enshrined in law, the Children Act 1989, which states that where a local authority:

> have reasonable cause to suspect that a child who lives, or is found, in their area is suffering, or is likely to suffer significant harm, the authority shall make, or cause to be made, such enquiries as they consider necessary to enable them to decide whether they should take any action to safeguard or promote the child's welfare. (Section 47)

The Act also goes on to state that:

> where the question of whether harm suffered by a child is significant it turns on the child's health or development, his health or development shall be compared with that which could be reasonably be expected of a similar child. (Section 31)

Therefore your judgements regarding children's welfare need to be based on an understanding of whether the issues presented by the child's health or development are reasonable in terms of how children of similar ages and backgrounds might present. Clearly, all children are different and individual, but any significant deviation from normative stages of development should always be fully explored, using colleagues from other disciplines where necessary in trying to build up a holistic view of a child within their family context. If you have family or friends with more than one child, you may have noticed that their development was at different rates and at different stages.

Reflective point

What reasons might there be for children developing at different rates within the same family?
    Draw on personal experiences from your family or from families with whom you have worked in a professional capacity.

Comment

If a child fails to demonstrate certain key stages of early development it should be a cause for concern, for example, hearing, vision and recognition. However, remember each child develops different aspects at different times. An example would be of a child who learns to walk early although learns to speak late. Equally, a child may learn to read early but remain in nappies until they are four years old. Thus, there is cause for concern only if there appear to be other underlying problems, for example, if the child appears to be unusually introverted and has poor eye contact. Lack of stimulating development can be responsible for slow progress, but is not necessarily a sign of potential child abuse. It could also be a sign of poor parenting skills which would also need to be addressed.

    As mentioned above, living with the effects of the 'toxic trio' of domestic violence, mental illness and substance misuse being in the environment will all have a deleterious effect on children's environments (Cleaver et al., 1999). Clearly, if a child has a disability this will also impact upon their environment.

THEORIES OF CHILD DEVELOPMENT

It is important for you to know the key theories that underpin much contemporary thinking about child development; various professionals having their own preferred theories and 'one size' not always fitting all. Part of social work's claim to uniqueness is that it does not label or compartmentalise children. Social workers, however, have to make individual assessments and may often find that other professionals do not agree with these assessments. Hence there is a need to be able to defend a decision from a theoretical, practice wisdom or evidence-based practice position. Many social workers say that they take an eclectic approach to theory, which is fine if it genuinely means that they have an good understanding of the various theories and have chosen to incorporate parts of these theories into their own worldview of child development. Eclecticism should not be an excuse for just knowing little bits about some theories. You will need to advocate for children and protect children in situations when there may be other professionals taking a quite different approach to the child's needs or risk. You therefore need to be confident in your theoretical understanding, which you will then use as a base from which to put forward a preferred plan of action or intervention.

Reflective point

Many of you will be familiar with what is often termed the 'nature/nurture' debate which Crawford and Walker (2003:10) succinctly summarised as follows:

> The nature viewpoint argues that our genes predetermine who we are and our characteristics are inherited … The nurture viewpoint argues that fundamentally our environment, experiences and the way we are brought up influence our development …

> How helpful is the nature/nurture question in helping you better understand the lives of the children and families with whom you will be working? Where do you personally stand on this debate?

To look briefly at the main theories concerning child development, we have ordered them as follows – sociological theories, biological and brain development theories, attachment theories and theories surrounding resilience in children.

SOCIOLOGICAL DEVELOPMENT THEORIES

Sociological theories (e.g. Vygotsky, 1978) emphasise the importance of our social and environmental backgrounds in shaping us as children. The interaction between children and their nurturing environment is seen as being a key determinant of how the child achieves their well-being, developmental stages and progresses in a positive manner towards the independence of adulthood. This approach is sometimes called the ecological approach to child development, and takes a holistic view of the child's wider environment.

BIOLOGICAL AND BRAIN THEORIES

A biological perspective looks at the genetic predetermination of behaviour and explores developmental stages around norms derived from large-scale studies of populations. Recently, there has been much interest in the biological factors concerning brain development and the effects of brain development on children's ability to function. Advances in medical research have meant that the study of brain development has become a more recognised discipline. Perry et al. (1995) and Cairns (2002) describe an impressive amount of evidence regarding the ways in which children's brains create a series of connections through the **synapses** within the brain. They argue that a child's experience in their early years largely determines how the brain will develop throughout life. Perry et al. (1995) say that it is the early years' experience that provides an organising framework which enables children to make sense of their relationships and their role in the wider world. If appropriate nurture is not available to a child in those early years, the belief of brain development theorists is that this necessary level of healthy functioning may never be attained because the brain cannot re-grow in certain key areas. A more positive perspective might be that children who have not had those early nurturing and stimulatory experiences may still develop but extra intervention and extra stimulation would have to be introduced to allow these children to develop in ways that enable them to have a more fulfilled or resilient life.

ATTACHMENT THEORIES

Attachment theory (Bowlby, 1980; Cairns, 2002) has recently had a resurgence of interest amongst a range of professionals, notably within the social work profession. Bowlby's (1980) traditional attachment theory rather fell from favour as it was seen as being politically incorrect in that its inference was that children developed best with mothers who stayed at home nurturing their children, not a theoretical base likely to appeal to feminists or a developing economy that demanded women in the labour force. The more recent work of Cairns (2002) and Golding (2007) sees attachment as not exclusively meaning attachment to a mother figure and is framed more within a requirement within a child's world to have one or more key figures, whether they are male or female, to whom the child can attach or bond. Klaus et al. (1996) define attachment as being an enduring affectionate bond between two individuals, that is, the need or feelings that a child has for a particular adult or number of adults. Fahlberg (2008) describes bonding as the process by which an adult grows to love a child and vice versa. Thus there are many attachment theorists and their interpretations of behaviours are varied and can also overlap. However, social workers should be aware of the key notions of attachment theory as such knowledge will help shape planning and thinking.

Attachment behaviour, the ways in which a child might develop a close relationship through responding to an adult, is seen by the attachment theorists as a way of ensuring physical and emotional survival. So attachment is about a child developing a secure base which they can draw on to cope in periods of being apart from those adult figures; secure attachment is seen as the desirable state for children to achieve. Insecure attachments take on a range of different presentations such as insecure, anxious, avoidant attachment/insecure avoidant attachment and disorganised attachment, each of which necessitates different caring strategies on behalf of the significant carers (Cairns, 2002). Merely to assess and then label a child's attachment status is not enough – the social worker's effectiveness is in putting in place interventions to address the specific attachment issue.

RESILIENCE

Theory is clearly one way that helps social workers make sense of children's behaviours and therefore to plan interventions that might help a child develop resilience.

Resilience is defined by Fonagy et al. (1994) as relating to normal development under difficult conditions, and the children who have contact with social workers often face the challenge of having to adapt in different ways to different life events and caring regimes. Gilligan and Manby (2008) identified three basic building blocks leading to development of resilience:

1   Secure base
2   Good self-esteem
3   Sense of self-efficacy.

If these building blocks are present, a child begins to feel competent in their environment and to be aware of their own strengths and limitations. Social workers might usefully look at areas in which interventions facilitate a more secure base in a child's life, their progress within education, their outside interests and their general social competencies. Resilience theory has influenced key policy initiatives such as *Every Child Matters* (DfES, 2003), whose main aims are those of enabling children to be healthy, safe, enjoy positive outcomes, to positively contribute to society and economic well-being. Many other initiatives such as Sure Start (DfES, 2003) have been designed around helping future generations of children become more resilient and less likely to present as children in need or children at risk of significant harm.

THE 'TOXIC TRIO'

Much recent UK policy has recognised the importance of giving children's development more prominence in welfare services. The *Common Assessment Framework* (DfES, 2004) and the *Framework for the Assessment of Children in Need and Their Families* (DoH, 2000b) clearly emphasise the need to assess children's development within the context of their parenting situations and the wider social environment in which they are living. Cleaver et al. (1999) found that parenting capacity is significantly affected by mental illness, substance abuse and domestic violence. Cleaver et al.'s phrase 'the toxic trio' is one you may often hear cited by professionals.

This is not to claim that all children whose parents have problems such as mental illness will result in children being vulnerable. However, it has been increasingly recognised (see Torbay SCB C18, 2009 and North Tyneside LSCB, 2010) that children with parents who have such problems in their own lives are increasingly at risk. Mental illness can often mean that parents are overwhelmed by their own problems and thus may neglect children both physically and emotionally. This can sometimes manifest itself in terms of emotional ill-treatment or sometimes even psychotic behaviours towards children, which can result in physical harm.

Similarly the effects of alcohol and drugs are increasingly recognised in contemporary practice and while having parents who are habitual drug takers does not necessarily equate with children being vulnerable, certain types of drug use do of themselves constitute a risk to children's development. Several serious case reviews (see Birmingham SCB, 2010 and Herefordshire SCB, 2009a) clearly show the tragedies that can result from parental drug use.

Parental capacity and the prevalence of domestic violence within families with children have also increasingly been recognised as factors that hamper the healthy development of children. Prior to research such as that of Silverman and Bancroft, (2002) and Hester and Radford (2006), social workers would rarely become involved in a family characterised by domestic violence unless a child had actually been injured as a result of fights between the parents or carers. Our knowledge now (Cummings and Davies, 2010; Mullender et al., 2002) suggests that children who grow up in environments characterised by domestic violence are less likely to do well themselves in terms of mental health, emotional well-being and their own adult relationships.

CHAPTER SUMMARY

There are many different theories relating to child development, mainly based on 'normative' children who are modelled in mainstream literature as having a broad range of supportive elements in their lives. Unfortunately, these supportive elements are often missing in the lives of many of the children who come to the attention of social workers. Children with delayed development, often combined with attachment difficulties, present their own challenges to a social worker who wants to be effective. Social work is about advocating and protecting children who have had poor developmental experiences, often being cared for by adults who had poor parenting themselves or whose problems such as poverty, mental health, substance dependency or domestic violence can eclipse their child's developmental and welfare needs.

If your work is informed by a credible and contemporary knowledge base about child development, you are far more likely to be an effective advocate or protector of children, able to appropriately challenge and add to the decisions/perspectives of others involved.

Ben

CASE STUDY 4.1

Ben is a three-year-old boy thought to have been conceived through an incestuous relationship between his mother and her father.

Within the first year of his life, Ben was classified as failing to thrive. Extensive medical investigations revealed he had a very rare condition in which he was unable to maintain the correct blood composition. His condition involved him being sick throughout the day and also having a significant number of very loose bowel motions. Because of the need to maintain the right blood composition, Ben was at risk of becoming very gravely ill if this did not happen. To achieve this Ben had to receive all of his nutrition through a gastrostomy feeding tube. He had a special milk formula given through the tube on three occasions during the day and then continuously over the night using a special machine. The feed was administered from 7.30 p.m. to 7.30 a.m.

Ben would drink fluids during the day through a feeder cup but would only hold finger food in his hands. He was still wearing nappies both in the day and in the night. He had started to walk but his gait was wobbly and he fell down on occasions. He also wore special boots to keep his feet in alignment.

Ben's understanding about the world around him appeared to be developing although he still had to learn to communicate verbally. At the time Kelly and his significant others were learning Makaton.

Ben's mother, Kelly, was 17 years of age. She lived in a house which was reported to be cold. She was said to be in debt, apparently owing rent of several hundred pounds, and that she also had no money to heat the house on some occasions. Other issues that had been raised regarded an alleged boyfriend who was at her house on a regular basis. He was known to use drugs and abuse alcohol. Kelly was known to have little routine in her life. Questions had been asked of her cognitive abilities.

In terms of Ben's development, can you identify areas in which his development is likely to fall outside normal parameters?

Do you think Ben's family life has had any influence on his development – if so why?

What theoretical perspectives did you use to justify your judgements?

Comment

Failure to thrive can affect the emotional and the communication development of children, as well as physical development. By the age of three years:

- Ben's speech should be understood by unfamiliar adults but will not be perfect
- He should be eating independently using spoon/fork/fingers and should be sufficiently socialised to be able to eat at the table
- He should be able to tolerate a range of different foods and textures
- He should have three meals a day plus three snacks. Fluids should be taken from an open cup
- His nutritional and fluid intake should usually be completed by early evening with a fasting period occurring overnight
- Toilet training may have been started or even completed. Ben should/could be dry over night and starting to identify when he wants to use the potty during the day.

Some children can be toilet trained earlier than three years. The process is dependent on the development of the central nervous system which transmits signals from the bladder to the brain to indicate the bladder/bowel needs emptying. This varies from child to child. As Ben receives his main source of nutritional needs during the night, this will hinder his ability to achieve bladder control and his ability to learn eating skills within the normal universal range.

Kelly's possible learning difficulty may inhibit her ability to understand Ben's emotional, social and cognitive needs, as well as learning to cope with his complex medical needs. If she is directing her energy towards trying to maintain a home for herself and Ben, this can leave her drained, with little reserves to meet Ben's needs.

Ben's care is very intensive and arguably too much for a single parent to undertake. The complexity of Ben's situation makes it difficult to establish the cause of his problems. The possibility of Ben being conceived through an incestuous relationship also indicates a possibility of a genetic cause to some of his problems.

Zane

Zane is 13 years old and lives in a high-rise block. He misses a lot of school in order to hang out with older youths from the area known to be into 'soft' drugs and petty crime. His father is currently in prison for alcohol-related offences of violence; his mother (herself a heavy user of alcohol and cannabis) is finding that Zane takes less and less notice of her.

Zane has recently been arrested for shoplifting and had a very small amount of cannabis on him at the time. When arrested, Zane said he was very unhappy at home and sometimes feels like jumping off the balcony where he lives.

What theories might help explain Zane's behaviour?

FURTHER RESOURCES AND READING

Bentovim, A., Cox, A., Bingley Miller, L. and Pizzey, S. (2009) *Safeguarding Children Living with Trauma and Family Violence: Evidence-based Assessment, Analysis and Planning Interventions*. London: Jessica Kingsley Publishers.

Birmingham SCB (2010) *Serious Case Review Under Chapter VIII 'Working Together to Safeguard Children' In respect of the Death of a Child Reference BSCB/2008-9/2* (www.lscbbirmingham.org.uk/images/stories/downloads/executive-summaries/BSCB+2008-9+2+SCR.pdf).

Brandon, M., Schofield, G. and Trinder, L. (with Stone, N.) (1998) *Social Work with Children*. Basingstoke: Macmillan.

Davies, D. (2011) *Child Development: A Practitioners Guide* (Social Work Practice with Children and Families). New York: The Guildford Press.

Humphreys, C. and Stanley, M. (2006) *Domestic Violence and Child Protection, Directions for Good Practice*. London: Jessica Kingsley Publishers.

Joseph Rowntree Foundation. Very useful site concerned with the root causes of social problems and how best to solve them (www.jrf.org.uk).

Merthyr Tydfil Local Safeguarding Children Board (2010) *Serious Case Review Executive Summary Child 'A'*. This case gives insight into the 'toxic trio' in a scenario that also examines challenges in working together, especially when parents are hard to engage (www.merthyr.gov.uk/NR/rdonlyres/DD0FFB06-B3FD-482D-98E3-38779C5C29E1/0/ExecutiveSummaryPublished140710PDF.pdf).

Sheridan, M.D., Sharma, A. and Cockerill, H. (2007) *From Birth to Five Years, Children's Developmental Progress*. London: Routledge Taylor and Francis Group.

5

COMMUNICATION: HOW TO IMPROVE YOUR SKILLS

Key Points of Chapter

- What are effective communication skills with children across age groups?
- The need to keep a child focus in all your communication work
- Communicating with parents and carers
- Diversity and the effective use of interpreters
- Special considerations for children with communication difficulties
- How to work with collusive or **resistant families**
- The use of '**Authoritative Practice**' as part of your skills repertoire
- Confidentiality – the myths and realities of keeping appropriate boundaries

Proposed Professional Capabilities Framework areas covered in this chapter

- Professionalism
- Values and Ethics
- Diversity
- Rights, Justice and Poverty
- Knowledge
- Critical Reflection and Analysis
- Interventions and Skills
- Contexts and Organisations

(Social Work Reform Board, 2010 – see Appendix 1)

Draft Standards of Proficiency for Social Workers in England covered in this chapter

1 Be able to practise safely and effectively within their scope of practice
2 Be able to practise within the legal and ethical boundaries of their profession
5 Be aware of the impact of culture, equality and diversity on practice
6 Be able to practise in a non-discriminatory manner
7 Be able to maintain confidentiality
8 Be able to communicate effectively
9 Be able to work appropriately with others
10 Be able to maintain records appropriately
11 Be able to reflect on and review practice
13 Understand the key concepts of the knowledge base which are relevant to their profession
14 Be able to draw on appropriate knowledge and skills to inform practice

(Health Professions Council, 2011 – see Appendix 2)

INTRODUCTION

As a social worker working with children and families, a vital skill is being able to communicate effectively. Communication is not just about talking; people can communicate their thoughts and feelings in many ways and for children who may be less sophisticated communicators, being aware of the often subtle ways in which they make their views known helps to ensure a fuller picture is obtained.

All too often in recording, social workers will write 'child too young' in relation to wishes and feelings. However, even babies can cry, smile, flinch and make various facial expressions and are generally very successful at gaining the attention of those who care for them and letting it be known if they are unhappy, distressed or fearful.

Several key inquiries and serious case reviews (e.g. Birmingham SCB, 2010; Laming, 2003) have remarked on the absence of the child in the case being reviewed. There is a strong message now that the child must be clearly central to your actual day-to-day work, not just central in your legal and ethical considerations. Colleagues such as teachers and foster carers may have closer relationships with children but social workers also need to know the children with whom they work as individuals, and not just 'cases'. In addition to skills in direct communication, an effective social worker also needs to be able to communicate with others involved in children's lives and we will look at issues of communicating within and outside your organisation, including current practice around confidentiality.

THE ROLE OF OBSERVATION

Observations of the interactions between children and their parents/carers are extremely important. Hence, it is necessary to see the family when the children are present or in the case of babies, when the baby is awake.

Reflective point

If you are not a parent or do not have younger siblings/nephews and nieces, how might you arrange to get experience that will develop your skills in working with children of different ages?

Comment

To take the example of a family with a baby, your observations should include watching what a parent does when the baby is distressed, how the child is handled, the tone of voice that is used and the sort of language that the parent uses, or even if the parent talks to the baby at all. A good social worker will make a note of whether there is good eye contact made and whether the interaction overall seems to be genuinely interactive and affectionate, or only of a task-centred nature. Toddlers are more able to let you know verbally how they feel but there will still be a limit to what you can elicit in this way.

Children often demonstrate their distress through challenging behaviour and with young children there is usually a reason why they present with 'behaviour problems'. Look out for 'wariness' or 'over-familiarity'. Both can be significant as young children will not usually be immediately comfortable with strangers. Some caution would be expected initially until a person becomes familiar to the child. However, if a young child is very tactile and comes to you straight away, perhaps sitting on your knee and being very 'touchy-feely' this should also alert you to possible attachment issues. If a toddler makes you feel uncomfortable with the nature of his or her touching or kissing, for example, rubbing your legs or kissing on the mouth, then the possibility of inappropriate exposure to sexual activity or knowledge would have to be considered. This would also be the case where words of a sexual nature were used in ways that would suggest that a child knew what they meant, for example, the word 'fuck' is unfortunately a word that many young children repeat from hearing adults and older children but this becomes more than a 'naughty' word if accompanied by body gestures that suggests the act of sexual intercourse (Howe et al., 1999).

Slightly older children can be seen away from home with parental consent. This provides the opportunity to communicate with the child in different settings and with different people in order to make comparisons regarding how they present and where they seem more comfortable and able to speak openly. Children will usually be fiercely loyal to their parents and carers and they will be very reluctant to be negative; they may have been told not to say anything and they should never be 'quizzed' as this is unhelpful in terms of evidence gathering in respect of any possible legal proceedings, and it may put them in a difficult situation at home.

Reflective point

What might constitute 'quizzing' a child? What indicators might children of different ages give that they are uncomfortable to continue talking about a situation?

GATHERING INFORMATION

Information from children should be gathered in a child-friendly way, taking into account their development and emotional age. Some ways of gathering evidence include:

- Using games or puzzles
- Finger and hand puppets
- Craft equipment

- Soft toys
- Music
- Face paints, hats, masks
- Story books/joint story telling
- Life path – using diagrams to illustrate key points in a child's life
- Life (story) book – compilation of key events in a child's life, using mementoes and photographs
- 'Feelings faces', lists of emotions.

Use and presentation of yourself is at the core of any play activity designed to elicit information – a child needs to feel at ease in your presence (Fahlberg, 2008; Koprowska, 2010). Being able to establish a relationship with a child is critical and you would do well to consider what working practices/interpersonal skills you could use to enable a child to gain an understanding of you and your role as a social worker (Koprowska, 2010). You will perhaps find that parents/carers block your attempts to engage with their children, in which case your concerns will be heightened. There may be genuine reasons for their reluctance to engage but they must also accept your role and professional responsibilities to see their children, alone if necessary. Social workers who are refused access to children have the option to apply for a court order and should never settle for glimpses of children, no matter what the attitude is of the adults (see Birmingham SCB, 2010).

Reflective point

How might you use your skills to encourage a reluctant parent/carer to allow you to speak to their children in private?
  What approaches might you take?

Teenagers can be difficult to communicate with and can provide their own unique challenges. Some teenagers may not have the verbal skills to communicate effectively with you because of the traumas they have experienced in the past. The majority of children who have emotional and behavioural problems have communication difficulties, but often these are not recognised by professionals. Some work in helping the young person recognise their emotions may prove to be beneficial in such situations. Feelings faces and body maps are structured methods used to enable a child to identify emotion by drawing an expression on a face that corresponds to a word written beneath or by marking on an outline of a body where they feel an emotion. Such exercises can be used as prompts to talk about feelings or equally help the child to understand and manage their feelings.

A young person's ability to develop their communications skills is improved when they are not constantly in a state of high emotional anxiety (Koprowska, 2010). A useful approach to developing a relationship and opening up communication channels is to transport the young person to an appointment. The intimacy of the car can help to break down some of the barriers that may be present or perhaps help the young person talk to you while having something to eat (note: this does not always have to be at a fast-food restaurant!). Such approaches may introduce the concept of eating and visiting different places to those usually frequented by the young person. A valued aspect of such occasions is that they can afford the opportunity to view the young person and decipher the messages they are projecting through their body language, eye contact, tone of voice, ability to concentrate or keep still, whether they are jittery or not; even their body smell can send messages that may prove to be helpful within the wider communication context.

Maintaining confidentiality will help facilitate the communication process between the young person and social worker, but honesty is a key factor within this situation through informing them that any information that compromises their safety will have to be passed on (for an example of the most tragic consequence of professionals not passing information on, see Birmingham Safeguarding Children Board (2006).) The voice of the child must remain central in all the work that is undertaken; all too often social work records focus on adults and their needs rather than on the child. Victoria Climbié, for example, was rarely spoken to in the little contact she had with the social worker before her death and she was never formally interviewed in French, her native language:

1   During the 211 days that Victoria's case was held by an allocated social worker employed by Haringey Social Services, she was seen by that social worker on only four separate occasions.
2   On none of those occasions did the social worker spend any more than 30 minutes with Victoria.
3   On none of those occasions did the conversation between the social worker and Victoria extend much further than 'hello, how are you?'
4   The amount of time that the social worker spent discussing Victoria's case with those who were responsible for supervising her work amounted to no more than 30 minutes in total. (Laming, 2003: 196)

COMMUNICATING WITH PARENTS AND CARERS

There is no doubt that communicating with parents and carers, especially where there is resistance or hostility, can be extremely difficult and stress inducing for social workers. Management support is needed so you will always need to make sure that your manager knows exactly what you are doing and knows about any anxieties you might have.

'Cold Calling'

A common practice scenario is 'cold calling'. Imagine a referral has been made by a family member, who wishes to remain anonymous, regarding two young siblings who are being neglected. The information is vague but, if true, it would be a cause for concern. The referrer has indicated there may be drug use and prostitution occurring in the property. You have been allocated the task of going out to share the referral with the mother, who is a single parent.

- What would your first considerations be?
- What information would you need before visiting?
- Who would you tell where you were going and what time to be expected back?
- Think of a range of strategies you could use, depending on how your visit is received?
- How might you 'draw the line' if a family member became verbally abusive to you?
- How might you conclude a visit?

The following sections provide comments relevant to the above case study.

PREPARING FOR HOME VISITS

Hopefully, your response to the above scenario would have considered the possible criminal content of the information, meaning that it must be shared with the police who may undertake a joint visit with you. This visit will determine if a joint or single agency investigation needs to be undertaken. A decision may be made for a single-agency assessment to be completed and it is important to keep in mind that there is currently no evidence to support the concerns that have been raised. For staff safety, initially a joint first visit with another worker would be undertaken because of the lack of information to confirm there is no risk to staff. At this point in the investigation there is uncertainty regarding whether violence or other risks, such as the presence of firearms, exist within the household. Your office should always know where you are, and have in place a system for knowing that you have successfully completed a visit and how long you are likely to be.

Prior to the visit, checks must be made to see if there is any historical information regarding the family. Contact must be made with the family so they are aware of your forthcoming visit and at this point in time you will be able to ascertain if an interpreter is required or any other form of support to aid communication.

ARRIVING AT THE HOME

On arrival at the home an honest explanation must be given to the family regarding the reason for your visit. At this point in time you have no authority to enter the house without a court order and a number of different possible reactions can be expected. The family will probably be shocked and defensive, possibly aggressive and tearful, when they realise the full implications of why you are there. At this point they may refuse you access to the house. It may be the case that the family has fallen out with a family member who has threatened them with 'social services' and they therefore have been expecting your visit.

Whatever the initial reaction of the carers, safeguarding of the children is your main priority and depending on the reaction of the parents, the situation may be assessed to be satisfactory to proceed. If not, then support should be sought from your manager and the police if necessary. If the visit proceeds, then parents are informed about issues such as record keeping, sharing information and consent being sought in order that information can be obtained for you to speak to their children. Their rights are also explained regarding how they can access data which is kept on the system about them and their children, and also how they can make comments, compliments or complaints about your intervention if they so wish.

The parents will be informed of the referral details, what has been said and why this is of concern to you. The house will be inspected with their consent, which will include seeing the children, preferably on their own, along with their bedrooms. This will feel very intrusive to the family but it is important for the social worker to remain calm and polite throughout, as well as being sensitive. At this stage it is unlikely you will have any substantiated facts and will be totally reliant on the family's cooperation, therefore it is important to keep them briefed about everything that needs to be done and fully engaged in the process.

Of course, if you are presenting someone with some information about themselves which is embarrassing or unpalatable then their natural response may well be to lie about it. You should expect this to happen quite often as the conversations you will be having will often be about difficult subjects. Parents too often know the responses they should be making and may not necessarily be totally truthful. It is hard sometimes to know what is accurate and what is not, but a picture will develop as you liaise with other professionals who know the family. This will help put things into context. If families are being untruthful, they should be challenged and told that such actions will not help their situation or that of their children. Laming (2003) and Munro (DfE, 2011b) both emphasise the need for social workers to be vigilant and look beyond superficial or obstructive responses, and while too cynical a mindset that sees child abuse in every scenario is not healthy, it is clearly not appropriate to always see the best in people, especially people who present as plausible and articulate. A 'healthy cynicism' is perhaps the best initial approach to take to new referrals until a fuller account has emerged.

Although it is vital that you see and speak to children alone, you will need to speak to them and their carers together at some point, primarily to observe the way in which they interact. It is important to watch carefully not only the verbal communication but also the non-verbal communication between them.

WORKING WITH RESISTANT FAMILIES

There has been considerable recent interest with regard to the skills needed to work effectively with resistant families. The report into the death of Victoria Climbié used the phrase 'respectful uncertainty' (Laming, 2003: 205) to describe the attitude professionals need to strike in trying to spot an abuser. The recommendation was that all professionals needed to be much more sceptical and mistrustful about face value explanations. Laming's subsequent report into the death of Peter Connelly (Laming, 2009) found again that professionals had been over-optimistic and overly trusting of the parental explanations for Peter's conditions. Laming suggested that an authoritative approach to intervention with resistant families that challenged poor parenting, while at the same time encouraging parents to embrace change, was the appropriate way forward for work in the safeguarding arena:

> professional expectations on parents are too low and many children may be experiencing unacceptable levels of neglect and emotional deprivation, without testing whether parents would improve their parenting if offered constructive challenge and support. (DfE, 2010: 22)

Some parents/carers are very plausible and articulate; some can draw you into their own view of the world; while others may seek to over-identify with your own circumstances as a woman/black person/young person. Just because a parent/carer seems co-operative with the process and appears to accept your interest as being best for the child, does not necessarily mean that this co-operation is genuine. That is, the 'disguised compliance' of carers can create an illusion of co-operation which places children at a much greater risk than is actually thought.

Conversely, in his 2009 report, Laming advises:

> Signs of non-compliance by parents, or indeed threat or manipulation, must form part of the decision to protect a child. (2009: 30)

Inquiries into tragic deaths such as that of Peter Connelly have drawn attention to 'highly resistant' parents and carers (see Haringey LSCB, 2009), highlighting problems of intimidation, bullying and often obstruction of social workers. Such behaviour was particularly evident in the serious case review concerning the circumstances of child HC:

> There is a great deal of evidence that HC's mother and her male partners were intimidating and verbally aggressive to staff from different agencies including Health Visitors and Social Workers. They were also highly manipulative, and they often managed to subvert the work being done to try and help the children develop and thrive. The household was often chaotic whilst professional home visits were being carried out, and the scale of neglect and poor parenting would have seemed overwhelming to those trying to provide a service to HC and the siblings. (Herefordshire SCB, 2010: 3)

It is also possible that you may over-identify with adults who are victims of various forms of oppression, such as domestic violence, or feel overly empathic towards a parent with disabilities or debt problems, rather than concentrating on the welfare of children which is the reason for your involvement. Some parents will attempt to intimidate you (see also Birmingham SCB, 2010); whereas others may adopt a passive, sullen or downtrodden, hopeless stance to detract from the likelihood of you placing any demands or expectations on them. Others will meekly agree with everything you say and promise, without any hint that they have no intention of complying, to do everything you have asked for in respect of their childcare. Passivity might, however, be related to a learning disability or a depressive illness or may stem from a genuine state of helplessness brought about by being the victim of domestic violence – these are the difficult areas in which you will be expected to use your professional judgement.

Reflective point

How might you use your skills to attempt to connect with a parent/carer who is:

- Aggressive?
- Dismissive?
- Disinterested?

How would you keep appropriate boundaries if a child or adult wanted to know about your marital status/where you live/whether you had children/what football team you support?

GENDER

Most social workers communicate mainly with women; the men in families are either not engaged with or are intimidating when engaged (see Birmingham SCB, 2010). This means that most social workers develop expertise and skills in communicating with women, not men, despite the fact that men are often central to the promotion of children's welfare. The vast majority of children and families social workers are also women, and it is understandable that such social workers will not wish to engage with men who may be oppressive, aggressive and violent. However, there is a professional responsibility, together with a managerial responsibility, for safe working practices which mean that such engagements should not be avoided. Social workers often enter volatile situations without any back-up protection that other professionals such as the police have and the fact that most social work interaction takes place in people's homes, unlike, say, many health professionals' contacts, gives all the more reason for practices such as joint visits to be commonplace rather than exceptional.

Reflective point

Consider the statement below from Lisa, 23 years, a newly qualified social worker:

> We have the Youth Offending Team (YOT) also based in our building as well and we have had a few visits by armed police as young offenders try to enter the building with guns or knives. This has been a real eye opener to the realities of Social Work/Youth Work in an inner city deprived area. I have spoken to colleagues whom I have met on the NQSW support group who work in Duty and Assessment and Care Management, who visit homes where there are guns 'sitting on the television' and where police will not go alone. Yet, social workers who are new to the profession are simply expected to visit without any support.

> If you were asked to visit a household where colleagues had told you that there were guns 'sitting on the television' what might your response be?

WORKING WITH INTERPRETERS

Most towns and cities in the UK now have sizeable communities of different cultures and ethnicities and for many of these adults and children English will not be their first language. The services of an interpreter are essential in such situations.

Some of our newer communities are very small and families may be extremely wary of speaking to you via someone from the same community as they may feel that other members in that community will get to know about issues which are very private to them. You will need to make sure that the interpreter is not someone who is known to them, as it must be an independent person who will not collude with the family and who understands child-centred practice. Increasingly, the view in the UK (e.g. Laming, 2003) is that any 'politically correct' stance taken of not challenging standards, disciplines and behaviours because they might be the norm in country or culture of origin is unacceptable and possibly against best child-centred practice also. A recent experience from practice involved a Somali mother who asked her general practitioner (GP) to recommend the best surgeon to carry out her young daughter's circumcision. The GP referred the case to children's social care, having had to explain to the mother that what might be considered acceptable and even best practice in her culture was considered both abusive and illegal in the UK.

As stated above, undertaking a visit to a family with an interpreter who is from the same country, or is known within the community, can present a barrier to engaging with the family due to their concern that confidentiality may not be maintained. Such barriers need to be recognised if the situation allows and another interpreter sought (Coulshed and Orme, 2006). Such issues must be recorded within the case file along with the actions undertaken to rectify them. A statement must also be made regarding any safeguarding issues and why the social worker has decided a visit can be delayed for a short period of time until a new interpreter had been identified.

Any professionals who have been contacted and who have been part of this decision must also be recorded in the case file.

In some cultures, such as certain Muslim cultures, women may feel reluctant to speak about domestic violence to an interpreter because of her role within a cultural setting (Coulshed and Orme, 2006). It is important not to stereotype all Muslim women in this category, as second and third generation Muslim women may adopt some Western values. Each case must be judged individually. In some situations Muslim women may use the social worker to help them escape from domestic violence. However, it is often the case that women may not engage with male social workers or interpreters unless their husband is present. An effective social worker will attempt to obtain such information when making the initial telephone contact to arrange a home visit.

It is important to use the first language of the family if communication is to be effective. This can be difficult to achieve at times, especially when one considers that not only are there a number of languages but there are also a significant number of dialects to each language. For example, a Romanian family may speak to you in a gypsy dialect that is different from mainstream Romanian language.

It is also important to find an interpreter who is able to understand and translate all written correspondence. Such safeguards can take time to put in place and may be problematic, but it is a social worker's professional responsibility to ensure that all efforts have been made to allow the family to fully participate in any assessment/investigation processes. By denying them this opportunity, the social worker is violating their rights and giving them the right to object and argue that they have not had the opportunity to understand what was happening, with any consequent delays possibly undermining the safeguarding of the children.

Prior to undertaking a visit, there is also a need to prepare the interpreter by explaining to them (Coulshed and Orme, 2006):

- The reasons and expectations of the visit
- That confidentiality must be maintained
- That a position of neutrality must be adopted, along with an appropriate emotional tone
- The need to ensure accurate information is transmitted to the social worker.

Using an interpreter can be time consuming and therefore you will need to allow more time for each visit or meeting. If at all possible, try to use the same interpreter throughout the intervention. To facilitate this it is advisable to book in advance to ensure that the interpreter is available.

The social worker will need to intervene if it appears the above conditions are not being met. Central to the interview with the parents and children is the assessment of risk, and in order to achieve the most effective communication, particularly where English is not the first language, interviews are best carried out in short spells, otherwise understanding can become lost. For families born outside England, the systems that social workers work within may not be the same as in their country of origin. The family may come from a country in which the state does not intervene in 'private family matters' and, if this is so, the social worker will need to spend more time explaining processes and possible outcomes so that the family is fully informed and clear that they are now subject to English laws and policies.

Some of the above preparation and sensitivities also apply to working with children and families who cannot verbalise due to disability or illness (see next section).

COMMUNICATING WITH PEOPLE WHO CANNOT VERBALISE

There are likely to be people you work with who are unable to speak, hence you will need to be creative about how you communicate with them. Preparation is important if, say, you are going to visit a child who is unable to communicate verbally and in such instances help and advice can be sought from other professionals beforehand. The need to communicate with children is essential in determining whether the child is safe or not. Social workers should not just believe what children have to say at face value but should be prepared to dig around a little more. Sadly, for many children who have been abused by a person whom they should trust and feel safe with, there is a fear that they will not be believed. This is a common technique used by adults to silence the children they abuse (Horwath, 2010). Disabled children are proportionately more likely to be abused than non-disabled children due partly to the extra vulnerabilities that come with their disability (Higgins and Swain, 2009). Their behaviour is often viewed as part of their disability and therefore concerns are not always recognised. Furthermore, social workers may view the child as being unable to communicate, will rely on a parent/carer for information and will not challenge them. Inappropriate emphasis can also be placed on support for the carer instead of support for the child. There is also evidence to suggest that professionals believe a child with a disability will not make a reliable witness and that any such children who make a disclosure may not be believed (Wilson et al., 2008).

The availability of the communication methods below should dispel the myth that children with disabilities are unable to communicate and fellow specialist professionals should always be approached to give advice on their usage (Wilson et al., 2008):

- British Sign Language – language for the deaf community
- Braille and Moon – method of reading by touch
- Deafblind manual alphabet – words are spelt out on to the hand
- Blissymbolics – symbols system where symbols can be accessed through a communication board/computer
- Makaton – language programme for children with learning disabilities
- Picture exchange communication system – uses pictures to sign
- Lip reading
- Finger spelling.

Non-verbal children can let you know how they are feeling by the way they behave. Any sounds they make may be accompanied by behaviours which could possibly indicate distress, but you will need to put this into context and speak to those who know them as signs of distress could be for other reasons, such as the very change in routine that your presence brings.

Body language is always important, but is even more so with non-verbalising children. You may observe particular movements such as foot tapping, head shaking/nodding: some children may pace the floor or even display some self-harming, such as picking their skin, biting themselves, banging their head or pulling their own hair. Any of these presentations may be unusual for you but may be 'normal' for that particular child so it is very important that a full picture is put together and that you communicate with all who are involved with the child or young person.

Facial expressions can also be very telling as can other body gestures. For instance a child may make abusive gestures or alternatively might wave or beckon to you. A child might run away when you come to see them or hide or run towards you; these are all things that have significance and need to be analysed in conjunction with the other information that is available. For example, if a two-year-old child of a lone female parent is accommodated in a foster home, the child may well show anxiety at the sound of a male foster carer's voice – such behaviour does not necessarily equate with the child having been abused by a male.

When asking young children 'how' questions, their ability to understand will depend on their age and level of cognitive understanding and it is important not to ask leading questions or display emotions when using words that might lead to an 'expected' response. Koprowska (2010) states that by the age of three a child is able to understand 'why?' questions, whereas by the age of five this has expanded to 'when?' questions, with children aged eight years being able to largely understand 'what, who and where?' questions.

CONFIDENTIALITY AND COMMUNICATION

There remains much confusion about the issue of confidentiality when working with children and families, particularly when information is shared outside an organisation. The reason for this continuing confusion is partly historical and partly due to a reluctance/the incompetence of professionals in understanding the new, child-centred approach to confidentiality as clearly laid out in the government guidance *Information Sharing: Practitioners' Guide: Integrated Working to Improve Outcomes for Children and Young People* (DfES, 2006).

There are common law provisions around confidentiality but where the welfare of a child is at stake, the **paramountcy** principle of the Children Act 1989 (see Chapter 3), overrides any confidentiality considerations and professionals have both a legal and moral obligation to share information appropriately on a 'need to know' basis. Despite the widespread fear of being sued in our ever more litigious society, no professional has ever been sued for sharing appropriate and relevant information about a child, although many have been criticised for failing to share such information (see Birmingham SCB, 2006; Laming, 2003). Information can also be shared where there is an overriding public interest in such disclosure. All organisations processing such personal and sensitive data must, however, comply with the Data Protection Act, 1998, and follow the 'Seven Golden Rules of Information Sharing' (Department for Children, Schools and Families (DCSF), 2008b: 11):

1 Remember that the Data Protection Act is not a barrier to sharing information but provides a framework to ensure that personal information about living persons is shared appropriately.

2 Be open and honest with the person (and/or their family where appropriate) from the outset about why, what, how and with whom information will, or could be shared, and seek their agreement, unless it is unsafe or inappropriate to do so.

3 Seek advice if you are in any doubt, without disclosing the identity of the person where possible.

4 Share with consent where appropriate and, where possible, respect the wishes of those who do not consent to share confidential information. You may still share information without consent if, in your judgement, that lack of consent can be overridden in the public interest. You will need to base your judgement on the facts of the case.

5 Consider safety and well-being: Base your information-sharing decisions on considerations of the safety and well-being of the person and others who may be affected by their actions.

6 Necessary, proportionate, relevant, accurate, timely and secure: Ensure that the information you share is necessary for the purpose for which you are sharing it, is shared only with those people who need to have it, is accurate and up-to-date, is shared in a timely fashion, and is shared securely.

7 Keep a record of your decision and the reasons for it – whether it is to share information or not. If you decide to share, then record what you have shared, with whom and for what purpose.

ENDINGS

We discussed earlier in this chapter the difficult issues that can arise when first meeting a family and we will now look at the issue of effective endings of involvement with a family. Most social work today involves time-limited contact and, perhaps apart from working in a fostering team, you are unlikely to experience relationships with children that last for some years. Nonetheless, endings of even short-lived professional relationships are important, as exemplified by the following reflection from Myra, a social work student on placement. Her account is both succinct and poignant:

Following a 'direct observation', one of the families that I worked with submitted feedback that will continue to influence my future work. We were still in the middle of our work together when my placement finished, and I realised that I had not prepared them for my premature departure. The mother commented that we had developed a level of trust that had enabled the family to start a 'journey' that might ultimately resolve their difficulties, but I would not now be around to complete the 'journey' with them. This made me realise how much of a commitment we demand of the people we work with without necessarily making a reciprocal commitment ourselves. I realise that the moment we ask people to place their trust in us, we have absorbed responsibilities that transcend common-place notions of 'work'. I hope that I never again commence (or conclude) interventions with the sincere but casual attitude that I had adopted on this occasion.

CHAPTER SUMMARY

Communication skills are key to effective social work – with toddlers, teenagers or resistant parents. There are a range of practical communication skills that you can develop and use in practice. Use of self and knowing your own motivations, strengths and weaknesses are essential if you are to be an effective communicator. Your own values and experiences will influence your judgements and you need to be aware of your own contribution to the processes of communication within families. Authoritative practice, where you are sure of your ethical, professional and legal grounds, is a positive way of dealing with the complex challenges in working with families who will be variously authentic or deceptive in their commitment to bringing about change.

CASE STUDY 5.2

Alesha

Alesha, aged seven months, came to the attention of children's social care when her parents, Nazim and Taslim Khan, visited your office asking for financial help, saying that they had just moved to your city and were experiencing problems with receiving their benefits. They told you that they had experienced racial harassment from their previous neighbours and that Alesha had been made subject to a child protection plan when she was about three months old. The parents were not clear about the reasons but gave the impression that neighbours had 'grassed them up' out of racist intentions.

As duty social worker, your statutory checks reveal that Alesha was subject to an ongoing plan due to neglect – poor weight gain, poor hygiene in the house and a lack of stimulation generally. Taslim had extended family in her previous home area but because of the heavy drinking and aggressive outlook of her husband, Nazim, they rarely visited. Such support was even less likely now that they have moved 100 miles away, Nazim saying that they moved because a mate had offered him a restaurant job on good wages.

Both parents are from a Pakistani Muslim background but have become largely westernised and are not accepted in mainstream Muslim culture due to Nazim's heavy drinking and criminal record. He has three offences for violence and three years ago he received a suspended sentence for involvement in a robbery in an off-licence. Taslim appears to have mild learning disabilities and is very passive and speaks very little, allowing Nazim to talk for her.

In the office setting, although Alesha seems well dressed and reasonably clean, you notice that there is little interaction between the parents and the child, who sits quietly in her buggy. Your contact with the family's previous local authority has revealed a history of domestic violence, usually drink related (Taslim was once hospitalised with a broken arm in early pregnancy with Alesha). Apart from occasional restaurant jobs, usually as a waiter, Nazim has rarely worked and left school with no qualifications at the age of 15. Taslim also has no qualifications, has never worked and was in a violent relationship prior to meeting and marrying Nazim two years ago. There were two children from this previous relationship, one having died shortly after birth due to a heart problem and the second child being brought up by a relative under a private fostering arrangement, with children's social care having had concerns about the child's welfare in a domestic environment characterised by violence.

The family have secured a small flat in a large Victorian terrace, which is owned by the restaurant owner friend of Nazim's. After discussions with management, you agree an emergency payment from Section 17 of the Children Act 1989 and arrange to visit to assess the family's ability to safeguard Alesha.

You have also discovered by contacting the previous local authority that Taslim was very sporadic in seeking antenatal care, but that the pregnancy progressed well. Concern had been expressed at the initial visits by the health visitor about the home conditions, especially the state of Alesha's feeding bottles and what was described in records as 'an air of hostility' from Nazim. Alesha remains rather small (below the fourth centile). Some reports said that the house was too cold in the winter months for such a young baby and neighbours once reported seeing her left in the garden in a buggy, crying for over an hour in very cold weather.

Imagine that the above case is passed on to your team and you are allocated as the social worker. Consider the following points:

- What communication skills would you need to be effective within this family situation?
- How you would effectively communicate with the child?
- Would you see the parents separately or together?
- How much would you need to know about the family's religion?
- What would your anxieties be in meeting the family for the first time?
- What would you do if you approached the flat and heard Nazim verbally threatening to beat his wife?

What other agencies are you likely to communicate with in respect of the above? Consider the issues of confidentiality involved, using the suggested template below:

1   Is there a legitimate purpose for you or your agency to share the information?
2   Does the information enable a person to be identified?
3   Is the information confidential?
4   If the information is confidential, do you have consent to share?
5   Is there a statutory duty or court order to share the information?
6   If consent is refused, or there are good reasons not to seek consent to share confidential information, is there a sufficient public interest to share information?
7   If the decision is to share, are you sharing the right information in the right way?
8   Have you properly recorded your decision?

Note: questions taken from *Information Sharing: Practitioners' Guide: Integrated Working to Improve Outcomes for Children and Young People* (DfES, 2006).

FURTHER RESOURCES AND READING

Birmingham Safeguarding Children Board (2006) *Serious Case Review Under Chapter VIII 'Working Together to Safeguard Children', In respect of the death of Case Reference:*

BSCB/2005-6/1 (www.lscbbirmingham.org.uk/images/stories/downloads/executive-summaries/BSCB+2005-6+1+SCR.pdf).

Department for Education and Skills (2006) *Information Sharing: Practitioners' Guide: Integrated Working to Improve Outcomes for Children and Young People* (www.london-scb.gov.uk/files/library/caf_practitioners_guide.pdf).

Department for Children, Schools and Families (2008) *Information Sharing: Guidance for Practitioners and Managers* (https://www.education.gov.uk/publications/standard/publicationdetail/page1/DCSF-00807-2008).

Department for Children, Schools and Families (2008) *Integrated Children's System – Enhancing Social Work and Inter-Agency Practice* (https://www.education.gov.uk/publications/standard/publicationDetail/Page1/DCSF-RBX-01-08).

Department for Children, Schools and Families (2010) *Working Together to Safeguard Children. A Guide to Interagency Working to Safeguard and Promote the Welfare of Children*. London: The Stationery Office (https://www.education.gov.uk/publications/standard/publicationdetail/page1/DCSF-00305-2010).

National Children's Bureau. Originally created as part of a project funded by the Department of Education, the NCB provides information to improve practitioners' skills of communication with children during assessments (www.ncb.org.uk/cwc).

Triangle. An independent organisation that provides a range of specialist support enabling communication with disabled children and young people, including opinions and advice to statutory agencies and the courts on assessment of needs (www.triangle.org.uk).

Wilson, K., Ruch, G., Lymbery, M. and Cooper, A. with Becker, S., Brammer, A., Clawson, R., Littlechild, B., Paylor, I. and Smith, R. (2008) *Social Work. An Introduction to Contemporary Practice*. Harlow: Pearson Education Limited.

6

ASSESSMENT: YOUR ROLE IN THIS COMPLEX DYNAMIC

Key Points of Chapter

- Assessment is a complex, ongoing dynamic process not a 'one-off' event
- The *Framework for the Assessment of Children in Need and their Families* (DH, 2000b) is your key generic guide to assessment. This framework is grounded in theory, research findings and practical experience
- Special considerations need to be made for children with communication difficulties
- Preparation is very important for effective assessment and issues of diversity must be sensitively handled
- You must have a sound understanding of the thresholds appropriate to the involvement of a range of agencies
- Families need to be engaged in the assessment process – be wary of families who are resistant or wholly compliant. Most families have strengths within them – try to find these strengths and build on them. You should make real efforts to capture the views of any men in the family during an assessment, and not be satisfied with input from women only
- It is essential that you capture the views of the child during your assessment and do not allow others to speak on their behalf. Assessment must always be focused on the child and not the adult
- Working with other agencies presents both difficulties and benefits – ensure that there is a mutual understanding of your contributions and question when you are unsure
- Effective use of skills such as communication, observation, reflection and evaluation should help ensure outcome-led assessments

Proposed Professional Capabilities Framework areas covered in this chapter

- Professionalism
- Values and Ethics
- Diversity
- Critical Reflection and Analysis
- Interventions and Skills
- Contexts and Organisations

(Social Work Reform Board, 2010 – see Appendix 1)

Draft Standards of Proficiency for Social Workers in England covered in this chapter

1 Be able to practise safely and effectively within their scope of practice
2 Be able to practise within the legal and ethical boundaries of their profession
5 Be aware of the impact of culture, equality and diversity on practice
6 Be able to practise in a non-discriminatory manner
7 Be able to maintain confidentiality
8 Be able to communicate effectively
9 Be able to work appropriately with others
10 Be able to maintain records appropriately
11 Be able to reflect on and review practice
13 Understand the key concepts of the bodies of knowledge which are relevant to their profession
14 Be able to draw on appropriate knowledge and skills to inform practice

(Health Professions Council, 2011 – see Appendix 2)

INTRODUCTION

An assessment is the collection and analysis of information which is relevant to an identified purpose, and is an ongoing process which actively involves children and families with the intention of helping social workers to understand people within their own environments (Coulshed and Orme, 2006; Coulshed et al., 2006). Assessment is a core component of the work undertaken by social workers, and is the first part of the care planning process as well as being the first point of contact with children and families (Cocker and Allain, 2008). Central to the role of assessment within children and families services is ensuring that the needs of the child are met and the child is protected from harm (DCSF, 2010).

An assessment has several phases which will lead into the intervention stages of planning, action and review. These stages can broadly be seen as (DH, 2000b: 29):

- The acquisition of information
- Exploring facts and feelings
- Putting meaning to the situation
- Reaching an understanding, with the family, of what is happening and what the impact on the children is
- Drawing up an analysis of the needs of the children and the parenting capacity of the children's carers.

Coulshed and Orme (2006: 25), view assessment as being core to effective social work practice and they identify the following CORE skills:

- Communication
- Observation
- Reflection
- Evaluation.

Appropriate questioning is a crucial skill if social work with children and their families is to be effective, Trevithick (2000) suggesting that a range of techniques might usefully be employed in order to effect best communication. Open questions give an opportunity for children and families to explore the complex issues in their lives; closed questions enable precision and accuracy; circular questions explore the same issue with different family members in order to find common ground for moving on. Techniques such as paraphrasing, capturing the essence or feel of a conversation; clarifying and summarising to ensure that all participants are in agreement about what has been said and the giving and receiving of feedback about how the process of communication is unfolding are key areas for skills development. Trevithick (2000) goes on to highlight other key areas where effective skills are needed such as prompting, probing, use of silence and appropriate self disclosure, the latter skill being one that develops with experience and is used to establish some degree of common ground or shared type of experience in order to build rapport. The importance of ending contacts sensitively and the closing of cases are also skills that will develop over time, such skills being essential if the children and families with whom you work are to feel respected.

FRAMEWORK FOR THE ASSESSMENT OF CHILDREN IN NEED AND THEIR FAMILIES

The nature of assessment work changed in 2000 with the introduction of the *Framework for the Assessment of Children in Need and their Families* (DH, 2000b, see Chapter 4, Figure 4.2). The overall aim of this assessment framework is to safeguard the child and address their welfare needs (Horwath, 2010), and the document is grounded in theory, research findings and practical experience. It encompasses the following three domains, which are now embedded in social work practice:

- Child's developmental needs
- Parenting capacity
- Family and environmental factors.

These three domains are further split into subheadings that give guidance to social workers about what discussions they should have with families. Underpinning the *Framework for Assessment* is an ecological approach which acknowledges that the economic situation and the environment in which children live can affect parenting capacities and how they respond to their children's needs. Analysis of the information gathered across agencies is structured around the interface between the above three domains and provides the opportunity for **strengths-based** approaches in assessing the needs of children (DH, 2000b).

Reflective point

Think about the last assessment you were involved in that involved children. If, for example, your assessment involved a child who self-harmed, what knowledge base did you call upon in order to effectively safeguard that child?

- How central do you think the welfare of the child was to that assessment?
- Was the assessment based on child development theory?
- Did the assessment demonstrate an equality of opportunity approach?
- Was the assessment truly carried out in partnership?
- How could that assessment have been improved?

TYPES OF ASSESSMENT

There are many different types of assessment; the first one a social worker is likely to undertake is the initial assessment. This involves a brief assessment of each child who is referred to children's social care. The aim of the assessment is to determine whether a child is in need and which services, if applicable, are required. A further aim of the initial assessment is to determine if a more detailed core assessment is required. Currently, an initial assessment has to be completed within ten days of referral and the child seen within timescales that are determined by the nature of the referral.

The assessment should be a planned process and should identify information that needs to be obtained as well as information that should be shared with the parents. A key aspect of the assessment process is seeing the child alone and assessing the parents' ability to safeguard the child (DCSF, 2010). Initial assessments involve a range of professionals drawing together and analysing the information obtained, along with making a decision as to whether a child is in need according to Section 17 of the Children Act 1989, or whether they:

> have reasonable cause to suspect that a child who lives, or is found, in their area is suffering, or is likely to suffer, significant harm. (Section 47, Children Act 1989)

Incorporated in the initial assessment is an assessment of the risks the child may be exposed to in their environment. Children at risk are also children in need; the two categories cannot be viewed as being mutually exclusive. The *Assessment Framework* underlines the importance of the welfare needs of children being responded to as soon as possible, regardless of whether there are child protection concerns or not (DH, 2000b).

Social work has been criticised for being defensive and risk averse. The effective social worker is not a risk-averse social worker but one who can incorporate effective management of risk by using the skills and judgements that are expanded on in this chapter. In terms of safety for social work staff, the need to ascertain information from other professionals also includes potential risks to staff. Safe or lone working should be supported by organisational policies to support staff in their work.

A core assessment is undertaken when there is a Section 47 child protection enquiry but can also be done whenever situations are seen to be complex. There is currently a timescale of a 'maximum of 35 working days' (Section 3.11, DH, 2000b) within which the assessment has to be completed. The aim of this assessment is to determine what action needs to be undertaken to safeguard and promote the welfare of the child. This involves assessing the capacity of the child's parents to respond to their needs within the wider family and community context (Horwath, 2010). The initial assessment will provide the focus for any subsequent core assessment, but the latter assessment process must cover all aspects of the *Assessment Framework* (DH, 2000b). The social work profession continues to learn lessons regarding the assessment process, some of which were identified by Lord Laming (DCSF, 2009), who stated there is a need for assessments to be child-focused, sensitive and comprehensive. He also identified the need for staff to have time to make sense of the information they have gathered, including time for reflection, going on to suggest that social workers should adopt a position of stepping into a 'child's shoes', in order that they gain a greater understanding of the difficult position in which children sometimes find themselves.

Central to the role of undertaking any assessment with the child and family is working with them so that they are able to identify their own risks. Such a process is viewed as empowering as it supports children and families in identifying their own strengths and to develop strategies to improve their situation. The importance of a strengths-based approach to children and families is increasingly recognised within social work, while balancing this positive perspective with the need to intervene to address any issues of concern (DCSF, 2009; Saleebey, 1996).

PREPARING FOR THE ASSESSMENT

The first aim of any assessment is to obtain clarity about its purpose, the anticipated outcomes and why an assessment has been requested. Following the allocation of a case, the social worker should:

- Always read a child's file and make best efforts to track such information down if it is believed to exist. Scrutinising a referral and any available background information might include:
  - critically analysing whether the child is at risk or is likely to suffer significant harm
  - reading any assessments which have already been done previously
  - reading any computerised information which is available

- Finding out what is known and what areas is there little or no information about
- Finding out what are the previous concerns
- Assessing whether the family previously engaged well with agencies
- Discovering the family's known strengths
- Analysing whether any patterns emerge from looking at the history of the family. A chronology will help you to understand this
- Finding out which other agencies are involved with the family, both children and adults
- Once you have sufficiently scrutinised such issues and reviewed any research that could be relevant to the assessment to be undertaken, you would then contact the family and arrange to see them at their home address; if they have major objections to this you could arrange a first meeting elsewhere as a starting point but the home environment will have to be assessed so future meetings will need to be at home. Make sure that the family knows that you will want to speak to the children alone to gather their views
- You should always ensure that due consideration is always given to equal opportunity considerations –
  - Use an interpreter to help to arrange the initial meeting, if needed
  - Determine if the child or family has any particular requirements to be taken into consideration such as: disability, culture, ethnicity, race and faith
  - If there are gender issues, perhaps in relation to particular cultures, ensure that this is dealt with from the beginning. For example, women from certain cultures may be unwilling to be alone in the company of an adult male and this situation may have the potential to put them at risk in the future
- It is also important that from an early stage in your preparation you think about appropriate sharing of information and about the likely timescales for intervention, especially if barriers are encountered.

GATHERING INFORMATION

This involves the use of a range of tools such as scales and questionnaires, but these should not be used in isolation. Such tools are designed to act as an aid and information should be obtained from a range of sources.

A useful approach is to undertake a chronology as it is able to identify the key life events in the child, bringing to the forefront the significant experiences and patterns that can be buried in a raft of information. A chronology should be used to inform all types of social work assessment. (For an example of an initial assessment, see Case Study 6.2, and for an example of a detailed chronology, see Case Study 6.3.)

Reflective point

Think about your own life course. What were the key chronological points that a professional making an assessment about your welfare/health should take into account as being significant?
    Why were these times in your life important?
    What might prevent you talking about some of these times with a professional?
    What skills do you have that could be used to help a child speak openly to you?

Talking about family histories can identify reasons for current behaviours and influence the way parents interpret the needs of their child. Serious case reviews have identified that little attention had been given to the past lives of families. Such information should include memories of how the carers were parented and how they have dealt with stressful situations within their own lives. Previous and present support systems should also be explored (Horwath, 2010).

Observation can provide a great deal of information as it allows you to informally witness interactions first-hand between the child and the carer in their own environment. More formal observations will include the observation of tasks such as feeding or bathing the child. It is important that the carer gives their consent to the observation and that you give a clear explanation for your need to observe. For example, if the child is failing to thrive you clearly need to be vigilant and inquisitive while also taking into account that the carer may feel self-conscious and nervous in your presence.

Special assessments are often requested in order 'to provide specific understanding about an aspect of the child's development, parental strengths and difficulties or the family's functioning' (DH, 2000b: 42).

ENGAGING WITH THE FAMILY

The object of your assessment is to secure positive outcomes for the children and perhaps their parents/carers when you have finished the process. An assessment is not only an information gathering exercise, but should include the family from the beginning, and is an interactive way of creating opportunities for change facilitated by the social worker. The reason why the assessment is being undertaken should be explained at the onset of the assessment process. This provides clarity about what is expected from the family and what the social worker's role entails.

Consent from the parents will need to be obtained at the outset so that other professionals can be contacted to gain a wider view of the family's situation. Again, it is relatively unusual for people to refuse to give consent, but it does happen, so a decision will be required regarding the risk the children are exposed to along with deciding if the family will accept interventions from other agencies. For children where there are significant safeguarding concerns, consent and confidentiality has to be weighed against the child's best interests. Key factors that have to be taken into account include the necessity to take action and the proportionality of action to take. The social worker and manager have to use their professional judgement to weigh up what may happen against what might not happen (DCSF, 2008b; DH, 2000a).

The Human Rights Act (1998) states that everyone has the right to respect for their private and family life, therefore a respectful approach to the sensitivities of the family situation should influence your practice. Much of statutory social work is nowadays characterised by brief relationships with families and communities although some settings such as fostering and adoption or children's centre work are likely to provide opportunities for longer-term work which may better suit certain people's preferred way of working. Even short-term relationships with families can be meaningful and effective. Relationship building with families can take some time, which may prove difficult given the timescales in which the work has to be undertaken, but there may be colleagues from a number of agencies who already have a good relationship with a family who could provide a route into the household. For example, a mother who has a mental health problem and who is very reluctant for new people to enter her household, but who sees her **community psychiatric nurse (CPN)** on a regular basis may be more accepting of the social worker visiting if a joint visit was arranged with the CPN. The reality of many assessment situations is that parents and children are suspicious of social work involvement. Often such involvement is viewed as stigmatising and a sign that parents are not coping, and taking part in an assessment can be intimidating for both the child and family. Parents may feel they are being interrogated and the assessment process can evoke strong feelings for the parents, while practitioners can be nervous about how a family will respond to them (Wilson et al., 2008).

Some important messages have come out of recent childcare inquiries regarding the need for social workers not to over-identify with the problems of parents and carers when it is the welfare of the child that is paramount. Social workers were particularly criticised in the case of the death of Peter Connelly in Haringey for having believed his mother's version of events without question (Haringey LSCB, 2009). Lord Laming's memorable phrase 'respectful uncertainty' (2003: 205) does not mean that we should approach all families as if they were abusers but that we should always have this possibility in mind, regardless of a family's history, background and economic standing.

ESTABLISHING HELPING RELATIONSHIPS

In order to maintain a 'good helping relationship', de Boer and Coady (2007: 35) defined two approaches, the first of which should adopt 'the soft mindful and judicious use of power'. It is important to understand the balance of power in the relationship between you, the social worker, and the family you are visiting as it is possible that you will be received with some hostility; therefore it is also vital that at the outset you provide clear reasons for your involvement. In order to be most effective, it is important not to bring any preconceived judgements from information you have already seen, and to adopt a non-judgemental and respectful approach to the family. Clear communication will help the family have a good understanding of what is happening. If you can facilitate an open atmosphere where exchanges can take place, this is more likely to be effective than adopting a procedural or dominant way of working. If you are to maintain a trustful relationship, you must ensure that you are reliable to your word and responsibilities, which include the basics such as turning up on time and returning telephone calls. It is the small things that can make all the difference to the building of an effective working relationship.

The second approach advocated by de Boer and Coady (2007) involves a more humanistic attitude that challenges the more traditional style of working. By utilising a down-to-earth style as opposed to the more 'professional' style, a comfortable relationship can be encouraged and maintained with the use of small talk and setting realistic targets and goals. It is important to understand the family in the context of their social life, past and present, as well as to show empathy to their difficulties, which can be aided through a sensible awareness of self-disclosure. Social workers often see themselves as powerless in the face of top-down directives and **managerialism,** but to many families and children, you hold all the power and this is a dynamic you should not underestimate.

REMAINING CHILD-FOCUSED

Although there is a body of literature emphasising the importance of being family-focused (Barlow and Scott, 2010; Wilson et al., 2008), it is critical to your assessment that you communicate with the children in the family. The tensions that can sometimes arise due to a social worker working within a family context can be resolved by co-working the case so that the parents and the children have their own workers. The children could be any age from pre-birth up to 18 years, therefore a range of communication strategies will be required. (Communication with children is discussed in greater depth in Chapter 4.)

You will need to tell the children, whatever their age, who you are and why you are in their home. Their initial engagement will depend on their experiences of being listened to, being interpreted correctly, being judged or misunderstood, being denied, being punished and what their attachment capabilities have been.

Again, there will be a tension between completing your assessment within timescales and having sufficient time to build up a rapport with the child who will need to trust you and be able to feel safe, understood and accepted. It may be that one of the pieces of intervention following an initial assessment, which you will need to complete in seven days under current guidance, may be further work with someone the child relates well to in a venue where they feel safe, to ascertain in more depth what their wishes and feelings are.

Research studies have shown that children and young people often know what their needs are and how these can be met, and that children and young people can generally tell people about these if they are given the time and space to do so (Butler and Williamson, 1994). They will need to be reassured that their opinions will be taken into consideration, and the Children Act 1989 states that the wishes and feelings of the child must be taken into account. This provision has been further reinforced in the Children Act 2004, which places a duty on local authorities to acknowledge the feelings and wishes of a child. To further reinforce this principle, the Children and Young Persons Act 2008 gives independent reviewing officers greater powers to intervene on a child's behalf in ensuring their wishes and feelings are heard – including the power to involve the Children and Family Court Advisory and Support Service (**CAFCASS**) at a much earlier stage. An independent reviewing officer's role is to improve the outcomes for looked after children by ensuring a high-quality planning process is maintained, taking into consideration the individual wishes of each child. CAFCASS is a government organisation that works under the regulations set by the family courts in order to:

- Safeguard and promote the welfare of children
- Give advice to the family courts
- Make provision for children to be represented
- Provide information, advice and support to children and their families (CAFCASS, 2011).

In terms of a social worker's view regarding the ability of the child to make decisions on their own behalf, this is a complex matter. From a legal perspective a child is deemed to be a child up until they reach their 18th birthday. Legally, a child can consent to medical, dental or surgical treatment when they reach the age of 16. A child can obtain a driving licence when they are 17 and are deemed to be able to undertake moral reasoning by 10 years, therefore making a child criminally responsible for his or her actions. For situations where there is no legal provision, some guidance comes from case law, otherwise known as Gillick *v*. West Norfolk and Wisbech (1985). This case involved a family in which the court ruled that the parents did not have to be informed or give consent for their daughter, who was under 16, to receive contraceptive advice from the GP. Lord Templeton ruled that a parent's legal right was a dwindling right which the courts would not uphold against the wishes of the child. This principle applies to other fields including children's rights within social work. Central to determining the child's competence is the assessment of their cognitive, intellectual and emotional characteristics. All will affect the child's ability to make a decision. Furthermore, a young person who makes an unwise decision does not indicate a lack of competence – the freedom of choice includes the right to make mistakes (Davis, 2009).

For younger children freedom of choice must also be an option for them which is linked in to their developmental stage as a starting point. Again, this is a difficult situation as children who have been subjected to abuse can have poor cognitive and emotional development, which must be taken into account in the process of establishing the wishes and feelings of this group of children (Iwaniec, 2006).

The effects of 'the system' on children can be very powerful and workers must show respect for the child's views and how important these are, along with working in an open and honest way and not making promises that cannot be delivered.

INCLUDING THE VIEWS OF OTHER PROFESSIONALS

Professionals involved in assessment processes include teachers, school or nursery staff, health visitors, foster carers, school nurses or other specialist healthcare professionals such as CAMHS (**Child and Adolescent Mental Health Service**), and agencies such as the Youth Offending Service (YOS). There may also be a variety of other professionals working with the adults in the family from organisations such as housing, police, probation, substance misuse teams and mental health services along with the family. Much of the public and fellow professionals' misunderstanding about social workers stems from a lack of knowledge about their specific role and about when social workers might get involved with a family. An example of a strategy designed to clarify this issue can be seen in the following threshold standards that have been developed by Worcestershire Safeguarding Children's Board and Worcestershire Children's Trust Board (2011) to help delineate the types of cases in which it is realistic for statutory social work teams to prioritise. This guidance is preceded by a statement that children's needs can change over time and that different levels of response will be accordingly appropriate.

THRESHOLDS FOR INTERVENTION

THRESHOLDS IN WORCESTERSHIRE

Thresholds have been developed based on a continuum of need and services in order to promote early identification of concerns by **universal services**. This approach utilises a four-tier model that takes into account the different stages of need and types of intervention (see model below). Within each tier of the model there are specific planning processes and a range of services available. Children and young people can access services from different tiers at different times in accordance with their changing needs, while continuing to receive universal services throughout their childhood.

TIER 1: UNIVERSAL SERVICES

Universal services are those provided to all families and children from health, education, and other community, voluntary, and private services such as leisure, play, housing and early years. The majority of children and young people make at least satisfactory overall progress in all areas of their development within effective inclusive universal provision.

TIER 2: TARGETED SERVICES TO MEET ADDITIONAL NEEDS

Some children and young people have additional needs or experience barriers to progress that cannot be met through universal services alone and where targeted services, which complement and build upon the work of universal providers, are required. There are a variety of early intervention services available including children's centres, early intervention family support teams, professionals supporting access to learning, and some voluntary and community services. Some children will need additional support from a service without which they would be at risk of not reaching their full potential. In other cases it may be that needs are unclear and information needs to be shared, or that a co-ordinated approach by a number of agencies is necessary, leading to the initiation of an assessment using the CAF.

TIER 3: SPECIALIST SERVICES TO MEET COMPLEX NEEDS

In tier 3 children and young people will have complex needs to the extent that their health, development and well-being will be impaired without intervention. At this level children and young people will need to be supported through multi-agency plans which are co-ordinated by the appropriate lead agency, for example, children's social care services, YOS, education services, community health services and CAMHS.

TIER 4: SPECIALIST SERVICES TO MEET
CRITICAL/ACUTE NEEDS

At this tier a child or young person's health or development has been impaired and they have suffered or are likely to suffer significant harm and have critical/acute needs. Examples would include children who are subject of a child protection plan, looked-after children, children who require a placement in a residential special school, children placed in a long-term hospital setting, or in a secure unit or Youth Offenders Institution (YOI).

Significantly, this threshold guidance is followed by a statement that such processes still need to be underpinned by the exercise of professional judgement, and a child-centred approach should guide all threshold decisions.

> **Reflective point**
>
> Do you think that threshold guidance such as the above is a helpful way of approaching the multiagency responsibilities towards our children?
> Do you envisage any problems in operationalising such a policy?
> If so, what skills/support might you call on to resolve any such problems?

THE COMMON ASSESSMENT FRAMEWORK

The CAF was introduced in 2004, as required by the Children Act 2004 and outlined in the *Every Child Matters* Green Paper (DfES, 2003), as a tool for early intervention. This approach, which is dependent on adults and children concerned being agreeable to undertake such an assessment, is relevant to Tier 2 above and would therefore not normally be led by a social worker. The CAF approach has much to commend it in its concept of the 'lead professional' who co-ordinates the issues around a family and in its very message, which is that all agencies have responsibilities towards children and families. The phrase 'Don't faff with a CAF' is a handy way of reminding you that CAF is not about child protection and neither is it a prerequisite to have had a CAF undertaken before making a referral to children's social care. The CAF should be used for children with additional needs, where practitioners require further multiagency understanding of a family. The use of CAF as a step down in respect of a child coming off a child protection plan is a recent proactive use of this system, whose effectiveness continues to be subject to evaluation (e.g. Easton et al., 2011). Findings to date suggest that where schools and health professionals embrace the spirit of CAF rather than see all family problems as being the sole domain of children's social care, then much positive work has been carried out. Conversely, where such professionals see their roles as being very specialist and do not want to work outside such boundaries, the opportunities that CAF presents to children and families are denied. Everybody is busy but what, for example, is the point of trying to teach maths to a child whose mind is preoccupied with his mum's mental health distress or the fear of eviction?

> **Reflective point**
>
> What has been the experience of CAF in your area of work?
> Ask colleagues across your network what their understanding is about CAF and try to find out whether there is any evaluation locally about the effectiveness of CAF and its impact on referral rates, children moving on to child protection plans or even children perhaps becoming accommodated.

Try to enquire as to why your colleagues think that the rates of success have been high or low?

How might you be able to make a difference to the way in which CAF has currently impacted in your locality?

MULTIAGENCY ASSESSMENT

Consulting with the array of professionals known to the family can help facilitate a balanced assessment particularly when one considers that the child and parents can present differently in different situations. Serious case reviews have identified failing to work in a multiagency context, which has resulted in harm or worse to children who were meant to be protected or supported by children's services. According to Lord Laming, 'some agencies still think they are helping out social care rather than thinking that safeguarding is everybody's responsibility' (DCSF, 2009: 36). Working across organisational barriers continues to be problematic and, as previously stated, assessments are undertaken in a multiagency context, therefore it is important to have an understanding of the different roles of each professional. Although a great deal of information can be obtained from this form of working, it also presents challenges in itself. Everyone involved in the assessment process should have clarity of purpose about the questions that need to be answered. Evidence rather than opinions or unsubstantiated information should form the basis of assessments. The expediency of the assessment will be dependent on the complexity, severity and immediacy of the child's situation. Holistic assessments must lead to objective professional judgements, with clear decision making and co-ordinated planning. There is also a need to distinguish between meanings attached to the professional's understanding of the situation and that of the child and family (Wilson et al., 2008). Greater understanding of how social workers undertake assessments has identified the need for staff to adopt a position of objective consideration and investigation of what has occurred, in preference to the tendency towards reassurance and justification that all is well. More importantly, relationship-based work adopted by social workers should not be for the benefit of the parents or for the benefit of the relationship itself, it is the child's needs which must be kept at the forefront of all relationship-based work (DCSF, 2009).

It is important to retain objectivity and integrity when undertaking the assessment process, particularly if professionals collude either against a family or in favour of them. Reasons why this may happen range from professionals feeling their concerns are not being taken seriously, or because they may have grown weary of a particular family, or because they feel the family deserves another chance. This conflict situation can prove to be challenging and can undermine the aim of the assessment process.

NEEDS VERSUS OUTCOMES

Traditionally, assessments have been needs led (some would say resource led), which has meant that the social worker, alongside other professionals and the family, has completed an assessment, identified the needs and offered services to meet those needs. The ever-expanding **personalisation** agenda, (Gardner, 2011) which started in the adult services, but is now more prevalent in children's services in respect of children with disabilities, has championed an assessment process that concentrates on outcomes rather than needs. The premise of this approach is that services will be tailored to what the child wants to achieve rather than the child or young person being fitted into available service provision.

This personalised approach is not being used in mainstream children's social care to any significant degree, but it does deserve a mention particularly as, in the current political climate, personalisation suits all political ideologies, and is viewed as being able to result in more cost-effective service provision as well as individualised care. Personalisation can also be interpreted as an alternative to the employment of social workers, whom many in government see as having 'failed' children.

A 'personalised' assessment looks at the outcomes identified for the child or young person and identifies how these will be achieved. These assessments have gathered momentum, particularly for young people with disabilities and are in transition to adulthood. An outcome-focused approach for social workers is a very different approach, which some have found to be extremely challenging, particularly as it is not easily quantifiable. Positives in the process are that the child or young person are kept central to, and more in control, of the process. However, from the social worker's perspective it takes longer to complete the assessment process. A great challenge in any social worker's growth and development is their ability to recognise issues of power and control, both within themselves (use of self) and within their role. In other words, part of effective working as a social worker is recognising and minimising the power differential between the child, young person, family and social worker (Koprowska, 2010).

DIVERSITY AND ASSESSMENT

The assessment process is by nature a complex one but there are many added complexities which social workers need to consider when they are trying to engage families. The following sections provide a consideration of some of those diverse issues.

ASSESSING THE UNBORN CHILD

An assessment may be requested regarding the circumstances of an unborn child, possibly because:

- Children were previously removed from one or both of the carers
- There are worries about parenting capacity, possibly in relation to domestic violence, mental health, learning disability or home environment
- There is known parental substance misuse
- There is an adult in the family home who poses a risk to children
- There are concerns about the mother's ability to protect the child
- A carer/s is known to social care; they may have been looked after and professionals may have expressed concern regarding their parental capabilities.

Evidence included in this form of assessment includes ante-natal, medical and obstetric history, and any actual or potential complications as well as compliance regarding the mother accessing services. A significant factor is also the age of the mother and the extent and quality of her support network if she is very young.

The parental relationship needs to be examined along with the effect a new baby will have on the main carer. Previous relationship problems, outcomes of any previous involvement of children's services including extended family members who have been in the care system or subject to a child protection plan need to be identified. A possible difficulty is assessing the potential parental capabilities of a mother or father if they do not already have children. Along with investigating the family and community networks, the assessment needs to include the capacity for change if this has been identified as a need for the welfare and safeguarding of the unborn child. Social and family networks also need to be explored, as well as parenting style, capacity for change, positive experiences, and hopes and fears for the future.

SITUATIONS OF DOMESTIC VIOLENCE

According to Cleaver et al. (1999) it is difficult to quantify the extent of domestic violence, although evidence suggests that 'adult partners who are violent toward each other are also at an increased risk of abusing their children' (Cleaver et al., 1999: 20). This statement is, however, difficult to measure, as other studies have found that mothers living in abusive relationships believe that their children are unharmed.

Both parents must be included in the assessment process if they are jointly taking responsibility for bringing up the child. This will include any new partner who becomes part of the mother's life during her pregnancy, inclusive of a new partner who does not appear to be part of the household. The assessment includes the non-abusive parent and their ability to protect their child if applicable. It is important that both parents gain an understanding of the previous abuse, and to establish whether both would be able to identify any future risks or areas of vulnerability which reduce their ability to protect the child.

Intricate to the assessment is gaining an understanding of the parents' knowledge of how to care for and their understanding of a child's needs. If support has been made available to help improve this area, then the assessment should include whether any learning has taken place. A further aspect is gaining an understanding of the attachment between their own parents and whether they are demonstrating an attachment to the unborn child or not.

MEN AND THE ASSESSMENT PROCESS

All too often men are absent from assessments in relation to children. This can happen because fathers may not be living in the same household; partners who are in the household are not seen as being important because they are not the father; the father does not seem to be very involved or whoever the adult male is may be a frightening figure and it is easier not to engage with him. Cleaver et al. (1999) have identified that men are absent figures in child protection investigations, suggesting it is in the man's best interests to remain invisible in order to protect himself. Also, in child protection enquiries in which the father was the perpetrator of the abuse, it has been found that social workers directed their interventions at the mother. A factor that could be influential in this situation is an understandable reluctance on the social workers' part to address difficult and potentially violent situations.

There is an argument that to empower other family members while involving the man is complicated, as he will often exercise the power within the household and this may need to be limited to increase the power held by the other family members. Men, however, can be a valuable resource in the family and it is unhelpful to overlook them during the assessment process as they may play a substantial role in planning if the family is in need of extra support. It is also essential to include men where they are thought to be 'perpetrators of abuse' as you can gain a good understanding of their views, what their future actions are likely to be and how this might impact on their children.

ASSESSMENT AND MINORITY ETHNIC GROUPS

Since discrimination of all kinds is an everyday reality in many children's lives every effort must be made to ensure that agencies' responses do not reflect or reinforce that experience and indeed, should counteract it (DH, 2000b: 12). The effectiveness of assessing families from different minority ethnic groups will depend on the ability of the social worker to work in a way which is both anti-oppressive and which recognises cultural difference. The aim will be to identify and meet the needs of children from these groups. This can be achieved by working in partnership with the families and supporting them to identify their own strengths and needs (DH, 2000a).

The social worker should be aware that, although there is much agreement in mainstream literature about the developmental needs of children, these are primarily based on **eurocentric** concepts and may not always be directly applicable to people from other cultural groups. The specific identity needs of children from minority ethnic groups must be considered because their knowledge about their origins and their culture will be different from children in the indigenous population.

When assessing parenting capacity it is important that as a social worker you are sensitive to culturally relevant differences, without making the criteria 'less stringent' (Banks, 2006). The assessment process may be compromised if culture is ignored as it is impossible to meaningfully assess any child outside of their cultural context. However, the social worker must be aware of their own response to cultural difference and beware of taking a restrictive view of this. Social workers from the same or similar backgrounds to the families with whom they work can also discriminate in a number of ways. Use of self is again critical here and you must always reflect on your own experiences and prejudice in this difficult political arena.

Reflective point

- What are the minority groups in the community where you work?
- What prejudices might exist in you, your family, your colleagues and your friends about these minorities?
- How much knowledge do you have about the value systems in these minority groups?
- Do you have enough knowledge to make effective assessments on their children? If not, how can you acquire such knowledge?

The use of language is important and the way that things may be described to you; for instance, words such as smacking, beating, licking and whipping to describe physical punishments may be used and interpreted very differently by different people. It is important to confirm actual behaviour and actions rather than subjectively interpreting a phrase used.

There should never be an over-reliance on cultural explanations as there is a danger that facts can be ignored and family dysfunction can be interpreted as arising from the culture rather than the behaviour. There is a balance to be struck between taking a stance that race/colour/faith/sexuality is not an issue for you (because you are so committed to equality of opportunity) and seeing the issue of race/colour/faith/sexuality as the overriding issues that dominate assessment and all other work with children and families. The politically correct debate has often been detrimental to children in need or at risk and has also not helped the image of social work. Social work is rightly proud to have at its core a commitment to equality and social justice, but the critical and open debate that we need to be having in our workplaces and communities about 'politically correct' issues, especially those of race and faith, is not happening. Many professionals and citizens are afraid of saying 'the wrong thing' and this cannot be a healthy state of affairs. With regard to children in need of adoption, government guidance (DfE, 2011a) has declared that it is no longer acceptable to make children in need of adoption wait for the right ethnic match. The appropriate child-centred policy is now to match children with prospective adopters who can meet their needs, with matching of ethnicities and cultures being secondary considerations.

KEY ISSUES IN THE ASSESSMENT OF CHILDREN WITH DISABILITIES

Disabled children are likely to warrant having an assessment solely because of their disability and this will often be linked to their parents/carers' ability to cope with the extra demands on their time and parenting skills due to the greater level of care these children require. For this group of children, assessment is the route to receiving service provision through Section 17 of the Children Act 1989, which identifies a disabled child as being a child in need.

Children with disabilities and their families are subject to multiple assessments from other professionals, therefore a wealth of information may already be available. Core assessments are highly relevant for children with disabilities with good assessments possibly leading to positive changes. The assessment process must also include the needs of the parents/carers. Challenges within the assessment process may include obtaining the views of the child, many of this group of children having difficulties in communication. It is essential that, as a social worker for the child, you find out how they use their communication tools so that they can be involved in the decision-making process. Parents/carers of this group of children will often need extra support but, at the same time, it is still the child's needs that are being assessed and not those of the parents/carers. For the needs of the carers there is a separate assessment process to support them. The Carers Equal Opportunity Act 2004 places a legal duty on local authorities to inform carers of their right to an assessment of their needs that takes into account their work and leisure activities (Brammer, 2010).

When assessing children with disabilities, factors that need to be taken into account include the fact that such children tend to be more socially disadvantaged, and there is also a strong identifiable relationship between poverty and childhood disability. Social workers also need to explore their understanding of disability and access information to help them understand the child's condition (DH, 2000a). From a safeguarding perspective, children with disabilities are at increased risk due to their extra needs which make them more vulnerable; for example, living in residential settings, their specialist communication needs and their requirement for intimate personal care in some situations (Foley et al., 2001). Further issues that may need to be taken into account if the parents also have a disability, is their own right to an assessment of their care needs and service provision under the Community Care Act 1990 (Brammer, 2010).

SOME COMMON MISTAKES AND HOW TO AVOID THEM

- Do not underestimate information given by family, friends, neighbours, as this may be as important as or more important than information from other sources
- Do not ignore the child, always listen to children and pay attention to what they say. Make sure that you have been given appropriate access to all of the children in the family and that you have used a communication method which they can understand. Consider what the evidence is to either support or refute what the child has said
- Do not focus all of your attention on the presenting problem, make sure that you make a holistic assessment and that you do not miss other concerns
- Do not be pressured by 'high status' referrers, think clearly about the information you have and whether you would see it differently if it came from a different source
- Do not assume that everyone understands what you say. Double check with the family, including the children, that they know what is happening and what will happen next
- Do not allow assumptions and pre-judgements to lead to misinterpretation, think about what the evidence is to support or to refute your assumptions
- Do not misinterpret parental behaviour, think about the reasons for their behaviour and whether it is co-operative or not
- Do not assume that the family do not need any ongoing support just because you have assessed the children as 'not being at risk'. Consider if they need support and who should provide that support before closing the case
- Do not collude with a family because they are aggressive or frightening, make sure that you are safe and ask for the support you need to ensure this, because if you are frightened the children may be too and you need to make sure the children in the household are safe
- Do not forget to take into account the strengths that families have and the resilience factors in respect of their children that can be built on.

CHAPTER SUMMARY

Assessment accounts for a large part of what social workers do in their working lives, especially when they are in statutory settings. As the above chapter has demonstrated, the skills needed for effective assessment are complex. Use of self is critical, knowing who you are – your strengths, the effects of your background and your own moral/value base. Knowledge of your organisation, its remit, its culture and the legal framework in which you are acting is essential. You need, with support and guidance from management and colleagues, to establish facts, make judgements, form a range of relationships and to be accountable in a variety of ways for your actions. Good assessment is at the heart of good social work and if you can hone your assessment skills, you will be well on the way to being an effective social worker. Case study 6.1 will help you reflect on what you might do in the situations presented and the skills and strengths you might draw on.

The Richards Family

Mrs Richards is a Black African Caribbean woman with three children aged eight, five and three. She has few friends and no family in the neighbourhood. Her husband is in prison, where he is nearing the end of a three-year sentence for dealing in cannabis. Her eight-year-old daughter, Millie, and five-year-old son, Dwayne, are having problems at school with being bullied and sometimes falling asleep in the day time. The three-year-old daughter, Leanne, is attaining all her standard developmental milestones. Mrs Richards says people 'look down' on her and recently she withdrew Leanne from nursery because of this belief.

Mrs Richards is struggling financially and has turned up at your office asking if all three children could go into foster care in order to give her a break as she is mentally and physically exhausted and needs to get the house cleaned up for her husband's imminent return.

How would you approach the assessment of this complex situation?

What techniques might you use to empathise with Mrs Richards and yet ensure that the children were at the centre of your considerations?

What does your intuition tell you about this case and what critical thinking will you need to do before formulating any plan?

Will you involve Mr Richards at all in your assessment?

Initial Assessment of Connor Harvey, 16 years

Please read the initial assessment on the following pages, which is based on a real-life situation. Critique this assessment in terms of its fitness for purpose and consider how you might discuss its contents with Connor and his father if you were allocated this case.

Chronology of John Smith

Read the chronology (pp. 104–10) and consider whether you would find it useful if you were allocated John's case.

Do you think that this chronology is recorded in ways that would be helpful to John if he ever wanted to know about his background?

Case Study 2 – Initial Assessment

Referral and Assessment Service
Nowhere
Tel:
Fax:

Initial Assessment

Details of Child: Connor Harvey

Family Name	Harvey	Given Names	Connor
Actual DOB	30-June-1995	Gender	Male
Ethnicity	White Irish	Primary Language	
Primary Address	3 Cosy Nook Anytown	Telephone (Mobile Phone)	
		Mobile	
		CSSR Case No	
Secondary Address		Current Address	

Initial Assessment Dates

Date Referral Received	29-Sep-2010
Initial Assessment Commenced	30-Sep-2010
Initial Assessment Due	08-Oct-2010
Initial Assessment Completed	04-Oct-2010
Was the Child/Young Person seen during this assessment?	Yes
If the child has not been seen, can this assessment be completed?	
If the child has not been seen and you are authorising this assessment to be completed, please give a reason for your decision:	

(Continued)

(Continued)

Reason/Information

Reason for initial assessment, including views of child/young person and parent/carers	Connor is not living at home and is refusing to go back, despite Dad wanting him home. Connor has depression and is under CAMHS. Dad has concerns that he is not taking his medication for depression. Dad is concerned that Connor is smoking cannabis and taking speed. Not attended school this academic year. No one has known where or who he is living with until today. Connor is living with an unknown male called Joe Brown who is 18 years old. Connor has been in school today and has bruises to face and chest and is unwell with a possible chest infection. There are concerns over his hygiene and general well-being. Connor has been giving Joe money but this has now stopped and Connor now has no money.
Date(s) child/young person and family members seen/interviewed	*List is empty*

Agencies contributing to initial assessment:	Role	Key Agency	Professional	Contributed	Details
	SCH	East School	–		

Child/Young Persons Development Needs

Health

Child's Needs	Connor is in good physical health although on first meeting he was reported to be suffering from headache symptoms following a drinking spree the night before. Whilst Connor has not raised any significant health concerns, information presented to the department would suggest that Connor is currently experimenting with drugs and alcohol on a frequent basis which has also contributed to the relationship he will experience with his father and family. Referral had been made for Connor to seek support around alcohol and substance misuse but he has not engaged with this service. Connor has the tendency to disengage and avoid professionals so he can do as he pleases. He has also received support (counselling) from CAMHS due historical concerns of presenting with anxiety, isolation and depression. At the time of writing this assessment Connor's mental health has deteriorated and he has been admitted to ward 14 at Anytown Hospital following concerns raised around self harm and threat to suicide. Connor will be assessed by a specialist clinic on the 12th November 2010. Connor very much struggles to manage his situation and circumstances which is compounded by the underlying mental health issues that he presents with.

Education	
Child's Needs	Connor is enrolled at East School. His attendance has raised concerns as this is reported to be poor. Connor also presents with additional learning needs and does have an individual educational plan. Connor is also required to attend College on a part time basis; again attendance is reported to be poor. Despite this it has been noted that when Connor does attend school he engages well. He has a good working relationship with his Learning Mentor at school who will also offer additional support outside of school. It is felt that Connor's behaviour has deteriorated since associating with a group of friends that he met at college. Whilst Connor's behaviour is not reported to be a concern within school when he attends, his interactions with older boys have placed him in a difficult situation both practically and emotionally. There are ongoing feuds that Connor will become involved in with his peers.

Emotional and Behavioural Development	
Child's Needs	Connor presents as a young person who will very much fluctuate with his moods, personality and responses, which will often cause his behaviour to be sporadic and unpredictable. Connor has been engaging in anti social behaviour where he is also known to be experimenting with alcohol and substances. His actions have led to further interventions when he has been reported missing; failing to return home for a period of time, disengaging and avoiding professionals, as well as presenting with attention seeking behaviour. Whilst Connor is aware of his circumstances he does not appear to take responsibility for his actions and will become resistant whilst also laughing at his actions which causes concerns for others. At the same time Connor is recognised to be a likeable person as his character can also be humorous and this draws attention from others; Connor very much sees his support networks as being his friends, despite their non allegiance to him. This further demonstrates that Connor can place himself in vulnerable positions in order to be liked by his peers, which has created further difficulties in his relationship with his family who have reported Connor coming back home late into the morning intoxicated, also bringing friends who are intoxicated resulting in altercations with his older siblings.

(Continued)

(Continued)

Identity	
Child's Needs	Connor is a young person of White Irish background. He will meet his own identity needs with very little resistance from his father. Connor has spoken about his sexuality and is in the early stages of experimenting with relationships though he has not disclosed any sexual/personal relationships he has with others when discussed further with him by professionals including social care and Police. Connor is fully aware that he is not of age to have a sexual relationship with another person as he is underage.
Family and Social Relationships	
Child's Needs	Refer to sections above. Connor's relationship with his immediate family members can become very fraught as a response to his actions and behaviours which will add to the stresses that the family are experiencing with him. Connor very much takes the lead in his relationship with his father often dictating what he wants to do. Father equally lacks self confidence and self esteem to follow through with behaviour management strategies.
Social Presentation	
Child's Needs	Connor can at times be observed to be well presented. This will deteriorate if he has not been living at home, spending time with friends, often experimenting with alcohol and substances. Connor is also reported to be self harming and will easily revert to self harm as a response to his situation and if he is not able to get what he wants.
Selfcare Skills	
Child's Needs	Connor is able to undertake all of his selfcare.
Attributes of Parents/Carers Capacities	
Attributes of parents'/carers' capacities which affect their ability to respond appropriately to the child/young persons' needs	Father is noted to be suffering from depression/anxiety/OCD which he is taking medication for. Father does struggle with implementing boundaries with Connor; this relationship is very much led by Connor and not father. Father lacks self esteem and confidence in his relationship with Connor, which has in turn led to Connor pushing boundaries.
Should a referral be made to adult services?	No

Family and Environmental Factors	
Family history and functioning	Father has been the primary carer for Connor since he was six months old. There has been infrequent contact between Connor and his mother. Whilst father is noted to be the primary carer for Connor this relationship is led by Connor himself, he is reported to have taken a lot of responsibility at a young age in caring for his father in response to his mental health concerns.
Wider family	Connor does have a good range of support networks around him, including paternal grandmother who will support both father and Connor. Connor also has an older sister who lives independently and whom he has lived with. Again this relationship can easily become fractured due to Connor's actions.
Housing	Family address is private rented; home conditions very clean and well furnished. no concerns. Connor has his own room which was observed to be clean. no concerns identified.
Employment	Father is not in any employment.
Income	Father in receipt of all relevant benefits for himself and Connor.
Family's social integration	Connor will isolate himself from his family due to his interactions with his peers which will take the main focus.
Community resources	CAMHS/ SCHOOL. Connor however will not always engage with professionals and will also avoid contact from professionals.
Analysis	
Analysis of information gathered during the initial assessment	Concerns have been raised as to Connor's mental health which is impacting on his presenting behaviour and actions. Whilst father will give into Connor's needs and requests very easily, father is not considered to be a risk for his son. Father does require additional support from agencies; family mediation has been offered to Connor and father via CAMHS. However Connor's mental health concerns have taken priority and this requires further intervention by the appropriate service. There are no risks associated with Connor returning home. Social Care will need to continue to monitor the case and offer support where identified.

(Continued)

(Continued)

Decisions	
Is the child/young person a child in need as defined in the Children Act 1989?	Yes
If yes, please tick which child in need category(ies) is/are appropriate:	
a) a child whose vulnerability is such they are unlikely to reach or maintain a satisfactory level of health or development without the provision of services	Yes
b) child whose health or development will be significantly impaired without the provision of services (is suffering or is likely to suffer significant harm)	
c) disabled child	
If the child is disabled, please record the types of impairment(s) (using the children in need categories)	
If the child's name is not on the disability register, have the parents consented to it being placed there?	

Further Action	
Initial Assessment Completed	04-Oct-2010

Action Taken	
Strategy Discussion	No
Legal Action	No
Core Assessment	No

Place into Accommodation	No
Provide Short Term Services	Yes
Specialist Assessment	No
Referral to Other Agency	No
Other Actions	No
Private Fostering Arrangement Assessment	No
No Further Action	No
Reasons for this Action Taken	To continue to monitor. CAMHS have a vital role in Connor's mental health which is an outstanding concern for all involved. There is a clear need to assess Connor's mental health and then look at what support needs to be offered, this will also depend on Connor's engagement.
Other agencies – please specify	
If development needs are identified in a child/ young person and services are not to be provided or are not available, please explain why:	
If an Initial Assessment was not completed within seven working days, please give the reason(s) why	
Signatures	
Name of Social Worker completing assessment	Jane Harris
Signature:	
Name of Manager	Sam Green
Signature:	

(Continued)

(Continued)

Initial Plan

Planning

Plan Revision	1.0
Plan Effective From	04-Oct-2010
Plan Effective To	01-Dec-2010

Child's Developmental Needs

Needs & Strengths	Outcomes	Service Provisions
Connor to engage in support services that are being offered to him including CAMHS and Family Mediation (via CAMHS service)	Unmet	
Connor to continue to take his medication as prescribed and recommended by his GP/CAMHS for depression and anxiety. Connor needs to ensure that he is not mixing his medication with alcohol/drugs; Connor is aware that this will have further implications on his ability to experience stability. Connor also needs to engage with CAMHS with review appointments when they are arranged.	Unmet	
Connor understands that every time he is absent from the family address for a period of time he will be reported missing. Connor also clearly understands that legally he is still required to be living at his home address despite his wishes and feelings. Connor is informed that every time he is absent he will be brought back to family address.	Unmet	
Connor needs to experience stability in the care he receives from his family members. Concerns raised where Connor has been self harming and also threatening to self harm. There are concerns about Connor's mental health issues which are also impacting on presenting behaviour.	Unmet	

Parental Capacity

Needs & Strengths		Outcomes	Service Provisions	
	Unmet			
Father needs to remain consistent with the messages he relays to Connor.				
	Unmet			
Father to receive additional support around his capacity to manage Connor's behaviour. In addition the relationship between father and Connor also needs addressing. Family mediation has been identified via CAMHS.				

Recorded Feedback

The completed Initial Assessment should be discussed with the child/young person and their parents/carers.

Person		Discussed	If no, when	Given	If no, when
Connor Harvey, 16 years					
Jack Harvey, 18 years	Brother				
Don Harvey, 50 years	Father				
Dianne Harvey	Sister				
Janice Knowles	Mother				

Case Study 3 – Chronology

Name: John Smith	Date of Birth: 13.01.2008	Cowleyshire Children's Social Care

GUIDANCE NOTES: *In line with the Laming Report this chronology is a means of showing significant events, sequences of events, and the age of the child when they occurred. The information should be used to inform assessments – in particular, the possible impact of events, taking into consideration the age and developmental stage of a child – and to build up a record of a child's history.*

A range of significant events can be recorded - moves, changes of carers, birth of siblings, new members joining the household, specific achievements etc. Events may be significant from the perspective of the worker even if the child/family does not regard them as so, or significant from the perspective of the child and their carers.

This form should be completed in such a way that should a child in later years request access to their records, they would recognise the special and significant times and this should lead them to locate the information they seek.

Age of Child	Date	Event	Source
Unborn	3.07.2007	Referral received by Social Care from community midwife to inform that Janet was pregnant. Initially she was going to have a termination but later decided not to. Three older children, Jane, Julie and Jo are all subject to Care Orders. Janet is an adult who poses a risk to children owing to wilful neglect of her first child. Janet is now divorced from her husband and is in a relationship with Ben Jones who is a known prolific perpetrator of domestic violence.	
	11.08.07	Concerns expressed by Susan Harrison, Perinatal CPN as she was unable to assess Janet when she visited because she had smoked cannabis the previous night and on the morning of the visit. Susan Harrison has arranged for the consultant psychiatrist who specialises in pre-birth concerns to complete an assessment. Appointment defaulted. Susan Harrison was concerned that Mother would be unable to care for the children.	

24.11.2007	Initial Child Protection Conference: Background information: Jane born 1997 and became the subject of child protection conference following an incident whereby she sustained a suspicious burn to her hand. After further concerns a Residence Order was granted to maternal grandparents in 1998. Julie was born in 1999 and was made subject to a child protection conference. This was owing to the previous concerns around Jane. Several referrals were made to social services in relation to Janet not being able to cope with meeting Julie's basic care needs. This culminated in Julie becoming under-weight and dehydrated and presenting with suspicious bruising. Janet was convicted of wilful neglect. Janet and her partner at the time were assessed within a Residential Unit but this was not successful. Julie was also placed with maternal grandparents and was made subject to a Residence Order. Jo was born in 2002 and her name was placed on the child protection register under the category of neglect. There was an agreement that Jo should be placed in foster care while assessments in respect of parents were undertaken. Jo later went to live with her paternal aunt.
30.01.08	Home visit made by social worker. Janet talked about how she had a positive relation-ship with all of her children.
10.02.08	Review Child Protection Case Conference, John currently in foster care. The social worker presented information to the conference and reported that the older children had contact with their mother, that there was an emotional bond between them and that the relationship between Janet and Ben was supportive with no evidence of domestic violence. Owing to the positive information around Janet engaging with services the plan was for John to return home to his mother's care.
May 2008	No concerns around commitment to contact with older siblings. Emotional bond apparent for both parents with John. Janet and Ben are mutually supportive of each other. Janet engaging with CPN and family assistant.

(Continued)

(Continued)

02.06.08	Child minder assigned owing to Janet feeling increasingly tired.
06.08.08	John's name was removed from the Child Protection Register.
28.11.08	Case closed to social work input.
15.12.08	Emergency Duty Team referral. Ben was arrested for a domestic violence incident against Janet; the incident was witnessed by Jane who called the Police.
20.12.08	Referral received from Sandra Hobbs – Benefits Advice Officer. Mrs Hobbs visited the family and was told by Janet that she is having suicidal thoughts and is not taking her medication. Janet appeared to be neglecting herself and was in soiled clothes with matted hair at time of interview. Mrs Hobbs was raising concerns around the children's safety.
21.12.08	Case re-allocated to a social worker. When she spoke to the health visitor and childminder they were also raising concerns around John's development.
12.02.09	Home visit by social worker. Janet said that she and Ben had separated and that she had not seen him for three weeks. A parenting course was suggested to Janet but she was not keen to go saying that she had done these before and knew what to do, she said she would think about it.
06.03.09	Planning Meeting: John to start playgroup, Janet attending the parenting course, concerns about John's speech – the older children all have learning difficulties.
15.03.09	Janet unable to take John to playgroup as she had a medical appointment.
21.03.09	Janet could not take John to playgroup as he had been ill.
28.03.09	Janet saying John is still not well enough to attend playgroup.
19.04.09	Janet phoned the social worker, she is worried about Ben as he has been calling around the house. She says she has been ignoring him and said that she had thrown his clothes onto the street.
26.04.09	John did not attend the playgroup.

Date	Detail
03.05.09	Janet phoned the social worker and said that she had seen Ben at the bank and he had been very aggressive towards her. He had informed her that he could see John whenever he liked. Janet said she told him that she needed to ignore his calls and that should he arrive at the property she would call the Police.
07.05.09	Care Proceedings started.
11.05.09	Home visit by social worker. Janet was at home with John, she said that John was not interested in toys and preferred the TV. Janet was advised that she try and get John interested by playing with him – Janet said that she would need a portage worker to be creative and try to gain his interest. It was agreed that a portage worker would be identified and would assist Janet in playing with John.
11.06.09	Home visit to Sam Harvey (Jo's paternal aunt). The purpose of the visit was to discuss the issue of contact between Janet and Jo. Sam said that Janet had stopped seeing Jo. She said that Janet had tried contact once a month for two hours but this did not prove successful and that Janet had not had any contact for two years.
05.08.09	Case transferred to another social worker.
10.08.09	Home visit completed by new social worker. Home conditions of a good standard.
12.10.09	Mother again engaging with nursery, attendance was good. Portage work had started.
12.11.09	Educational Psychologist reported: John's speech is significantly delayed. John diagnosed as having global developmental delay.
24.12.09	Home visit by social worker, the home environment was clean and tidy. Present during the home visit was a male friend of Janet who appeared to be a frequent visitor.
09.01.10	Phone call from police to report that Janet's friend who was now staying at the home address is of serious concern to the Police for offences including: Assault on ex-partner. Assault on unknown female. He has been detained under the Mental Health Act. Conviction for theft.

(Continued)

14.03.10	E-mail from Emergency Duty Team to report that Janet had contacted them to report that her ex-partner had broken the terms of his non-molestation order.
	Social worker made a visit to Janet – she showed her the broken window where Ben had broken in. She said that he was drunk but she had to let him out through the house and out of the front door.
	Home conditions: front living room was particularly untidy, kitchen was grubby.
15.03.10	Telephone call received from police who expressed concern that Janet had not contacted the police immediately. If the police had been called and Ben was on the premises there would have been a clear breach of the Order and he would have been arrested. Instead of locking her back door she had allowed him through the property. When this was reported on the 12th July Janet said she was not available to make a statement.
	Again on the 13th July she was not available to make a statement. Police were concerned that once again, and despite clear advice Janet had not acted appropriately. Police suggested a strategy meeting given the most recent incident and also the concern about Janet's new boyfriend being a part of the household.
17.03.10	Social worker contacted Janet to advise her that the Local Authority were becoming increasingly concerned about her ability to protect the children.
	Later that day Janet made a statement to the Police.
08.05.10	Full Care Order issued by the Family Proceedings Court, John to remain living at home with his mother.
07.07.10	Home visit by social worker to collect John from Janet's house for contact with Ben. The living room was very untidy and it was determined that a 19-year-old friend of Janet's was staying with her and sleeping on the floor, her boyfriend was also staying.
	Contact with Ben and paternal grandmother was observed to be positive.
	On returning to the property Janet wished to have further discussion with the social worker. She relayed that she was upset about John's recent diagnosis. She said the consultant had predicted that he would become particularly difficult for her to manage. Janet said that she was already finding his behaviour at home difficult.

	The social worker had not observed any particularly difficult behaviour. On the contrary John is usually quietly and happily occupied even if he does seem sometimes to be in his own separate world. The issue is more that Janet does not make the effort and does not seem to find much pleasure interacting with the children. The social worker went over the reasons as to why other adults should not be in the house. He then became aware of another man in the kitchen washing the dishes, Janet was unclear about who this was.
03.10.10	LAC Review Concerns shared about Janet allowing other adults into the home.
02.11.10	Telephone call from Janet to Social Care – she said that she is having problems with harassment from her neighbours who she says are calling John names.
13.12.10	The Police made a visit to the property owing to a neighbour reporting that she heard John crying all night. Janet said that John had chicken pox. There were also concerns expressed about John being left with inappropriate adults.
17.02.11	Janet refused to allow access to workers who had come to speak to her about a parenting course which had been organised for her.
17.04.11	Concerns expressed that Janet's boyfriend seems to undertake a lot of the caring of the boy, the social worker spoke to Janet about this and she did not think there was any problem. John was seen and seemed well and cheerful, he was playing with Janet's boyfriend.
03.05.11	Janet had informed her CPN that she has major problems getting John to sleep but there is a male family friend who comes to look after him when she goes out. When he does this he makes a bed downstairs and the two of them sleep together. The CPN also stated that there was a man present during the visit but he did not come out of the kitchen.

(Continued)

		The social worker spoke to Janet about this and she denied that John slept in the same bed but said that her boyfriend slept on the chair when John slept in the living room. She accused the CPN of calling her friend a paedophile.
	4.06.11	Janet was having suicidal thoughts which she initially denied but eventually admitted and said this was out of frustration. She agreed to work closely with her CPN.
	10.02.11	John's nursery expressed concerns to Social Care about John watching horror films; he had been speaking explicitly about them. They also said that when John came into nursery he was hungry and went straight to the snack bar and was rifling through other children's lunch boxes.
	15.03.11	The social worker contacted Janet to say that given she had admitted that her boyfriend was staying in the family home a risk assessment would need to be completed and a CRB undertaken and that this would need to be done prior to the Local Authority agreeing that he could remain. Janet said that she wanted the assessment undertaken as soon as possible.

FURTHER RESOURCES AND READING

Brammer, A. (2010) *Social Work Law*, 3rd edn. Harlow: Pearson Education.

Cleaver, H., Unell, I. and Aldgate, J. (1999) *Children's Needs – Parenting Capacity: The Impact of Parental Mental Illness, Problem Alcohol and Drug Use and Domestic Violence on Children's Development*. London: The Stationery Office.

Cocker, C. and Allain, L. (2008) *Social Work with Looked after Children*. Exeter: Learning Matters.

Davis, L. (2009) *The Social Worker's Guide to Children and Families Law*. London: Jessica Kingsley Publishers.

Department for Children Schools and Families (2009) *The Protection of Children in England: A Progress Report*. London: HMSO (https://www.education.gov.uk/publications/eOrderingDownload/HC-330.pdf).

Department for Education (2011a) *Adoption Guidance, Adoption and Children Act* 2002, First Revision: February 2011. London: HMSO (http://media.education.gov.uk/assets/files/pdf/a/statutory%20guidance.pdf).

Department of Health (2000b) *Framework for the Assessment of Children in Need and their Families*. London: HMSO (www.dh.gov.uk/en/Publicationsandstatistics/Publications/PublicationsPolicyAndGuidance/DH_4008144).

Horwath, J. (2010) (ed.) *The Child's World, The Comprehensive Guide to Assessing Children in Need*. London: Jessica Kingsley Publishers.

Koprowska, J. (2010) *Communication and Interpersonal Skills in Social Work*. Exeter: Learning Matters.

NSPCC (2009) Gillick Competency and Fraser Guidelines. This factsheet discusses the seminal case that addressed consent laws for the under 16s (www.nspcc.org.uk/inform/research/questions/gillick_wda61289.html).

Parker, J. and Bradley, G. (2010) *Social Work Practice. Assessment, Planning, Intervention and Review*, 3rd edn. Exeter: Learning Matters. This is a very good resource for assessment tools such as genograms and ecomaps.

Trevithick, P. (2000) *Social Work Skills. A Practice Handbook*. Buckingham: Open University Press. This is a detailed and practical handbook that goes into depth with regard to communication skills. Many practical extracts from social work interviews are given to illuminate skills.

7

SAFEGUARDING, CHILD PROTECTION AND YOUR CHANCE TO MAKE A DIFFERENCE

Key Points of Chapter

- Safeguarding represents a preventative approach to keeping all of our children safe
- Child protection largely concerns formal processes with children whose care has reached levels of concern that might suggest that they are at risk of 'significant harm'
- There is a great deal of evidence out there about how to safeguard children – read it!
- There are clear definitions of child abuse – physical, sexual, emotional and neglect. These need to be contextualised with the child's environment
- Professional judgement has a core role in child protection – it is not all about meeting deadlines and ticking (electronic) boxes
- You must promote best ways of working in your organisation and challenge your practice

Proposed Professional Capabilities Framework areas covered in this chapter

- Professionalism
- Values and Ethics
- Diversity
- Rights, Justice and Poverty
- Knowledge
- Critical Reflection and Analysis
- Interventions and Skills
- Contexts and Organisations
- Professional Leadership

(Social Work Reform Board, 2010 – see Appendix 1)

Draft Standards of Proficiency for Social Workers in England covered in this chapter

1 Be able to practise safely and effectively within their scope of practice
2 Be able to practise within the legal and ethical boundaries of their profession
3 Be able to maintain fitness to practise
4 Be able to practise as an autonomous professional, exercising their own professional judgement
5 Be aware of the impact of culture, equality and diversity on practice
6 Be able to practise in a non-discriminatory manner
7 Be able to maintain confidentiality
8 Be able to communicate effectively
9 Be able to work appropriately with others
10 Be able to maintain records appropriately
11 Be able to reflect on and review practice
12 Be able to assure the quality of their practice
13 Understand the key concepts of the bodies of knowledge which are relevant to their profession

(Continued)

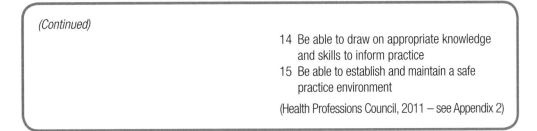

(Continued)

14 Be able to draw on appropriate knowledge and skills to inform practice

15 Be able to establish and maintain a safe practice environment

(Health Professions Council, 2011 – see Appendix 2)

INTRODUCTION

Most of the headlines about social workers, for example, about social workers failing again (Donnelly, 2009), relate to reported cases whereby social workers have known of a child's circumstances but that child has been seriously injured or even killed. While it should never happen that children who are subject to the attentions of social workers and other professionals experience such a fate, the harsh fact of society has always been that adults will abuse and kill children. The job of social workers is to ensure as far as possible that children are protected but also that individuals, cultures and communities are allowed to bring their children up in ways that they believe to be appropriate so long as these ways accord with English law.

Much recent interest in the world of safeguarding has revolved around situations whereby social workers have been unwilling to challenge cultural norms (Laming, 2003; Birmingham SCB, 2010) but increasingly the expectation is that social workers will look at the child first and not at cultural considerations first. It is important to recognise that the responsibility of protecting children rests primarily with their parents and carers and then with the social workers. This responsibility is also increasingly shared across professionals, safeguarding being everybody's business. The use of the term safeguarding has emerged in recent years (DfES, 2003) and led on from a common usage of the phrase 'child protection' which in turn had derived from terminology such as 'non-accidental injury' and 'battered babies'. The term safeguarding is designed to give a more preventive feel to looking after our children and to emphasise that such roles are part of all citizens' duties and responsibilities, not just the responsibility of a limited number of social workers in our communities. Safeguarding as an approach would encompass considerations such as safe caring policies within foster homes, safe play areas in our towns and cities, speed restrictions around schools, healthy eating initiatives, sport for all initiatives as well as incorporating the sharp end of safeguarding, which is child protection. The term child protection is generally seen to apply when concern has been raised about whether a child is at risk of significant harm and when a referral posing this question has been made to a statutory authority such as children's services. A child protection case would necessarily encompass the formality of meetings, adherence to policies and possibly legal proceedings.

LESSONS LEARNT FROM KEY INQUIRIES

There have been a series of recent enquiries into the death of children at the hands of their carers (e.g. Birmingham SCB, 2007; Laming, 2003) and to be an effective social worker, you should read these enquiries at source and not rely on others' interpretation of them.

Reflective point

Read one of the key enquiries online and make a note of how your understanding of the 'facts' of the matter change.

Ask colleagues what they understand about the case in question and share your learning at a team meeting or in a memo.

Comment

We believe that there will be at least one significant part of the enquiry you read that differs from your understanding of the 'facts'. If you take the initiative, even as a student or an NQSW, you can claim a small step in promoting research awareness/evidence-based awareness across the profession. It remains an unacceptable state of affairs that many qualified social workers do not know the details of key enquiries and research findings, despite their ease of availability through the internet. Intuitive, experiential, practice wisdom is worth very little without underpinning from such rich sources. Traditionally, social workers have not kept up to date with such core intelligence, partly because they think their situations are 'unique', partly because much research/enquiry outcomes are critical (in a negative way) about social workers and partly because of time pressures. There is now a requirement that registered social workers must evidence at least 15 days *post-registration training and learning (PRTL)* every three years to ensure their continued registration. In reality this is administered with a very light touch and leans towards the tokenistic rather than the meaningful for many social workers. Hopefully, you will not be driven by minimal requirements but by a desire to be part of a changing, learning culture that embraces new knowledge and learning in the search for professional effectiveness.

Reflective point

Choose a serious case review from one of the many safeguarding board websites across the country. When reading the review ask yourself – could that have been me, my team, and my practice being reported on?

Why do you think that the findings of many serious case reviews are similar?

THE VICTORIA CLIMBIÉ INQUIRY

The tragic death of Victoria Climbié has become well known to the public as well as being a seminal case that highlighted major shortcomings in multiagency child protection work and its associated systems. Victoria was a Black African child, eight years old at the time of her death, who was systematically tortured and neglected in the most horrific ways by her privately arranged carers over the eight-month period that she was in their 'care'. As mentioned above, as a social worker, you must read enquiries such as Victoria's at source and not rely on hearsay, media or trade journal coverage.

Victoria's situation was quite unusual in that she was sent to Britain from the Ivory Coast in Africa, ostensibly for a better life and education. Her parents had arranged for Victoria's great aunt, Marie-Therese Kouao, to care for her. Victoria initially met up with Kouao in France and then moved to London with her, where she lived in a variety of accommodation across different London boroughs with Marie-Therese Kouao and her boyfriend Carl John Manning, whom she had met some months after arriving in England. Although Victoria never actually made it to school, she was not hidden away and was seen by many professionals during her 11 months in the UK including three housing authorities, four social services departments, two police child protection teams, NSPCC officers and staff within two hospitals. However, nobody actually knew Victoria, who was never formally interviewed by any professional in her native French language and whose 'carer' was largely allowed to speak on her behalf, giving a one-sided and untrue account of Victoria's wretched life.

Lord Laming (2003) led the Victoria Climbié inquiry and he formed the view that it was not particularly the systems which did not protect Victoria. It was the lack of skills within those systems at fault and poor practice was seen throughout interventions with Victoria and her family. He blamed inadequate interagency working, ineffective and inept management and people deferring to adult needs rather than protecting the child. He believed that the answer lay in 'doing relatively straightforward things well' (Laming, 2003: 13).

Victoria was a Black African child and her carers were both black as well as many of the staff who were involved with her. *The issue of race was raised in relation to Victoria and the question asked:*

'If Victoria had been a white child, would she have been treated any differently?' (Laming, 2003: 12)

Neil Garnham QC said in his opening statement:

Assumption based on race can be just as corrosive in its effect as blatant racism ... racism can affect the way people conduct themselves in other ways. Fear of being accused of racism can stop people acting when otherwise they would. Assumptions that people of the same colour, but from different backgrounds, behave in similar ways can distort judgements. (Laming, 2003: 12)

Lord Laming made 108 recommendations to social care, healthcare and the police, as well as some general recommendations as a result of the Victoria Climbié inquiry.

THE PETER CONNELLY INQUIRY

Like Victoria, Peter was not hidden away and he was actually on the Child Protection Register when he died in August 2007 at 17 months of age at the hands of his 'carers', one of whom was his mother. The family was seen 60 times in eight months by social workers, police and doctors.

Lord Laming found failings in the information sharing between agencies, poor training and support for overstretched frontline staff and he also believed that 'red tape' was hampering social workers, overlain with a culture that emphasised process and targets. He felt that the IT systems introduced were over-complicated and that recording systems were lengthy with an unhelpful 'tick box' approach. Greater skills for social workers in recognising child developmental problems and greater awareness of manipulative, collusive carers were also issues for the skill base of the social work profession that emanated from this inquiry.

In his progress report, *The Protection of Children in England* (DCSF, 2009), Lord Laming also pointed out there are some real challenges in the recruitment and retention of child protection workers and a lack of personal accountability among senior management. Social workers reported that they often felt their training does little to prepare them for working with families in crisis and that child protection social work was sometimes seen as a 'Cinderella service' (Laming, 2009: 44). Lord Laming concluded that child protection issues had not been given the priority they deserved in the six years since the Victoria Climbié tragedy.

LEGISLATION AND CHILD PROTECTION

Safeguarding children in the UK is based on legislation under the Human Rights Act 1998, an Act which guarantees certain basic freedoms and rights for individuals. Within the UK the key Act that underpins safeguarding children is the Children Act 1989 (see Chapter 3) and the key principle of this Act relevant to child protection is that the welfare of the child is paramount.

The key policy that flowed from the Victoria Climbié report was *Every Child Matters* (DfES, 2003) and the subsequent Children Act 2004 made further structural changes in the way in which children in the UK were to be safeguarded. The Children Act 2004 sought to introduce greater accountability among professionals and to encourage agencies and professionals to work much more closely together in terms of their approaches to safeguarding children. The main initiatives under the Children Act 2004 are listed below:

- Establishment of **local safeguarding children boards**, which replaced the old area child protection committees. These boards have a much wider remit with regard to ensuring that local workforces are trained and equipped to safeguard children. These boards are responsible for standards and also for carrying out serious case reviews into any situations in that locality wherein a child has become seriously injured or died
- Appointment of a Children's Commissioner in March 2005 to protect and promote children's rights
- Merger of children's social services departments at managerial level with education departments to form the Integrated Children Services (ICS), each local authority having a director of children's services with responsibilities across what had previously been two

separate departments. Within the ICS, children's social care teams are responsible for social work with children and families

- Appointment of a minister for children in 2005, which gave greater status and national prominence to the safeguarding of children and young people.

Some other initiatives suggested by the Children Act 2004, such as a national electronic database of children, were not brought to fruition due to issues of cost. Since the initiation of ICS, there has unfortunately been criticism (see DfE, 2011b) that these departments are unwieldy and impenetrable and that their associated IT and communication systems are unduly bureaucratic and hinder rather than help efficiency within safeguarding.

CHILD PROTECTION AND SAFEGUARDING CHILDREN

Much social work with children is concerned with safeguarding their welfare while at the same time promoting their welfare. Much of the media image of social work stems from work carried out, or not carried out, by social workers in child protection settings. Professional judgement, knowledge of child development and the ways families operate should be at the heart of all child protection and safeguarding work. The various forms and procedures should serve to complement this essential professional judgement. Since the death of Victoria Climbié (Laming, 2003) there have been many procedural changes to the way in which child protection is addressed, the new terminology of 'safeguarding' having been introduced as part of the policy *Every Child Matters* (DfES, 2003) and the Children Act 2004 with the intention of promoting the message that safeguarding is everybody's business, not just the business of social workers.

Working Together to Safeguard Children (DCSF, 2010, Section 1.20) defines safeguarding and promoting the welfare of children as:

- Protecting children from maltreatment
- Preventing impairment of children's health or development
- Ensuring that children are growing up in circumstances consistent with the provision of safe and effective care
- And undertaking that role so as to enable those children to have optimum life chances and to enter adulthood successfully.

Essentially, safeguarding has more preventative connotations than child protection, the latter being a part of safeguarding, but safeguarding being everybody's business from neighbours, friends and family through to professionals in the field of childcare. Initiatives such as the provision of safe play areas, designated people at schools, and television story lines about the risks of internet grooming all are part of safeguarding. Some social workers, particularly those based in outreach or children's centres will have a significant part to play in preventative strategies, whereas many social workers employed in statutory settings will be primarily occupied with protecting children who have reached the threshold of 'significant harm' or about whom serious concerns have been raised.

DEFINITIONS OF CHILD ABUSE

There are four categories of abuse defined in *Working Together to Safeguard Children* (DCSF, 2010), which is an interagency guide to working towards safeguarding and promoting the welfare of children, based on the Children Act 1989 and the Children Act 2004. The four categories – physical, neglect, emotional and sexual – are not mutually exclusive. Emotional abuse, although a category of abuse in its own right, is a part of all child abuse.

Physical abuse may involve hitting, shaking, throwing, poisoning, burning or scalding, drowning, suffocating, or otherwise causing physical harm to a child. Physical harm may also be caused when a parent or carer fabricates the symptoms of, or deliberately induces, illness in a child (DCSF, 2010).

Neglect is the persistent failure to meet a child's basic physical and/or psychological needs, likely to result in the serious impairment of the child's health or development. Neglect may occur during pregnancy as a result of maternal substance abuse. Once a child is born, neglect may involve a parent or carer failing to:

- Provide adequate food, clothing and shelter (including exclusion from home or abandonment)
- Protect a child from physical and emotional danger or harm
- Ensure adequate supervision (including the use of inadequate care-givers)
- Ensure access to appropriate medical care or treatment.

It may also include neglect of, or unresponsiveness to, a child's basic emotional needs (DCSF, 2010).

Emotional abuse is the persistent emotional maltreatment of a child such as to cause severe and persistent adverse effects on the child's emotional development. It may involve conveying to children that they are worthless or unloved, inadequate or valued only insofar as they meet the needs of another person. It may include:

- Not giving the child opportunities to express their views, deliberately silencing them or 'making fun' of what they say or how they communicate
- Age or developmentally inappropriate expectations being imposed on children, including interactions that are beyond the child's developmental capability, as well as overprotection and limitation of exploration and learning, or preventing the child participating in normal social interaction
- Seeing or hearing the ill-treatment of another
- Serious bullying (including cyber bullying), causing children frequently to feel frightened or in danger, or the exploitation or corruption of children.

Some level of emotional abuse is involved in all types of maltreatment of a child, though it may occur alone (DCSF, 2010: 1.34).

Sexual abuse involves forcing or enticing a child or young person to take part in sexual activities, not necessarily involving a high level of violence, whether or not the child is aware of what is happening. The activities may include assault by penetration (e.g. rape, buggery or oral sex) or non-penetrative acts such as masturbation, kissing, rubbing and touching outside of clothing. They may include non-contact activities, such as involving children in looking at, or in the production of sexual images, watching sexual activities, or encouraging children to behave in sexually inappropriate ways or grooming a child in preparation for abuse (including via the internet). Sexual abuse is not solely perpetrated by adult males. Women can also commit acts of sexual abuse, as can other children (DCSF, 2010).

Reflective point

Which of the following would you see as neglectful, bearing in mind that different professionals and the influence of your own background may have a significant effect on your judgement?:

- Leaving an eight-year-old alone in a house while you pop to the shops?
- Leaving a four-year-old alone in the house while you pop to the shops?
- Leaving a 10-year-old at home for three hours in the early evening while you go to your part-time job?
- Leaving a 10-year-old alone in the house for three hours in the evening while you go to your part-time job, with the 10-year-old caring for your five-year-old daughter?
- Sending a seven-year-old child to boarding school and only visiting once per term?
- Allowing your 16-year-old daughter to sleep with her boyfriend at his parents' house at weekends?
- A father telling his 10-year-old daughter to ring him at work if mummy has too much to drink and can't cook her tea?
- A five-year-old starting school who has never had any vegetables in their diet?
- A child who has clearly worn the same clothes three days in a row at nursery school?
- An eight-year-old child walking alone to the park to play with friends?

SECTION 47 ENQUIRIES

To look first at the legal frameworks surrounding child protection, Section 47 of the Children Act 1989 gives local authorities a duty to investigate and make enquiries in relation to the welfare of a child. When a local authority is informed that a child who either lives or is currently in its area of jurisdiction is either subject to a protection order or there is reasonable cause to believe that a child in that area is suffering, or is likely to suffer from significant harm, there is an expectation that a range of enquiries will flow.

Together with the *Framework for Assessment of Children in Need and their Families* (DH, 2000b, see Chapter 4), a Section 47 enquiry provides the key framework under which information should be gathered together and analysed. Such enquiries involve making statutory checks about children with various authorities and other professionals, including a check that the child's name and address is correct or perhaps similar to other known children. A decision will need to be made as to whether a child meets the threshold of Section 47, and whether services should be offered to try to lessen the degree of need in a child or whether the child needs to be considered under the child protection system, possibly even needing to be removed from their immediate environment. If your decision, in conjunction with your supervising social worker or manager, is that there is reasonable cause to suspect the child is suffering or likely to suffer significant harm, then you should arrange a strategy discussion which would involve social workers, the police and the referring agency together with any other relevant agencies. It is essential that the people attending a strategy discussion are of sufficient authority to be able to make key decisions. The purpose of the strategy discussion is to enable all available information to be shared with a view to making a multiagency decision as to whether a Section 47 enquiry should commence; whether there is to be a criminal investigation as part of the concern raised and whether a core assessment under Section 47 of the Children Act 1989 should be either started or, if it has already started, whether it should be brought to a conclusion.

The roles of each agency in terms of the presenting problems should also be discussed and any immediate actions should be decided at this strategy discussion, which could involve whether to immediately put services into a family or, for example if a child was in a medical setting, to decide how the child might be safely moved from such a setting. The strategy discussion is also charged with agreeing what degree of information should be shared with the family – the issue of whether to let the family know some or any of the referral information is a contentious one.

A core guideline in such situations is whether sharing such information with a family would place a child at increased risk, either in terms of abuse or family being given time to create their own alibis or remove themselves from the local area. Inappropriate sharing of information might also mean that any police investigations into any alleged offence would be compromised. A decision could also need to be made during part of the strategy discussion (which can take the form of a telephone conversation or a more formally constituted meeting) regarding whether any legal action should be taken. All decisions from strategy meetings should be recorded and shared with the relevant agencies and the outcome would clearly be put on that child's record. Section 47 enquiries can sometimes run in parallel with a police investigation, rather than having to take place after a police investigation and in some cases there may even be the need for more than one discussion.

Reflective point

Think of a strategy discussion you have been involved in or you have heard about from a colleague and ask yourself the following questions:

- Did it appear that people from the relevant authorities at the right level of seniority were involved in the discussion?
- Was a consultant paediatrician involved in the discussion?
- Was the discussion a balanced one with the child at the centre?
- Do you think there were any resource implications that may have steered the shape of the outcome?

SOCIAL WORK INTERVIEWS DURING A SECTION 47 ASSESSMENT

Social work interviews with a child are carried out by the social worker, sometimes with a police officer. The object of the interviews is not only to get clear information about what has transpired in the child's situation, but also to obtain as much information as possible that may lead to a police conviction. Guidance is given in the Ministry of Justice (2011) publication *Achieving Best Evidence*. Essentially, this guidance says that all joint interviews with children should only be carried out by staff who have undergone specialist training in this area, and recognises the sensitivities often involved, for example: asking children to discuss issues that may be very personal and delicate; children who may have some kind of mental health issue; and children who have problems in communication or perhaps children from different cultural, racial or religious backgrounds from those of the staff carrying out the interview. A child who is deemed competent can give consent to these interviews and, as discussed above, the permission of parents would not always be sought. Apart from interviewing the child and parents/carers, the wider family would also be involved and it may be that a fuller picture of a child's situation can only be built up through further observations of that child with parents or possibly doing some direct work with the child with a view to ascertaining what their wishes and feelings are. Additionally, specialist assessments may be needed, for example, psychological assessments, and it may be that further specialist help is essential.

The aim of effective child protection interventions is to bring about positive change in children's lives. Once a child is subject to a child protection plan, analysis and planning must follow in a child-centred fashion, as the next two chapters will discuss.

Reflective point

Think about some interviews with children that you have heard about or been involved with.

- Were those interviews carried out by professionals with relevant specialist training and experience?
- If the children were considered to be too young to be interviewed were appropriate observations carried out about their situation? Was there access to appropriate medical or psychological advice?
- Were the procedures explained to the adults and children involved in a way that was meaningful? How do you know?
- Was the recording of the investigation sufficiently robust to best serve the interests of the child or children concerned in any formal arenas, for example, court hearings?

CHAPTER SUMMARY

Safeguarding children is everybody's business, whereas the formality of child protection work is primarily the domain of social workers in partnership with fellow professionals. Our knowledge base regarding child protection is vast, yet year on year more tragedies related to children occur, with the children in question sometimes being known to social workers and often being known to other agencies.

If you have the knowledge, the skills and support to be able to practise authoritatively and to know how to communicate with children and adults in tense and difficult situations, you can be part of a new culture in social work that does not repeat mistakes of the past but learns from them.

CASE STUDY 7.1

Mary

Mary, a six-week-old baby girl, has been with foster carers, Jane and Jack Hardy, since birth, due to concern about her birth mother's violent partner.

During contact with her six-week-old birth daughter, Mary's mother draws the attention of the contact supervisor to a dark mark on the child's cheek which is about the size of a ten pence piece.

What steps would you take as the social worker once your attention had been drawn to this marking?

What knowledge/practice wisdom base are you going to draw on?

What should be the guiding principle of your interventions?

FURTHER RESOURCES AND READING

Barlow, J. and Scott, J. (2010) *Safeguarding in the 21st Century – Where to Now?* Dartington: Research in Practice.

Bentovim, A., Cox, A., Bingley Miller, L. and Pizzey, S. (2009) *Safeguarding Children Living with Trauma and Family Violence: Evidence-Based Assessment, Analysis and Planning Interventions.* London: Jessica Kingsley Publishers.

Higgins, M. and Swain, J. (2009) *Disability and Child Sexual Abuse: Lessons from Survivors Narratives for Effective Protection, Prevention and Treatment.* London: Jessica Kingsley.

Luckock, B., Lefevre, M., Orr, D., Jones, M., Marchant, R. and Tanner, K. (2006) *Teaching, Learning and Assessing Communication Skills with Children and Young People in Social Work Education.* Social Work Education Knowledge Review 12. London: Social Work Institute for Excellence (www.scie.org.uk/publications/knowledgereviews/kr12.asp). This is a very extensive piece of research that explores the ethical and emotional considerations in communicating with children and young people.

NSPCC website. This gives further examples of serious case reviews (www.nspcc.org.uk/Inform/research/reading_lists/serious_case_reviews_2010_wda76891.html).

Signs of Safety.net. This website draws on the perspective of everyday practice of social workers to address a positive form of child protection issues (http://signsofsafety.net/).

8

ANALYSIS: CRITICAL SKILLS FOR EFFECTIVENESS

Key Points of Chapter

- Children and families social work is complex and complicated. Even the briefest of encounters involves a vast amount of written and verbal information. Making effective use of this wealth of information necessitates the use of analysis
- Analysis is the key to effective report writing, verbal presentations and **reflective practice**
- You must find space to work in a reflective manner – being busy, busy, busy is not effective social work
- Effective analysis was missing in many cases examined as part of key enquiries and serious case reviews
- Statistics and research facts only tell one part of the social work story – reflective practice, using our **emotional intelligence** and analysis of children's developmental domains need to be explored in order to get the full story
- 'Respectful uncertainty' (Laming, 2003) is a key phrase to consider when you are attempting to analyse new families and new situations
- Information from persons thought to be of higher status should be analysed/questioned just as it would be from others
- Intuition has a role to play in effective analysis but this must be combined with critical thinking
- Self-awareness and emotional intelligence are crucial attributes for you to develop. It is not a mistake to have strong views but it is a mistake to have nothing else

---

Proposed Professional Capabilities Framework areas covered in this chapter

- Professionalism
- Knowledge
- Critical Reflection and Analysis
- Interventions and Skills
- Contexts and Organisations

(Social Work Reform Board, 2010 – see Appendix 1)

Draft Standards of Proficiency for Social Workers in England specifically covered in this chapter

1 Be able to practise safely and effectively within their scope of practice
4 Be able to practise as an autonomous professional, exercising their own professional judgement
6 Be able to practise in a non-discriminatory manner
8 Be able to communicate effectively
9 Be able to work appropriately with others
10 Be able to maintain records appropriately
11 Be able to reflect on and review practice
13 Understand the key concepts of the bodies of knowledge which are relevant to their profession
14 Be able to draw on appropriate knowledge and skills to inform practice
15 Be able to establish and maintain a safe practice environment

(Health Professions Council, 2011 – see Appendix 2)

INTRODUCTION

Analytic skills can be enhanced by formal teaching and reading. Intuitive skills are essentially derived from experience. Experience on its own, however, is not enough. It needs to be allied to reflection – time and attention given to mulling over the experience and learning from it (DfE, 2011b: 87). Following the information gathering part of the assessment there needs to be a move towards the processing of the information which has been collected; this needs to be analysed and evaluated, and then conclusions drawn which can be used in practice to support decision making. This process will underpin the compilation of any plan to safeguard or promote the welfare of a child.

This chapter will consider the benefits of intuitive thinking and analysis and also take a look at critical and reflective thinking in relation to effective social work practice.

WHAT IS ANALYSIS?

Analysis is the breaking down of information into smaller, more organised chunks and then considering the links between these and how they fit together. It is an objective process which helps us to better understand the information before us and it enables us to draw conclusions and make decisions about complex matters. Social workers are frequently involved in gathering together a mass of highly complicated, often contradictory and incomplete information, and can understandably find it difficult to sort through this information in order to make important decisions about families. Recent enquiries and serious case reviews (e.g. Laming, 2003; Birmingham SCB, 2010) have been critical of social workers' failures to analyse key information and in practice it is often difficult to see 'the wood for the trees' when reading through files and reports.

The main features of analysis are rigour, accuracy, a systematic approach and objectivity – a logical analysis of data which have been systematically collected. This approach, if used in a robust manner, will help prevent social workers from jumping to conclusions about families and reaching either an over-optimistic view or conversely an over-pessimistic view because of unchallenged hypotheses from others.

There can be a tendency for professionals in general (it is not just social workers who may be poor at analysis!) to form an impression about families very early on and then not change even if further information is contradictory. Such outcomes are all the more likely if we seek only to verify what we believe, rather than try to locate information that might disprove our views. It is often due to overload and tiredness that we revert to our 'gut instincts', but using analytical tools can help to give a more balanced view of a situation and make our judgements much more effective and fair to the children and families concerned.

Analytic reasoning is seen by (Munro, 2009) as being a time consuming activity, acquired by cultural and formal learning, which requires the application of formal knowledge and logic. Effective analysis is therefore difficult and challenging, especially given the complexities within social work scenarios.

INTUITION/EMOTIONAL INTELLIGENCE

Intuition is an emotional response to a situation; it is unconscious, automatic and cannot be avoided. Munro (2009) suggests that once we recognise this as being a vulnerability in ourselves and in others, then we can move on and try to recognise, and therefore reduce, the biases that will inevitably arise from this unconscious and automatic phenomenon. Intuition is a basic way of thinking that does not need to be taught, and because it is automatic it does not take the time that analytical reasoning does. Intuition can be used to help us to engage with people in an empathetic manner as it draws on internal life experiences as well as knowledge. Use of intuition by social workers in their interaction with people might also be termed 'emotional intelligence' (Goleman, 1995).

It would be taking an unacceptable risk, however, to rely solely on intuition or emotional intelligence for your professional judgement and decision making, although the practice wisdom that you build up over the years as a result of intuitive thinking is a valuable part of your extensive toolkit as a social worker. Thus any emotional response to a situation should properly be combined and tempered with the much more deliberate, logical and objective mode of analytical thinking.

Munro (2009) views intuitive reasoning as being an unconscious, automatic, emotion laden and biased process that draws upon a person's received wisdom about the way the world works for them.

Analytic and intuitive reasoning are both seen by Munro (2009) as having strengths and weaknesses and both play a part in our making judgements and decisions.

CRITICAL THINKING SKILLS

Critical thinking is made up of your having reasons for what you believe, critically evaluating your own beliefs and actions, and being able to present to others the reasons for your beliefs and actions (Cottrell, 2005). Critical thinking is not, as the term may suggest, a negative way of thinking – it is more about being questioning of ourselves, others and the information and issues we are presented with:

(a) We are often too easily persuaded by arguments from those who are seen to be 'authority figures'. For instance, if a paediatrician says, 'This bruise is consistent with the explanation given of the child hitting his head on the door', it is unlikely that other professionals will challenge this view.

(b) We can find it difficult to change our minds if new information comes to light which does not confirm our existing views.

(c) We can sometimes accept risk factor associations without questioning these enough.

(d) We can be too easily persuaded by arguments which cite generalised 'factual' data as being the determining factor in the individual decisions that have to be made.

By thinking in a more critical way, we would be more questioning about the information presented to us:

(a) The bruise seen on the child's head may well be consistent with the explanation given but this is a medical opinion and not a fact, and while it is consistent with the explanation there may be other explanations which could be just as valid. The injury will need to be seen in context with what other information is available.

(b) We can hold very entrenched views about families which are hard to change even when new information comes to light, so we need to be more open-minded in our approach and not be afraid to say we have changed our minds. Good critical thinkers will consider counter-examples as well as those which are compatible with their beliefs.

(c) It may be true to say that many victims of child abuse live in families where there are high levels of deprivation, where parents are young, possibly single, welfare dependent and living in poor housing, perhaps with a visiting partner. This type of information, however, is true of a large proportion of inner-city communities who are needy but non-abusing and there is little, in relation to this, which is of accurate predictive value in respect of child abuse (Parsloe, 1999). All information needs to be seen in context and this will be part of the contextual data gathered for analysis.

(d) Sometimes 'factual' data in the form of statistics can be provided stating that there are obvious associations between one thing and another. We need to have a healthy scepticism about these claims and look more critically at the issues. **Performance indicators** only measure quantity, not quality. The numbers of completed assessments for team A, for example, may be higher than for team B, but this does not indicate which team is doing assessments meaningfully and thoroughly.

In summary, critical thinkers:

- Evaluate arguments by exploring reasoning
- Do not uncritically accept what they are told
- Respect the views of others but question claims to authority
- Consider opposing views and alternative explanations
- Spot sweeping generalisations and would challenge claims such as parents who have been abused as children will go on to abuse their own children
- Do not speculate
- Are aware of their own biases
- Are wary of initial assumptions but make these explicit and examine their validity
- Use language thoughtfully – seek clarification where needed, are wary of 'labels', and do not use descriptors as explanations. For example, a critical thinker would state that X shows aggressive behaviour, not that X is aggressive.

It is not a mistake to have strong views but it is a mistake to have nothing else.

ANALYSIS – THE TOOLS AT YOUR DISPOSAL

Once the information gathering part of an assessment has been completed you need to know what to do with the information collected, which may often be a 'mish mash' of confusing and incomplete data gathered from a number of sources, some possibly more reliable than others. To analyse this information it will need to be broken down into manageable pieces and worked through methodically and carefully to make sense of what is there. This process will take time and effort but the end result should be objective and rigorous in a way that helps you to understand why things are happening, not just what is happening.

Several items in your social work 'toolkit' can assist in this process:

- First, there are our own personal skills in critical thinking, practice experience and emotional intelligence
- Second, there are our learnt skills in social work knowledge, theories and research
- Third, there are practice tools such as completed assessments, plans, genograms, chronologies and social histories. Supervision sessions, especially group supervisions, can also be used to 'test out' ideas and make sense of information.

'Signs of Safety' (Turnell and Edwards, 1999) is a solution and safety oriented approach to analysis, which can be useful in making sure that there is a balance between risk factors and safety factors. You need to combine the tools you have in order to make sense of the information we have gathered.

Reflective point

Situation 1

Imagine that you have a serious medical problem and you are seeking help from your doctor to consider treatment options. From the following list think about each criterion you would want your doctor to rely on when making decisions about your treatment:

- The doctor's intuition or 'gut feeling' about what might work
- What he/she has heard from other doctors in informal exchanges
- The doctor's experience with similar cases
- The doctor's demonstrated track record of success based on data he/she has gathered systematically and regularly
- What fits his or her personal style
- What is usually offered at the surgery
- Self-reports from other patients about what was helpful
- Research evidence
- What the doctor is most familiar with
- What the doctor has learned by critically reading professional literature.

> ### Situation 2
>
> Think back to a child or family you have worked with and, from the following list, reflect on each criterion you would *ideally* use to make your practice decisions. If you have not yet worked with any families, reflect on what you would ideally want to use:
>
> - Intuition or 'gut feeling'
> - Information, given informally, from other professionals
> - Your experience with similar cases
> - Your demonstrated track record of success based on data you have gathered systematically and regularly
> - What fits your personal style
> - What was usually offered at your place of work
> - Self-reports of other service users about what was helpful
> - Research evidence
> - What you are most familiar with
> - What you know by critically reading professional literature.

THE VALUE OF REFLECTION

Reflection, at its most basic, is simply considering or thinking about past events. Schön (1991) describes two processes of reflection:

- Reflection on action – thinking, after we have acted, about what we have done, how it went and how it may have been done differently
- Reflection in action – thinking, while we are acting, about previous experience and applying that experience to the current situation, 'thinking on our feet'.

Both of the above are a means to linking theory to practice, the first is something which needs to be planned for and is done after the event and the second is more about the professional judgement of an experienced practitioner. Reflection can be seen by some as 'airy fairy' social work but it is actually the sign of a focused, emotionally and procedurally aware practitioner who is not blasé, defeatist or arrogant about their practice. Rather, they constantly want to improve by looking back on what they have done, learning from this and doing a better job next time. The ability to be critically aware of self and why you acted the way you did, particularly when under pressure, is indicative of an effective professional. Use of self is more fundamental to social work than any other profession, and unless you can be open and self-critical, and able to see yourself as others see you, then you are not cut out for social work. You will hopefully learn about techniques for exploring self while on a social work training course but the learning does not stop there, learning about self is a life-long mission, never complete.

As Jones and Gallop (2003) point out, it can be difficult to find any reflective space in childcare social work. They suggest that this space may be found in individual case supervision sessions and that it needs to be protected as it is in danger of becoming 'squeezed out'. In reality, although all children's social care offices are, by their very nature, extremely busy, it is a false economy to limit the opportunities for reflection and to concentrate on doing and not on thinking about what we are doing. Inexperienced social workers, in particular, need to have a safe space in which to think about and discuss with others the situations they have been dealing with as these can be complex and sometimes frightening, aspects which can be overlooked by busy managers who have been in the job for a long time. If there is no 'reflective space' in the office we are working in we should create it ourselves and encourage others to join.

Reflective point

Think of ideas for finding 'reflective space' in a busy workplace.

If you work for an organisation with mobile and flexible working/'hot desking' how might you tackle the above challenge?

Beyond information gathering

Collecting information is one part of the social work task whereas critical thinking, interpreting, analysing and reflecting enable us to make sense of that information and to make decisions about how best to safeguard and promote the well-being of children.

Reflective point

The list below (Turney, 2009: 7) includes the skills and attributes which are necessary to support analytical, critical and reflective thinking. Reflect on those attributes that you believe you have, those you believe you do not have and those you think you can develop:

- Curiosity
- Open-mindedness
- The ability to manage uncertainty and not knowing
- Being able to question one's own as well as other's assumptions
- The ability to hypothesise
- Self-awareness
- Observation skills
- Problem solving skills
- Ability to synthesise and evaluate information from a range of resources
- Creativity
- Sense making
- Ability to present one's thoughts clearly, both verbally and in writing.

CHAPTER SUMMARY

Analysis is essential if any social work is to be effective. We can be faced with mountains of information about the complex lives and relationships of children and families but unless this information is analysed in ways that mean clear, child-centred actions follow, there are unlikely to be many positive outcomes from interventions. Reflective practice around analysis calls for a blend of intuitive and analytical reasoning, using both your emotional and technical intelligence.

FURTHER RESOURCES AND READING

Community Care website. This website has informative up-to-date articles covering most aspects of social work. These are often summaries that will direct you to the source material, especially when research findings are being reported (www.communitycare.co.uk/Home/).

Joseph Rowntree Foundation (2000) *Working with Families where there is Domestic Abuse.* This article focuses upon research findings regarding domestic violence (www.jrf.org.uk/publications/working-with-families-where-there-domestic-violence).

The Meriden Family Programme. This NHS programme supports families with sensitive issues and works with organisations to promote a high standard of mental health services by offering valuable research, publications and resources (www.meridenfamilyprogramme.com/resources.php).

Signs of Safety website. This website draws on the perspective of everyday practice of social workers to address a positive form of child protection issues (http://signsofsafety.net/).

9

EFFECTIVE PLANNING

Key Points of Chapter

- Effective planning for children will promote and safeguard their welfare
- Children must always be at the centre of your planning focus
- Effective planning invariably means working with other agencies – expect both to challenge and be challenged
- In order to be effective, plans must be reviewed in meaningful ways and any non-compliance followed up

Proposed Professional Capabilities Framework areas covered in this chapter

- Professionalism
- Values and Ethics
- Diversity
- Rights, Justice and Poverty
- Knowledge
- Critical Reflection and Analysis
- Interventions and Skills
- Contexts and Organisations
- Professional Leadership

(Social Work Reform Board, 2010 – see Appendix 1)

Draft Standards of Proficiency for Social Workers in England covered in this chapter

1 Be able to practise safely and effectively within their scope of practice
2 Be able to practise within the legal and ethical boundaries of their profession
4 Be able to practise as an autonomous professional, exercising their own professional judgement
8 Be able to communicate effectively
9 Be able to work appropriately with others
10 Be able to maintain records appropriately
11 Be able to reflect on and review practice
13 Understand the key concepts of the bodies of knowledge which are relevant to their profession
14 Be able to draw on appropriate knowledge and skills to inform practice

(Health Professions Council, 2011 – see Appendix 2)

INTRODUCTION

A child's plan is the end product of the assessment, analysis and decision making that has already been completed. The plan should give a clear picture of the child's situation and will detail who is involved with the child and their family and what actions will be taken by whom to address the identified needs. It is a multidisciplinary document.

The child's plan is the plan of intervention and will be very important to the family as it is a practical plan of action, which they have been involved in collating, in order to help them to make and to maintain changes. The family needs to understand what they have to do in order to achieve their goals and improve the lives of their children, so the plan needs to be clear and comprehensive. An example of a completed child's plan is included in Case Study 9.1 below.

TYPES OF PLAN

There are several different types of plan that may be used following assessment, depending on the child's situation. The SMART model (Doran, 1981) is a well-known business planning model that we suggest could be usefully adapted to the social work environment by turning it into the SMARTEST model by adding ethical, sustainable and theoretical elements as follows:

- **S**pecific: aims and objectives
- **M**easureable: outcomes and goals agreed with service users
- **A**chievable: goals and outcomes likely to succeed
- **R**ealistic: outcomes that focus on the core issues
- **T**imely: setting short time frames to review aims, objectives and outcomes
- **E**thical: based on person-centred, equal opportunity principles
- **S**ustainable: likely to be carried on when professional involvement reduces
- **T**heory: is theory based

The plans that you are likely to be involved with as a children and families social worker are:

- Child in need plan – this will be negotiated with the child, the family and all agencies who are involved
- Child protection plan – completed following a Section 47 enquiry and assessment (Children Act 1989) and a child protection conference
- Care plan – this will be prepared during care proceedings for approval by the court before a child can be made subject of a care or supervision order

- Care plan for looked after children – completed for a child who is accommodated by the local authority, the child may be the subject of a care order or accommodated via Section 20 of the Children Act 1989
- Pathway plan – completed for a young person in the care system in preparation for adulthood
- Transition plan – completed for a young person with a disability not in the care system, in preparation for adulthood
- Person-centred plan/essential lifestyle plan – an in-depth plan completed for a young person with a disability to inform future lifestyle options
- Common Assessment Framework plan – this type of plan may involve a social work role but would usually be completed by a 'lead professional' from another agency working with the child and is designed for children whose needs are at a lower threshold than might warrant statuary social worker intervention
- Plan of action – drawn up following a family group conference.

Sometimes there may be more than one type of plan. If, for instance, a child subject to a child protection plan became looked after they would need a care plan for looked after children. Depending on the circumstances, these two plans may need to run alongside each other and should complement, rather than contradict, each other otherwise the family will be unclear as to what is expected from them and may be 'set up to fail'.

WHAT SHOULD AN EFFECTIVE CHILDREN'S PLAN LOOK LIKE?

The actual format of the plan will depend on the electronic recording system used; however, all systems will follow the dimensions in the *Assessment Framework* (DH, 2000b, see Chapter 4). The format of this framework helps us to think about each aspect of a child's life and what the conclusions were from the assessment. A successful assessment should therefore mean that each need identified in the assessment will have an action in the plan.

It is important to present a detailed picture in your planning and to include the identified strengths, which can be built on, as well as the issues that need to change and improve. The plan should maintain a focus on the child, although there will usually be assistance offered to other family members, most usually the child's carers. Whichever plan is decided on, it should be drawn up with the full involvement and agreement of the family wherever possible. It is the job of the social worker to engage and secure the commitment of the family to the plan (Social Worker Retention Project, 2011).

The professionals involved in drawing up the plan must ensure that the objectives of the plan are reasonable and that the given timescales are realistic and will give the family a chance to make the necessary changes. There should not be too many actions because if a family is presented with too much all at once they can be overwhelmed and also feel that there is nothing which they are doing right. If they are faced with too much to do they may well do nothing. It is better to prioritise and identify what the immediate actions should be and when these have been successful other actions can be added.

It is also sometimes the case that individuals are simply not ready, for example, a young mother may have suffered abuse as a teenager and it has been identified that she needs counselling, however, if she is not ready herself to do this she may need to see that she can succeed at other things first and the counselling can be introduced at a later stage. Thus planning should always be needs and outcomes led rather than being resource driven. Social workers need to be creative around their consideration of resources and not forget that the family can be the greatest resource available.

The *Assessment Framework* (DH, 2000b: 4.36) recommends that the following areas of clarity are required in all plans for children:

- The objective of the plan, for example, to provide and evaluate the efficacy of therapeutic interventions
- What services will be provided by which professional group or designated agency
- The timing and nature of contact between the professional workers and the family
- The purpose of services and professional contact
- Specific commitments to be met by the family, for example, attendance at a family centre
- Specific commitments to be met by the professional workers, for example, the provision of culturally sensitive services or special assistance for those with disabilities
- Which components of the plan are negotiable in the light of experience and which are not
- What needs to change and the goals to be achieved, for example, the child's weight to increase by a specific amount in a particular period, regular and appropriate stimulation for the child in keeping with her or his development and age
- What is unacceptable care of the child
- What sanctions will be used if the child is placed in danger or in renewed danger
- What preparation and support the child and adults will receive if she or he appears in court as a witness in criminal proceedings.

Social workers need to be honest about the reasons for the plan, open about who does what and what the consequences may be for not doing this. They should use simple, clear language and interpreters/translators where needed, and be explicit about their concerns. All plans should be clear about how, when and where reviews will take place.

EFFECTIVE PLANNING MEETINGS

The most important people to invite to the meeting are the family members, including young people if they wish to attend. Otherwise the plan should be discussed with them outside of the meeting and they should be given the opportunity to say what they think would help them and what they think should be included. All agencies who are involved with the family should be invited, even if they do not have a specific task to do. This is because it is useful for everyone to be kept up to date with what is happening and to be part of the 'team around the child' (TAC).

It is, of course, difficult sometimes to get everyone together, for example, during the school holidays. At such times it may be necessary to speak to some people outside of the meeting. Some tips to remember when setting up meetings are:

- Choose a venue that everyone can get to
- Be clear about the time and place
- Remember to book a room for the meeting
- If young children are coming make sure they have something to do or someone who can help entertain them
- Remember to book an interpreter if needed
- Check dates so that they do not clash with cultural celebrations, birthdays etc. – if you do not know then you need to check when these are
- Make sure that you have allocated enough time and that everyone can stay
- If you expect there to be some contentious issues, be prepared for these in advance
- Make sure that everyone gets the opportunity to speak during the meeting, some people may need to be encouraged to take part more than others, but you do not want to miss their input
- If you want everyone to have a copy of the plan with them make sure you have access to a photocopier
- If some people are unable to attend make sure you speak to them beforehand for their views and send them a copy of the plan.

EFFECTIVE REVIEWING OF THE CHILD'S PLAN

All plans need to be regularly reviewed to see if the agreed objectives are being achieved. It is usual to review about every six weeks but this will vary depending on the type of plan and what it is for. If parts of the plan are not working well they will need to be amended – it is no use persisting with if it is clear that some things need to be changed.

It is essential to make sure that children are spoken to throughout the whole process, as it is important that we know whether things are improving for them and any changes which are being made are positive ones. During review meetings we need to check that not only are positive changes being made but also that they are being maintained. It is important to be aware that some families may engage superficially in order to get what they see as an intrusion into their lives out of the way. We therefore need to be sure that changes are 'real', and multiagency discussion should make this more apparent. Some tips to remember when reviewing plans are:

- Agree future dates, times and venues at the first review
- Be outcomes focused
- Make sure you know the child's views
- Be ready to change parts of the plan if needed
- If some professionals have not completed their tasks you need to address this promptly
- If the family is struggling with some tasks you need to be aware of this
- Remember that families may be reluctant to say if they are struggling
- Remember to praise people for their achievements – making changes is hard for us all.

Reflective point

The second review for the child's plan has been held and the health visitor, who has several tasks within the plan, has again not turned up.

What are you going to do?

Edward Lane

Think about a planning meeting you have been involved in which you did not feel went well and consider how you will approach the next one. See following pages (pp. 138–47).

CASE STUDY 9.1

CHAPTER SUMMARY

Effective planning calls for social workers to have a range of skills which need to encompass both procedural and interpersonal skills relevant to working with children and families. There are many different types of plan and complex families may have several plans relating to their children, hence it is imperative that these plans complement each other and make sense to families. The child must always be at the centre of the plan, not the adult. Plans need to be reviewed and changes made if individuals, including professionals, are not playing a full part in making the plan effective.

Details of Child: Edward Lane

Family Name	Lane	Given Names	Edward
Actual DOB	12-Dec-1997	Gender	Male
Ethnicity	White British	Primary Language	English
Primary Address	35 North Road ANYTOWN	Telephone (As recorded on System)	
		Mobile	
		Case No	
Secondary Address		Current Address	

Planning

Plan Revision	2.1.1
Plan Effective From	30-Mar-2011
Reason for Update	Children's Support Plan Review held on 20 March 2010

Revision Notes	Children's Support Plan Review held on 20 March 2010			
Child/Young Person's Development Needs				
Needs & Strengths	Outcomes		Service Provisions	
Strength		Partial		Current
Edward has a good sense of humour and can be polite and friendly.	That these traits can be encouraged and fostered.		Edward's family Other professionals who work with Edward	Starting: **10-Nov-2009** Ending: ___ Type: Y – Family Support
Unmet		Unachieved		Current
Emotional & Behavioural Development: Edward presents as very anxious and wants to please and would like people to think highly of him; however when he does not achieve this it leads to him being very upset. Mr Hall, Edward's class teacher, informed that Edward is sometimes 'socially awkward' making provocative, inappropriate comments in the changing rooms, this was the area that Edward most needs help with. Edward likes to make a cup of tea for his Mum, dealing with the process up to pouring the boiling water.	That Edward's levels of anxiety will reduce.		Referral has been made by social care for Edward to access a course which addresses issues of confidence and self esteem. Mother is happy for Edward to access this course and South School have agreed to organise transport from school for Edward on Monday mornings beginning 28/2/10 for six weeks.	Starting: **10-Nov-2009** Ending: ___ Type: Y – Family Support
Unmet		Unachieved		Current
Edward can be aggressive, sometimes he hits and kicks his siblings.	For Edward to be less aggressive towards other young people.		Dr Smith to monitor and review Edward's medication. Family to be kept informed of any incidents at school via the communication book.	Starting: **10-Nov-2009** Ending: ___ Type: Y – Family Support

(Continued)

(Continued)

Unmet	Unachieved	Current
Identity: Edward can be lacking in confidence and tends to have low self esteem; this has been noted at school and by the Community Learning Disability Team.	For Edward to increase his confidence and feel good about himself.	Edward to access a course to help him identify reasons for feeling good about himself. It is hoped that this course will also enable Edward to examine his relationships and communication skills. Parents to encourage Edward in this area. South School and Respite Provision to be made aware of this desired outcome. Starting: **10-Nov-2009** Ending: _____ Type: Y – Family Support

Unmet	Unachieved	Current
Social Presentation: Mr Hall, class teacher, commented that Edward's actions towards his peers are not always appropriate. Edward is sometimes 'socially awkward' making provocative, inappropriate comments in the changing rooms, this was the area that Edward most needs help with. However, in his class Mr Hall advised that Edward is liked.	For Edward to develop an appreciation of social context.	Agency support worker to help Edward access social activities for three hours once/fortnight. Starting: _____ Ending: _____

Partial	Unachieved	Current
Self care skills: Edward has some good basic self care skills, he can wash, dress, toilet and feed himself. Edward requires help with finer motor skills, for example, buttons, putting on socks and tying bows on laces or aprons.	For Edward to become more competent in putting on socks and doing up buttons.	Previous class teacher, commented that Occupational Therapy support for Edward in school might help to develop these skills. Starting: **10-Nov-2009** Ending: _____ Type: Y – Family Support

However Edward is over-sensitive to gentle touch but under-sensitive to dangerous sensations. For example, he is unaware of the danger of heat on a cooker or scalding water. Consequently his self care abilities are not appropriate to his age.		
Unmet	Unachieved	Current
Family & Social Relationships: Edward has a strong attachment to his Mum. Mrs Lane explained that Edward prefers to be in the same room as herself. When Edward is staying at his respite provision, he will telephone his Mum each evening, apart from Friday and Saturday nights when Edward knows that his Mum is at work. Dianne, Edward's sister, also commented that Edward really loves his Mum. Edward does not usually choose to have contact with his father and Mr Lane commented that Edward will often go upstairs when his father is at home. However Edward does sometimes go swimming with his Dad and brother. Dianne (Edward's sister, aged nine) described to social care how she and Edward like to play imaginary games together. Dianne also commented that it was hard to ignore Edward as he will punch, push, kick or swear. James, Edward's brother (aged 12), enjoys playing on the DS machine with Edward and going with all the family to play football in the	For Edward's relationships with family members to improve.	Support recommended for Mr and Mrs Lane to work with identified agency to improve their understanding of Edward's behaviour and identify strategies for managing his behaviour. Respite Provision to continue to provide short breaks for Edward and for his family. Sessional worker to continue to provide a short break for Edward and for his family alternate weekends. Course to provide help for Edward to understand his feelings and improve his relationships. Starting: _____ Ending: _____

(Continued)

Needs & Strengths	Outcomes	Service Provisions	
park. Sometimes James and Edward 'wind each other up' and resort to fists, but then both will 'back off'.			
Partial	**Partial**		
Mrs Lane explained that she did not believe Edward could put himself in another person's shoes. Edward works happily with his peers at school in his class group of seven or eight students. Mr Hall, class teacher commented that Edward is liked by his class mates.	While at Respite Provision, Edward was observed recently particularly 'looking out for' a visitor, Laura, and asking for the music channel to be put on the TV for her benefit. Edward was also observed playing cars with two visiting children aged six/seven.		

Health

Needs & Strengths	Outcomes	Service Provisions	
Unmet	Unachieved		Current
Edward has diagnoses of ADHD, ASD and has a moderate learning disability. He takes medication for ADHD.	To ensure that Edward is taken to all medical and dental appointments. To ensure that Edward takes his medication at the correct time.	Edward's parents to take responsibility. Dr Smith to review. Frequency of review needs to be identified.	Starting: **10-Nov-2009** Ending: ——— Type: Y – Family Support
Unmet	Unachieved		Current
Edward's general health is good. Edward eats well but due to the level of his activity, he finds it hard to maintain his weight. At Edward's 'extended stay' review at Overnight Respite on 1/2/11, it was agreed that Edward should not be allowed more than two bags of crisps in one day, mother felt that she was	For Edward's weight to increase but without causing tooth decay.	Responsibility of parents. Dietician at Clinic to review. Frequency of review needs to be identified.	Starting: **10-Nov-2009** Ending: ——— Type: Y – Family Support

in a difficult situation between the dietician advising snacks for Edward as he is so small and the dentist saying that snacks would damage Edward's teeth.		
Unmet	Unachieved	Current
Edward's sleep can be irregular and he can wake around 4.30am; Edward is active as soon as he wakes and this can disturb other family members.	For Edward's sleep pattern to improve. For strategies to be in place so that Edward disturbs other members of the family less frequently.	Mrs Lane to talk with Dr Smith about increasing or changing Edward's medication. Starting: **10-Nov-2009** Ending: _____ Type: Y – Family Support
Unmet	Unachieved	Proposed
Edward suffers with his nerves; he finds it hard to try new things.	To reduce Edward's levels of anxiety.	Edward's family to try to give Edward timely information about family activities. Overnight Respite to inform the family of Edward's short break dates giving as much notice as possible. Mr Hall, Edward's class teacher, has noted Edward's anxiety and will pass his experience of Edward in Year 7, on to new staff for Year 8. Starting: _____ Ending: _____

Education

Needs & Strengths	Outcomes	Service Provisions
Strength	Unachieved	Current
Edward told social care that his favourite subject at school is maths.	For Edward to be encouraged to continue enjoying and achieving in maths.	Edward's new class teacher for Year 8 to be made aware of Edward's interest. Edward's parents to encourage him in this area. Starting: **10-Nov-2009** Ending: _____ Type: Y – Family Support

(Continued)

(Continued)

Strength	Unachieved	Current
Mr Hall informed that Edward's reading was very good and his maths and PE were 'sound'. Edward has a very good memory for dates and sequences of events.	For Edward to use this skill and to feel appreciated and proud of his abilities.	Edward's new Year 8 class teacher to be made aware of this ability and provide opportunities for Edward to use it.	Starting: **10-Nov-2009** Ending: _____ Type: Y – Family Support
Strength		
Mr Hall informed me that there is a communication book which can be used to pass messages between home and school and that he would utilise this more in future as there were positive things he could say about Edward at school.		
Strength		
Edward is now in his second year at secondary school, Year 8. He is in a small, 'nurture' group with seven or eight other pupils and his teacher is Mr Hall. Edward appears comfortable with the other pupils and I observed him participating in a 'speech and language' focused lesson, partly outdoors and taking part in some reflective/thoughtful work indoors.		

Parental Capacity

Needs & Strengths	Outcomes	Service Provisions
Unmet	Unachieved	Proposed
Mrs Lane commented that she finds it difficult to understand Edward and hard to know how to deal with him. Mrs Lane has tried to	For Mrs and Mr Lane to feel that their relationships with Edward have improved.	Discussion to take place with the Community Learning Disability Team to determine	Starting: _____ Ending: _____

Unmet	Unachieved	Proposed
follow professional advice to always praise Edward but she finds that this will often cause Edward to react angrily. Mrs Lane has commented that it is very difficult to 'figure him out' and that Edward is 'very complex'. His Mum believes that this is not a new situation as it was the same at primary school and it is now at secondary school.	For Mrs Lane to be able to provide emotional warmth to Edward and for this to be received by him.	their recommendations as specialists in this area. Work with CLDT would necessitate Mr and Mrs Lane's and Edward's full involvement with professionals. Anger Management course to work with Edward. Outcomes and recommendations from this course to be shared with Mr and Mrs Lane and some follow up planning to be put in place.
Mrs Lane described Edward as not being affectionate. On the occasions when he will hug his Mum it appears this is usually because he wants something rather than an expression of affection. Mrs Lane says that sometimes she will feel disappointed by this lack of affection.		As above. Starting: _____ Ending: _____

Family and Environmental Factors (Birth Family)

Needs & Strengths	Outcomes	Service Provisions
Unmet	Unachieved	Current
Mr Lane is finding it difficult to find work at present. Work was very irregular ranging from none to 48 hours/week.		Mr and Mrs Lane have found details of the benefits they can apply for, should they wish. If Mr and Mrs Lane would like any further information around possible entitlements, please contact social worker. Starting: **10-Nov-2009** Ending: _____ Type: Y – Family Support

(Continued)

(Continued)

View of all Parties

Child/young person/family members/agencies who are party to the plan

Please state name, relationship to child/young person or role, agency, contact number.	Mr and Mrs Lane Edward's parents Mr Hall South School June North Key Worker Overnight Respite Susie at Anger Management Course Karen Jones Co-ordinator Care Agency Debbie Taylor Children's Social Worker

Next Review

Agreed date for the next review	08-Mar-2011
Lead professional/agency for this review:	Martin Smith Independent Reviewing Officer
If the overall aim and contents of the plan have not been discussed with any of the parties/agencies concerned, please give reasons:	
What steps will be taken and who is responsible if any party/agency wants to alter any aspects of this plan?	Janet Hogan South Social Care Office

Comments

Child/Young Person's Comments	Edward said that he likes ice cream and pizza while on short breaks at Respite Provision. Edward described his sessional worker as 'nice' and he said that he enjoys going out with her.

	Edward was clearly aware of the plans for short breaks football training every day in February half term, followed by a stay at overnight respite the following week, 25/2/2011– 4/3/2011. Edward appeared more relaxed about speaking to his social worker on her last visit and didn't need to 'let off steam' before speaking to me. Edward clearly communicated which lesson would follow our talk, enabling me to reassure him that I would return him to the correct place when we had finished.
Parents/Carer's Comments	
Other action(s)	

Recorded Feedback

Child/Young Person/Family Members/Agencies who may be party to the plan

Person		Discussed	Signed	Date Signed
Samantha Lane	Mother			
Dean Lane	Father			
James Lane, ≈ 12 years	Brother			
Dianne Lane, ≈ nine years	Sister			
Debbie Taylor	Allocated Case Worker			
Martin Smith	Independent Reviewing Officer			
Key Agency – South School	Key Agency			

FURTHER RESOURCES AND READING

CAFCASS (2011) (www.cafcass.gov.uk).

Department for Education (2009) *Early Identification, Assessment of Needs and Intervention – The Common Assessment Framework for Children and Young People: A Guide for Practitioners.* Leeds: Children's Workforce Development Council (https://www.education.gov.uk/publications/eOrderingDownload/CAF-Practitioner-Guide.pdf).

Department of Health (2000a) *Assessing Children in Need and their Families: Practice Guidance.* London: HMSO (www.dh.gov.uk/en/Publicationsandstatistics/Publications/PublicationsPolicyAndGuidance/DH_4006576).

Department of Health (2000b) *Framework for the Assessment of Children in Need and their Families.* London: HMSO (www.dh.gov.uk/en/Publicationsandstatistics/Publications/PublicationsPolicyAndGuidance/DH_4008144).

10 RECORDING: PURPOSE, IMPORTANCE, TECHNIQUES

Key Points of Chapter

- Clear and contemporary recording is critical to effective social work
- Recording must be done in the interests of promoting best social work practice, not merely compliance with deadlines/monitoring
- Your IT skills must be well developed
- The child must be visible, and central, to your recording
- You must use supervision and the practice wisdom of colleagues to help develop your skills in recording
- Always differentiate opinion from fact
- Be analytical and make judgements based on research and practice evidence
- Involve families and children in awareness of, and possibly as contributors to, your recording

Proposed Professional Capabilities Framework areas covered in this chapter

- Professionalism
- Knowledge
- Critical Reflection and Analysis
- Contexts and Organisations
- Professional Leadership

(Social Work Reform Board, 2010 – see Appendix 1)

Draft Standards of Proficiency for Social Workers in England covered in this chapter

2 Be able to practise within the legal and ethical boundaries of their profession
5 Be aware of the impact of culture, equality and diversity on practice
7 Be able to maintain confidentiality
8 Be able to communicate effectively
9 Be able to work appropriately with others
10 Be able to maintain records appropriately
11 Be able to reflect on and review practice
13 Understand the key concepts of the bodies of knowledge which are relevant to their profession
14 Be able to draw on appropriate knowledge and skills to inform practice

(Health Professions Council, 2011 – see Appendix 2)

INTRODUCTION

Recording is vitally important if social work is to be accountable, and recent years have seen a growth in the amount of recording required, most recording now being electronic in nature, and carried out by social workers themselves rather than by administrative staff. Recording, however, should primarily be concerned with promoting and protecting the welfare of children and represent a clear method of communicating key information about complex situations both within and outside of your organisation. Concern among the workforce about an increased managerial emphasis on compliance and concern about the way in which bureaucratic priorities have been increasingly taking social workers away from face-to-face contact with children and families have been echoed in the *Munro Report*:

> The level of increased prescription for social workers, while intended to improve the quality of practice, has created an imbalance. Complying with prescription and keeping records to demonstrate compliance has become too dominant. The centrality of forming relationships with children and families to understand and help them has become obscured. (DfE, 2011b: 8)

Commentators such as Ince and Griffiths (2011) and UNISON (2008) have also been very critical of the IT systems that have developed to support the Integrated Children's Services (ICS), echoing concerns about the dominance and complexity of computerised ICS systems which are also seen to take away the focus from professional judgements about children and families. Computerised systems have a major potential in helping the efficacy of the administration processes necessary to communicate effectively and thereby better safeguard and promote children's welfare by reducing administrative burdens. However, it cannot be right that many social workers, especially in statutory settings, are spending some 80 per cent of their time on administration tasks, many of which are computer centred rather than children centred (DfE, 2009). It is interesting to note that in recent times of economic constraint and budgetary awareness, many administrative posts have disappeared within public services, administration being seen as non-essential. The reality in social work is that social workers now carry out many tasks previously carried out by administrators, this situation having come about by stealth at a time when the virtues and efficiencies of mobile and flexible working have been promoted across public services. Interestingly, there have been no systematic evaluations of such new ways of working and much of the performance management/computerised culture within public services has remained unchallenged until very recently (see DfE, 2011b; Harris and Unwin, 2009).

Reflective point

- Are there any administrative jobs that social workers carry out in your organisation that could be more efficiently done by administrative staff?
- How might you make suggestions to rectify such situations?

- Do you think that some social workers take far longer than others to carry out certain administrative tasks?
- Are such differences in practice a good thing professionally, or should they be addressed by management?

WHY DO WE RECORD?

Case recording is the written proof of the work we do with children and families. It should offer a clear understanding of why we are involved in a child's life, what interventions have been made, the reasoning behind this and what the outcomes of those interventions have been. In essence, it is a record of our formal involvement and a way of recording plans and monitoring progress.

The child's views, wishes and feelings should be regularly sought and clearly recorded and it should be obvious that the record is about the child as the service user. There will, of course, be information from professionals as well as information concerning the child's carers but this should not be seen as more important and should not be given more time and space than what the child is saying.

The recording should tell the child's story and should clarify what happened that was significant, what decisions were made and why. We must be satisfied that if, in a few years' time, the child was to read the recording they would be able to follow what is written and understand what happened when they were younger. It should be clear to them that they are the central figure and that they and their family have been written about in a manner which conveys care and respect irrespective of their background or culture. Our recordings should always promote continuity and not leave unexplained gaps in children's lives.

Case recording should be viewed as part of the service which is provided to a child, while bearing in mind that the process is not the purpose. All the recording we do may be viewed by a variety of different audiences so it needs to be accessible not only to families but also to the courts (both family and criminal); those who may be inspecting, auditing or carrying out inquiries; colleagues who may be dealing with cases in our absence or taking over responsibility for a case; managers who are seeking information or providing supervision and a host of other professionals who will have access to various reports and plans that we write. It is clear that we are made accountable by our recording for our actions and that in our actions we are representing the local authority or independent sector organisation for which we work while at the same time promoting best practice, and hopefully providing a model of clarity, consistency, reflection, analysis and insight that will be effective.

Reflective point

How many reasons can you think of for keeping records about children and families?

Hopefully, your list is fairly extensive and it is perhaps illuminative to reflect on whether the records that you read/inherit from other professionals meet all of those reasons.

Case summaries are very important in all children's records and, although a file should always be read in depth, such summaries are most helpful starting points. Many of the families with whom you work will be complex and fragmented, often with different branches and surnames. Using pictorial, visual representations such as compiling a genogram or ecomap (see Appendices 3 and 4 for examples) can be a helpful way of getting a digestible picture of a family and its dynamics. Genograms, or family trees as you may know them, can provide the social worker with an understanding of an individual's family, and extended family, providing insight into relationships and family interaction. This visual representation, usually drawn by the child, can be used as a tool to help the social worker assess and implement effective interventions. Genograms are often used in conjunction with **ecomaps**. Ecomaps include a wider representation of relationships and support systems and may include people such as teachers, neighbours or friends. Both genograms and ecomaps are useful when compiling a chronology of key events in a child's life (Horwath, 2010). A chronology, a brief record of key events/milestones in a person's life can also help clarify understanding, some social workers finding that drawing a timeline with key events marked as high or low points also aids understanding a child's view of their situation (for an example of a chronology see Case Study 9.1).

We will now look at a series of problems as a means of exploring the necessary skills needed in the arena of social work recording.

RECORDING PROBLEMS AND SOLUTIONS

PROBLEM 1: IT IS DIFFICULT TO KEEP RECORDING UP TO DATE

Yes, it is a difficult and time-consuming challenge for all social workers; however, maintaining accurate and up-to-date records is of great importance. There is a strong link between recording and the quality of practice, and past enquiries such as that into the death of Victoria Climbié (Laming, 2003) have called for better maintenance of records. This helps us clearly identify when a child has been seen and what efforts have been made to be effective.

In a busy children's social care office there are a lot of interruptions and this can mean that our best intentions to catch up with recording can be thwarted; it is unrealistic to think that there will be a quiet period while we sit and complete this task. If recording does pile up, particularly in complex cases, we may have a tendency to avoid doing it because the job seems too much and so we seek out distractions.

PROBLEM 1: SUGGESTIONS FOR PROBLEM SOLVING

- Recognise that recording is an important task
- Recognise that recording is part of the service that we provide to a child

- Plan – allocate time to complete recording and minimise interruptions
- Record as you go along so that you do not become overwhelmed and you do not forget vital information
- Include recording in the time you allocate to any significant contact with a family/professional/ meeting.

Recording may not be fun but it will keep you free from unnecessary stress if completed regularly so it *is* well worth the effort.

PROBLEM 2: THE CHILD IS ABSENT FROM RECORDING

The child is the service user but it is unfortunately a very common scenario in children's social care teams to read through reams of recording, supposedly about a child, only to find the child 'missing'. This is not to say that the child is not mentioned at all; there may be numerous mentions but nothing about discussions with the child, what the child said, what the child's understanding of their situation is, what are their likes and dislikes and how they behave with their care-givers.

If the child is absent from our recording, it will indicate to the reader that no work has been done with that child and that their views may well have been ignored. It may be that sometimes we avoid talking to children about difficult issues in order to protect them but if they are to be involved in decision making we cannot avoid this reality. When speaking to children we need to be aware of their age and understanding and give them information sensitively so that they can form their own understandings.

Children may not want to talk to us and there may be many reasons for this. It may be that time is needed to form a relationship with the child; we will need to get the views of others who know the child better than we do and to carefully observe and record how the child behaves.

The recording may focus too much on the parents/carers and their needs. Many parents/carers that we work with have a lot of their own issues which will need support to overcome in order to be able to successfully care for their children. However, we must not be hijacked by these adult concerns and do need to spend time with children so that we can judge the impact of the parental issues on them.

PROBLEM 2: SUGGESTIONS FOR PROBLEM SOLVING

- See children regularly and on their own; giving the child a voice will support and protect them
- Involving a child fully and knowing that child well will enhance decision making and planning
- Plan sessions so that you are able to meet the child's needs and abilities; remember that each child in a family is an individual with their own needs and views
- Record what the child says in their own words, older children may even be able to make some of their own records and hence feel more a part of the planning
- Clearly mark the child's wishes and feelings within your recording so that they are easily found.

PROBLEM 3: FACT OR PROFESSIONAL JUDGEMENT?

As social workers we collect and analyse a lot of information, using this to make assessments and professional judgements. While doing this we may use social work theories, research and past experience as well as case histories. Therefore a substantial amount of what we record may be our own opinions and those of others. Sometimes we are not careful enough in differentiating what is fact and what is opinion and may give them equal weight. Opinions should not be recorded as facts but, in order to have some value, they should be recorded and backed up with supporting information.

Remember that initial views about a family are often based on the records we read so these must be as accurate as possible. Remember also that families may have access to their files and will be able to see the rationale and phraseology used in decision making. In summary, records should contain both facts and opinions but it should be clear which is which and opinions should be based on practice wisdom and sound judgement.

PROBLEM 3: SUGGESTIONS FOR PROBLEM SOLVING

- Sharing assessments and plans with families can make us more aware of what we are recording and is more likely to help us substantiate opinions
- Make it clear in your recording what is a fact and what is an opinion
- Record facts first and then analyse using any evidence you have, including research findings
- If a professional or a family member has given an opinion then record this as such.

PROBLEM 4: WHAT INFORMATION SHOULD BE RECORDED?

Social care files are now primarily electronic but there are still a lot of historical paper records in existence, some of which have many volumes and can be extremely difficult to read as they are handwritten, often not filed correctly and not always in date order.

There is sometimes a lot of unnecessary, unfocused information which does not need to be there and this makes it hard to locate what is significant. Narrative styles of recording can omit vital details and lack analysis. Although the physical size of files is now not an issue because of electronic recording, and information should be easier to locate, it remains important for you to know what information should be recorded. This is particularly challenging in the early years of a social work career especially as your recording may have a variety of audiences/purposes. As there can be a very diverse audience it can be difficult to know what to record. Over-recording is unhelpful and inefficient and it can undermine the privacy of the child of the family.

Under-recording can mean that evidence is missing and can, at worst, place children at risk. 'Defensive' recording is understandable when the social worker does not know what the future challenge to their practice may be. The spirit of the *Munro Report* (DfE, 2011b) has called for less defensive practice and a return to an emphasis on professional judgement and decision making, based on effective working relations with children and their families. It is difficult, however, to be entirely sure about what information it is 'safe' to omit and what information is crucial to include. Supervision has a key enabling role here.

Duplication of information may occur when prescribed proformas overlap but sometimes social workers repeat themselves because they feel more confident doing this than cross-referencing to other pieces of information on file.

PROBLEM 4: SUGGESTIONS FOR PROBLEM SOLVING

- Bring your concerns about depth/volume up in supervision. Ask whether there could be a team exercise comparing recording style and effectiveness
- Remain focused when recording and include the child's developmental needs, parental capacity and the impact of family and environmental factors. Make clear what services will be offered, why, what are the desired outcomes and how progress will be monitored
- Record significant information and say why it is significant: ensure that this significant information is visible in your recordings and not submerged under the volume of information that many complex cases hold
- Always have a clear plan of action for each child and use this as a structure for your recording
- Maintain your records and go through them regularly to update and maintain clear direction
- Cross-reference rather than recording duplicate information
- Learn the skills of précis writing
- Use chronologies in all cases to provide a summary of information and give a clear idea of any patterns which may emerge in the behaviour of families.

PROBLEM 5: USING LANGUAGE THAT PEOPLE CAN UNDERSTAND

The Data Protection Act (1998) gave people the right to see the information in their social work records. Access to files is sometimes viewed with suspicion by social workers who can feel guarded about what they record. Many documents are now shared as a matter of course with families, who have the chance to give their views and may disagree with some of what has been written about them. It can provide an opportunity to correct factual inaccuracies and any disagreements should be noted.

Sharing records can improve the working relationship between families and social workers and it can result in a better mutual understanding. As a result of sharing information with families, recording should be more accessible, focused and factual and any opinions explained.

PROBLEM 5: SUGGESTIONS FOR PROBLEM SOLVING

- Use plain language
- Refrain from using jargon
- Make sure that families are given a copy of your agency's Access to Records Policy
- Share early drafts of assessments, plans and reports with families, where possible, so that you can incorporate their views in the final document
- Encourage the family, especially the children, to contribute to the record
- Share final assessments, reports and plans with families and make sure they understand what they are reading
- Use interpreters and translators where needed.

PROBLEM 6: WHERE IS THE ANALYSIS?

Apart from serving many other uses, recording is a practice tool for social workers and managers and should be used in decision making. It is therefore much more than a diary of events. Case recording should support analysis and reflection and so social workers need to assess the weight of each piece of information, drawing on their understanding of the child's needs and the context in which the child lives and also their knowledge from research and practice.

When analysing information it is necessary to organise and evaluate information. There are tools that can be used to help the analytical process such as completed assessments, chronologies, genograms and social histories. Regular analysis means that recording becomes a proactive task which aids ongoing assessment, planning and the effectiveness of interventions.

PROBLEM 6: SUGGESTIONS FOR PROBLEM SOLVING

- Use analysis to explain why things are happening (not just what is happening)
- Use the tools you have to help you to organise and analyse information
- Use chronologies as a way of reviewing progress and evaluating the effectiveness of interventions
- Keep up to date with current research to inform your practice.

PROBLEM 7: RESPECTFUL RECORDING

As already discussed, failing to differentiate between fact and opinion can be disrespectful to families. The way records are written and language is used can be oppressive or discriminatory. Personal details which are wrong, such as mis-spelt names, undermines the confidence that families have in social workers 'getting things right'.

Maintenance of records and confidential information being securely locked away is, apart from policy and guidance, all about the importance we attach to the respect we have for families and the work we are doing with them. If we went into any office which held information about us we would expect it to be ordered and held in a safe place.

PROBLEM 7: SUGGESTIONS FOR PROBLEM SOLVING

- When you read your recording, imagine that you are the child being written about, what would you think of these records?
- Make sure that all personal details and spellings are correct, check with the family
- Maintain the records and ensure that any filing is done regularly
- Lock away all confidential information
- Consider the language you use when writing about children and families and make sure that it is always respectful and non-oppressive/non-discriminatory.

Reflective point

Read the following extracts and rewrite as you think they should be written:

John's mum is caring, she is chaotic though seems capable.

Samantha's dad is dirty, his flat is covered in half-eaten food and rubbish, Samantha's mother told me that he had been shoplifting but not been caught, they split up three months ago.

Jane is cooperative and willing to do anything I ask of her so that she does not have to have any more social care involvement. I need to look more closely at some concerns I have about her wider family and am worried that she might disengage.

ACTIVITY 2

- Read the following statement then imagine you are about to speak to the author of the statement as you will be taking over responsibility for this case:

Mrs Khan is a complex and neurotic woman who had very poor parenting herself and seems unable to provide for her children. She dresses inappropriately and has a very messy dirty household.

- Make a list of what you would want to ask and possibly raise about the content and style of the above notes.
- Write down what you think is the best way of telling the author what your concerns are.

ACTIVITY 3

- Read through a piece of your own recording and critique and then rewrite it.

TIPS FOR EFFECTIVE RECORDING

- Be clear about why you are recording
- Record as soon as possible after an event or observation
- Do not ramble! Use focused recording
- Make sure that the child is central in your recording
- Use genograms to clarify family relations
- Use plain language and avoid jargon
- Make sure that you get personal details and spellings of names correct
- Where possible stick to facts
- When giving an opinion ensure that this is separate from the facts and explain how you have reached this opinion
- Record in a way that you would be happy for the child and family to read
- Do not forget to date and sign records and reports, as necessary
- Keep chronologies updated
- Remember to use your recording tools for analysis
- Use research findings to back up your judgements.

CHAPTER SUMMARY

Recent government initiatives such as the Social Work Task Force (DCSF, 2009) and the *Munro Report* (DfE, 2011b) have been critical of the dominance of procedure and bureaucracy in today's managerially driven social work. At the same time, enquiries into the deaths of children and the findings of some serious case reviews have been critical of the level and depth of recording available and the ways in which it has been used (or not been used) to protect children.

It is difficult, particularly when starting out on a social work career, to know the right amount of recording to produce to be able to achieve the right emphases and balances. Remember to use supervision and the practice experience surrounding you to get a healthy perspective on recording. Always ask yourself whether the child's welfare is truly paramount in your recording endeavours?

FURTHER RESOURCES AND READING

Healy, K. and Mulholland, J. (2008) *Writing Skills for Social Workers*. London: Sage.

Horwath, J. (ed.) (2010) *The Child's World, Assessing Children in Need*. London: Jessica Kingsley. This comprehensive work has a strong child-centred perspective.

O'Rourke, L. and Grant, H. (2005) *It's All in the Record: Meeting the Challenge of Open Recording*. Lyme Regis: Russell House.

Social Care Institute for Excellence. Visit the Institute's website (www.scie.org.uk) for a very helpful NQSW resource – Outcome statement 8. Recording and sharing.

11 WORKING IN AND AROUND THE ORGANISATION

Key Points of Chapter

- Social work takes place in a wide variety of organisations, each with its own value base
- You need to find your 'fit' with an organisation
- Multidisciplinary working is a part of what you will do in any social work role – to make this effective, you need to develop a specific set of skills
- Your organisation needs to be clear about the types of situation that call for social work involvement
- Meetings, meetings, meetings – are they all really necessary?
- Foster carers – unique colleagues who should be valued and respected
- The need to know how teams work and what your most effective role is within teams

Proposed Professional Capabilities Framework areas covered in this chapter

- Professionalism
- Values and Ethics
- Diversity
- Rights, Justice and Poverty
- Knowledge
- Critical Reflection and Analysis
- Interventions and Skills
- Contexts and Organisations
- Professional Leadership

(Social Work Reform Board, 2010 – see Appendix 1)

Draft Standards of Proficiency for Social Workers in England covered in this chapter

1 Be able to practise safely and effectively within their scope of practice
2 Be able to practise within the legal and ethical boundaries of their profession
3 Be able to maintain fitness to practise
4 Be able to practise as an autonomous professional, exercising their own professional judgement
5 Be aware of the impact of culture, equality and diversity on practice
6 Be able to practise in a non-discriminatory manner
7 Be able to maintain confidentiality
8 Be able to communicate effectively
9 Be able to work appropriately with others
10 Be able to maintain records appropriately
11 Be able to reflect on and review practice
12 Be able to assure the quality of their practice
13 Understand the key concepts of the bodies of knowledge which are relevant to their profession
14 Be able to draw on appropriate knowledge and skills to inform practice
15 Be able to establish and maintain a safe practice environment

(Health Professions Council, 2011 – see Appendix 2)

INTRODUCTION

Many different types of organisation carry out social work with children and families. Almost all these organisations now work in various types of partnership in an attempt to best create relationships and deliver services to children, families and community. Indeed, one of the great advantages of a social work career is that you can choose to work across a whole range of statutory, voluntary and private organisations all with their own systems, values, processes and accountabilities.

Contemporary social work practice is characterised by a cornucopia of procedures, guidelines, policies and protocols. In many ways, the complexity of social work is unhelpful in that workers can get lost in the paperwork and meeting the requirements of system rather than meeting the needs of children and their families (DfE, 2011b). Consider the reflections of Louise, 28 years, on the systems in her workplace:

> A huge investment in time and money has resulted in the obligatory use of specialised computer software. My placement experience has demonstrated to me that very few practitioners regard the software as a tool for their use, it is instead perceived as a means of supervising their work and extracting performance indicators. An analysis of frameworks of power might conclude that this has resulted in a situation where the 'tail is now wagging the dog'.

Due to the frequent changes in and restructuring of organisations 'organisational memory' (Mid Staffordshire NHS Foundation Trust Inquiry, 2010: 374) is lost and not only do people within these organisations not know the people they are working with, they often do not understand the organisation's structure or its key procedures and protocols.

Some of you will enjoy systems work and be skilled at report writing, and doubtless will look to find a social work role, probably in a local authority, where such work is significant. Others among you will seek to avoid systems-oriented social work and will seek positions, perhaps in the charitable sector or in community development work, where you will have the opportunity to play to your strengths. Although charitable or private organisations are also regulated by inspection regimes and have to accord to certain performance measures (particularly when contracted under the local authority, e.g. private foster care organisations) one of their main advantages is that they do often have shorter lines of communication and are less shackled by paperwork/IT compliance.

The performance management culture (Harris and Unwin, 2009) has meant that many organisations have been increasingly concerned with league tables and performance measures that often bear no relation to the core job that they are supposed to be doing, that is, promoting and protecting the best interests of children and their families. Inspection regimes have been part of social work with children since the 1980s (Cree and Myers, 2008) and a range of audit systems also have a part in the scrutiny of contemporary social work. Professional autonomy has been challenged over the years, particularly by the Conservative governments of the 1980s and by New Labour when they were in government.

As discussed in Chapter 1, some social work teams now are virtual teams and do not have a specific office space. **Hot desking** and the use of mobile information technology has led to many social workers working in a far more isolated manner than ever before. Such a work style may suit some individuals whereas others will seek a workplace where there is a greater degree of collegiality. According to Habermas (2004), social interactions also form an important part of the communication process and facilitate relationship building and effective working relationships. The support systems that are available in the more traditional-type workplaces, where you have an allocated desk/office/peer support and managerial system, clearly offer a different type of experience to more modern work environments which do not have these characteristics. In terms of your own development and supervision, particularly as an NQSW, you will need to ensure that there are sufficient support networks and meetings for you to become a safe practitioner.

Reflective point

Are there likely to be any differentials in experiences for social workers who choose to work in a fostering support team in:

- A local authority?
- A private sector organisation?
- A charitable organisation?

What would motivate you to choose to work in one of these sectors?

MULTIDISCIPLINARY/MULTIAGENCY WORKING

Multidisciplinary working can have many advantages (e.g. Atkinson et al., 2007) including those of clear role boundaries, recognition of professional differences, an understanding about what other agencies might be able to contribute and the potential to clearly share aims and information, perhaps even sharing funding and access to resources. However, Trevithick (2000) argues that multidisciplinary working also has its disadvantages. For example, time spent contacting and debating issues with other professionals is time not spent with children and families themselves; and it is often assumed that the more professionals who can put their heads together to make a decision the better. However, it may well be that the tendency for groups to conform or to bow to the status of a dominant professional personality can in fact lead to inferior decisions being made in such scenarios.

Multidisciplinary working in children's services has increased considerably since the Children Act 2004, despite the fact that there is no conclusive research base to support the effectiveness of this way of working. There is some limited evidence that the multidisciplinary based CAFs are working (Easton et al., 2011; Laming 2009).

A national review of the workings of the ICS concludes with the mixed message that:

> although the evidence is limited on outcomes, overall the direction of travel is a positive one and, for children and young people, there would not appear to be any negative effects. It may not be possible to demonstrate a causal relationship between the provision of integrated services and positive outcomes for children and families for the reasons highlighted earlier. However, we can perhaps say that integrated working creates the conditions that make improved outcomes for children and families more likely. (Oliver et al., 2010: 44)

We know also that not working together with other professionals can produce poor practice and even tragedy (see Blackburn with Darwen LSCB, 2010; Haringey LSCB, 2009) and there is much to be gained from listening to and learning from other professionals' point of view. Some other professionals may want to focus on one aspect of a child, for example, their offending or their attachment behaviour, whereas your imperative is to always ensure that such focused interests are always considered as part of the child's holistic, family and community make-up.

Reflective point

Are there some situations with which you have become involved where you felt it was unhelpful to have to consult/arrange meetings with many different professionals?

Could those decisions have been made either just by your own organisation or by liaising with just one rather than many organisations?

EVERY CHILD MATTERS

Every Child Matters (DfES, 2003) gave out a clear message that safeguarding children was not just the business of social workers, but was an area of work that was everybody's business, from citizens through schools, medical professionals and law enforcement agencies. There is much material in serious case reviews and inquiry reports such as those of Lord Laming (2009) that state that agencies are not working well together and do not share information.

The evidence base that led to *Every Child Matters* (DfES, 2003) clearly painted a picture of families across the UK who received a whole range of assessments from multiple agencies, ranging from universal healthcare agencies through to Connexions through to social services and educational agencies, all using different languages and all with different thresholds for intervention. All also had their own version of key workers, and quite clearly such a cumbersome system was not seen as constituting an effective way to communicate with families who may already be in chaos or suffering the overwhelming burden of dysfunction within one or more of their members.

Together with this desire to simplify communication with families and to ensure that agencies work better together, there was a drive under *Every Child Matters* (DfES, 2003) to decrease the number of children who were receiving **targeted and specialist services** and to move towards a future whereby universal services dealt with the majority of UK's well children. Targeted services, for example, Sure Start services, were seen as best placed to work effectively with vulnerable children whereas specialist services, such as social work, were envisaged as working with children in acute need. Any child, at any stage in their life course, can move between stages. Perhaps a child could be safe and healthy within mainstream services but due to a change in family dynamics may then move into needing targeted support and may even need specialist services. With the provision of effective interventions, the aim would be to move that child back to universal services meeting all their needs.

EFFECTIVE USE OF MEETINGS

'Meetings – the practical alternative to work' is a humorous statement that might be seen pinned to office doors, but behind this humour lies a very serious message. Part of the bad press about social workers is that they are 'always in meetings'. While it is evident that in the spirit of partnership, **multiagency working** and fulfilling an increasingly complex range of legislative duties, social workers will need to attend a range of meetings the numbers of these meetings must be questioned. Analysis of how effectively meetings are run; how they are minuted; how many people need to be there in order to make a decision; and whether decisions are made at that meeting – are critical issues of professionalism that should be balanced at all times. There are different types of meeting – professionals meetings, strategy meetings, planning meetings, child protection conferences, team meetings and management meetings. All meetings will need to be managed effectively and there will be different views and possible criticisms to field and actions to negotiate. Meetings, however, are often characterised in our experience by inefficiency, and lack of clarity and purpose, and are jargon riddled and often unproductive.

If you are arranging or chairing a meeting, there are certain key organisational responsibilities that you must get right to ensure that the meeting is as productive as it can be. Book a suitable room and ensure that its location is accessible to all, having particular sensitivity to the travel and caring responsibilities of families and children. The timing of the meeting is also critical and it is useful to set a finish time to the meeting to enable people to attend. You might want to offer in your invite to the meeting that people unable to attend contribute a written report, rather than not have any input from a person who may hold a critical piece of information. You will also need to arrange for somebody to record the key action points from a meeting; the actual format of recording will be governed by the protocols within your organisation.

You should be clear in your mind about the purpose of the meeting from your point of view and also think about other people's agendas and what they might be seeking from a meeting. Sometimes meetings are straightforward but on other occasions something unexpected crops up, pieces of information or behaviours that may radically alter the shape and structure of the meeting. For example, you may be involved in a TAC meeting delivering a CAF plan and an issue arises which seems to suggest that there is a safeguarding concern. Quite clearly the meeting would need to be brought to a halt and it would need to be explained to the participants that the issues being discussed would now move into a different forum.

Many professionals are comfortable with meetings, and many spend much of their working life in meetings, productive or not. Many families and children will be very threatened by the strange surroundings and protocols of a meeting, and it is essential that the chair introduces families and children and ensures that they understand, in jargon-free language, which issues are being discussed and what contribution everybody is allowed to make. The potential outcomes of a meeting might also be clarified, not just for the sake of children and families, but also other professionals who may be less familiar than yourself with the actual subject matter of your meeting. It is still all too common that people introduce themselves with acronyms and jargon and do not fully incorporate families and children into their deliberations. Sometimes meetings can be patronising and talk down to families and children and sometimes they can just ignore them, making their presence tokenistic and enabling you to tick boxes but not to interact in any meaningful manner.

Multidisciplinary working requires a range of skills including ensuring that you are aware of the role played by others such as health visitors, school nurses, year heads in schools and police members of child protection teams. You also need to know the basic remit of their jobs and the jargon that they may use. Always ask in meetings if phrases are being used that you do not understand because you can be guaranteed there will be at least one other person in that room who also does not understand what is being spoken about. It is a sign of intelligence, rather than ignorance, to ask such questions.

Effective social work teams need a balanced mix of established staff and new blood, and ideally they should reflect some of the diversity in the communities they serve. Interdisciplinary working is very much a part of the working life of a social worker and in order to be effective you will need to know about the roles, responsibilities and authority of the fellow professionals with whom you will find yourself working. Many professionals attend meetings where they are unsure of the scope and purpose of the meeting, unsure of the roles of others present and unsure of the jargon and abbreviations that often characterise such meetings.

Reflective point

Do you know what the roles of health visitors and educational psychologists are in your placement/work area?

How might you find out how health visitors and educational psychologists could/should complement your child protection work?

When children and families are involved in formal meetings, the dynamics are even more difficult to deal with, and careful consideration must be given to how you might enable a family or child to have a meaningful, rather than a tokenistic or patronised role in a meeting or case conference. Careful attention should be given to preparing the family, letting them know who is going to be present, that they can withdraw at any point, what the timescale of any decision made is likely to be, and that their understanding will be checked on as the meeting progresses.

Chairing skills would include ensuring also that everybody has a fair say and that some people do not dominate the meeting. Issues of status are present at all meetings and a good chair will ensure that any meeting is child-centred and not status-centred. All professionals in an increasingly multidisciplinary world need to get better at understanding each other's unique contributions to the overall welfare of children and families. Meetings should always conclude with a clear summary of the outcome of the meeting and the next steps that will be taken. From a professional development point of view it is useful also to reflect on how well the meeting went; how well did you contribute or chair; and what might you do differently next time to ensure a more positive outcome.

Particular difficulties can arise when the family has communication difficulties due to impairments or English not being their first language, and the services of an appropriate interpreter (see Chapter 5) should be engaged. Additionally, you may need to meet with the child and family immediately after a meeting to clarify outcomes and options. Consideration of factors such as these should be taken into account when scheduling meetings and other diary commitments; ineffective chairing of meetings should always be addressed, either during or after the meeting, seeking managerial advice as necessary.

FOSTER CARE

Foster care is sometimes seen as a specialist element of work with children and families which mainstream children and families workers do not need to have a deep understanding about. This is quite an erroneous position to take and it is the professional responsibility of all social workers involved in any way with children and families to understand the responsibilities and roles of contemporary foster carers. Foster care is in rather a unique position, having developed from the kindness of strangers over the ages through to increasing regulation since the Second World War, and has now become the placement of choice for children and young people, particularly since **residential care** homes have been seen as costly, ineffective and at times abusive (e.g. Barter, 2003).

Foster carers carry out a range of roles ranging from short break carers for children with disabilities, kinship care, emergency or remand fostering, treatment or therapeutic fostering, and short and long term fostering. Some foster carers specialise in preparing children for adoption and the skills needed in all forms of foster care are to be respected and valued by social workers, many of whom may still see foster carers as having a less important role in a child's life than themselves. The reality is that foster carers know the children with whom you will be working in great detail and also see their carers or parents in unguarded ways that it is not always possible to do in professional settings.

Foster carers are increasingly expected to act professionally, and the Fostering Network (2010) has made a strong case over the years for foster carers to be remunerated and given equivalent status alongside professionals such as social workers. The debate around professionalism is a complex one and there are many definitions of professionalism that consider issues such as status, training, regulation and autonomy. It is our contention that foster carers are part of a 'hybrid' profession in that they have many of the ethical and statutory responsibilities that other professionals have, but in the unique position they hold, they are never 'not at work'. That their task is carried out not by one individual professional but by a whole family, puts them in a unique position. As a social worker, you should look for ways to build relationships with foster carers that enable them to best understand the procedures you are bound by and to ensure that their insights and experience are both valued and incorporated into children's planning and outcomes rather than being seen as some kind of lesser contribution when their opinions are sought alongside those of social, medical and police professionals. Foster carers are also at the centre of safeguarding issues, allegations in foster care (Jackson and Unwin, 2010) being a cause for concern. While proven allegations are rare, any foster carer who fosters for any length of time will be subject to complaints and allegations because of the contested and traumatic nature of the backgrounds of the children for whom they care and the various agendas around that make the environment emotionally very volatile. Unlike social workers, medical professionals or police professionals, however, foster carers do not have employment rights or trade union rights of representation and they are not catered for by employment legislation that would ensure levels of remuneration were guaranteed until a case was proven or otherwise. They are indeed very vulnerable and this vulnerability should be acknowledged and dealt with sensitively if you are involved in issues around foster carers and allegation issues.

Reflective point

Should you treat an allegation against a foster carer differently from an allegation against a general member of the public?

Comment

There is no doubt that allegations are part of the territory of being a foster carer and all allegations should be treated seriously but respectfully and swiftly investigated. This is because foster carers are your colleagues and a scarce resource through over-zealous or judgemental actions, particularly as we know that the vast majority of allegations made against foster carers are either unfounded or proven to be false. Foster carers will have their own fostering support social worker whose main role is to support them through their development and practice, but the fostering support social workers will also get to know the children for whom you are responsible as a children and families social worker. Again, you should ensure that you know them sufficiently well to be able to communicate meaningfully and in a child-centred way.

In looking holistically at the issues within foster care it is important that you also consider the health and welfare of any sons and daughters of the foster carers who have variously been constructed as invisible, vulnerable or valued (Jackson and Unwin, 2009) within foster care. Sons and daughters of foster children can be vulnerable in that they lose some of the attention from their parents when a foster child moves into the family and at worse will suffer emotional and sometimes even physical and sexual abuse from foster children who are placed.

Reflective point

Why might a child who is fostered make allegations?

Comment

Some of the possibilities are:

- The foster carer, or a member of their family, has actually abused the child
- The child has misinterpreted their actions or intentions
- The child or someone close to the child has a grudge and sees the foster carer as the person to attack
- The child may be seeking to pressurise the social worker into letting them move back to their carer or parent's home
- The child may see an allegation as a way of getting attention and kicking against the care system.

Foster care now takes place in local authorities, private foster agencies and in not for profit agencies (the last two are often aggregated into the 'independent sector'). Encouragement of foster care in the independent sector has been a feature since the 1980s, and independent agencies essentially developed because local authorities were seen as not giving sufficient attention and support to their own foster carers. This sector has grown considerably, although it is of course still supported by local authority money as it is the local authorities who pay for their children to be placed in independent sector placements, which may cost over three times as much as a local authority placement. Some local authorities have improved their services in response to this competition whereas others have allowed their services to wither away and are now virtually totally dependent on the independent sector. The theoretical benefits of the independent sector are that their priorities are fostering first and foremost; originally the independent agencies were small and often led by ex-foster carers, hence they were empathic and knowledgeable about the needs of foster children and their carers. Many of these small agencies, in line with the pattern of much capitalist entrepreneurialism, have now become part of bigger companies via takeovers and there is concern that business considerations may outweigh child-centred considerations.

Despite the far higher charges of the independent sector, there is no convincing evidence that the success of the independent sector with regard to stability of placements and the outcomes among children who are fostered are significantly any different from those in children within local authority fostering placements. The overall outcomes for children who leave care, whether they are fostered or in residential care, is still very poor when compared with mainstream populations of children, in relation to the likelihood of reaching higher education, achieving employment, achieving stability in later relationships and avoiding mental illness (Cameron et al., 2007).

RESIDENTIAL CARE

Residential care is now a comparatively small part of childcare provision and you will be unlikely to have many children accommodated within residential care during your career. Some older children prefer the greater anonymity that a children's home offers compared to the closeness of a foster home and may therefore do comparatively better in such a setting. It is important that you get to know the culture within any local children's home that you may be working with and forge a relationship with the key worker for the child for whom you are responsible. Children in care, whether they are in foster care or residential care, place great emphasis on wanting a social worker who they can talk to and who will stick around for some years rather than only dip in and out of their lives (McLeod, 2010). It is important that you do your utmost to keep up not only with your statutory level of visits to children in care but also that you maintain other contact, for example, telephone calls, birthday contact and ensure that the child sees your commitment to them as authentic and genuine, even though you may have many other children and families on your case list.

HOW TEAMS WORK

Much has been written about how teams work and here we look briefly at some of the seminal writing concerning teams which you may find useful when considering your most effective role within those teams. Belbin's (2010) team roles remains a very influential way of looking at team dynamics; the essence of his argument is that effective teams need a role balance with the right proportion of creative thinkers, shapers of ideas, and people who will do the grassroots job, together with those who will monitor and evaluate. If you have too many thinkers in a team then you may have lots of great ideas but no action and if you have lots of 'busy, busy' people who are running around in circles without direction or purpose then that team will also be ineffective. In recent years, social work and public service in general has seen a proliferation of monitoring/evaluation and this state of imbalance has been criticised by reports such as the *Munro Report* (DfE, 2011b). Another key writer on teamwork is Tuckman (1965), whose model of 'storming, forming, norming and performing' and its many fine tunings has also stood the test of time. Essentially Tuckman identifies that all effective teams should appropriately storm (push and pull for position/role/influence) before forming (starting to recognise strengths and weaknesses), before norming (finding the right balance of skills, roles and responsibilities), before (hopefully!) going on to perform their required duties, in your case as a social work team with children and families.

Effective team working can help to reduce the stressors that are often present within the contemporary work place. According to Wilson et al. (2008), team working is underpinned by good and effective communication, both formal and informal, including tackling awkward and difficult issues. Effective teams help organisations adopt a learning culture which should be of benefit to workers and also to the children, families and communities. An effective social work team will embrace reflective practice as a way of looking at itself and adopt practices in the light of effective reflection. Informal peer supervision, both from an individual and team perspective, provides the means whereby learning and growth can occur (Wilson et al., 2008). Zoe, 28 years, reflects positively below on the way she saw her team working:

> I worked in a team comprised of a diverse group of people. There were a number of people who had held careers in other fields before entering Social Work. It was evident that they brought insights to the team that were the product of their varied backgrounds. At the same time we had younger newly qualified workers who had come straight from college. They had particular strengths unsullied by the cynicism that occasionally affected older or more experienced workers. The open plan office encouraged debate and reflection, and created a mutually supportive environment in which people could wrestle with the contradictions that sometimes accompanied our statutory role. These various factors resulted in a synthesis of 'best practice', a situation that was ultimately to the benefit of the service users we worked with.

CHAPTER SUMMARY

There are a wide range of organisations in social work and you need to find one that best fits with your skills, values and preferred ways of working. You need to know how teams work and how you best perform in teams, much of your work being carried out alongside other organisations and with colleagues such as foster and residential care staff. It is essential that you develop skills in working with others and that you understand their roles and responsibilities. Being effective in meetings and in the way you use IT and other systems around your job is essential if you are to free up time to enable you to work directly with children and families.

FURTHER RESOURCES AND READING

Health Professions Council (2011) *Standards of Proficiency for Social Workers.* (England) Professional Liaison Group (PLG) (www.hpc-uk.org/assets/documents/10003381Item05-enc3-draftstandardsofproficiency2-SOPs.pdf).

Munro Final Report (DfE, 2011b) – This report recommends proposals for social work reform in order to meet the needs of children and families (https://www.education.gov.uk/publications/.../Cm%208062.pdf).

Social Work Reform Board website – A useful website that contains all the details of the workings of this government commissioned body set up in 2010 to reform social work in England. The Board has strong links to the *Munro Report* (www.education.gov.uk/swrb).

12

LOOKING AFTER YOURSELF

Key Points of Chapter

- The social work environment is a highly pressured one that calls for resilient workers
- You cannot deliver effective social work services if you do not have a good work/home life balance
- Some work environments are inherently unhealthy and should be challenged
- There is an onus on management to take responsibility for the health of their teams
- You have a personal/family responsibility for keeping yourself healthy by making a good work–life balance a reality
- There may be untapped strengths and resources in your teams
- Supervision and training have a critical role to play in your healthy and productive development as a professional
- Recent government-backed reports seek to bring about a learning and supportive culture within social work

Proposed Professional Capabilities Framework covered in this chapter

- Professionalism
- Values and Ethics
- Critical Reflection and Analysis
- Interventions and Skills
- Contexts and Organisations
- Professional Leadership

(Social Work Reform Board, 2010 – see Appendix 1)

Draft Standards of Proficiency for Social Workers in England covered in this chapter

1 Be able to practise safely and effectively within their scope of practice
2 Be able to practise within the legal and ethical boundaries of their profession
3 Be able to maintain fitness to practise
4 Be able to practise as an autonomous professional, exercising their own professional judgement
8 Be able to communicate effectively
9 Be able to work appropriately with others
11 Be able to reflect on and review practice
12 Be able to assure the quality of their practice
15 Be able to establish and maintain a safe practice environment

(Health Professions Council, 2011 – see Appendix 2)

INTRODUCTION

Change is the only constant in social work and an effective social worker is the worker who finds ways to manage change, despite the challenging, volatile and, at times, hostile environment in which you will be working. Jones saw social work as a:

> traumatised, even defeated occupation, the manifestations of stress and unhappiness in social services departments were various, serious and pervasive. … Many spoke of being emotionally and physically exhausted by the demands of their work. (2001: 550–1)

Ten years on, Munro makes the following recommendation:

> Local authorities and their partners should start an ongoing process to review and redesign the ways in which child and family social work is delivered, drawing on evidence of effectiveness of helping methods where appropriate and supporting practices that can implement evidence based ways of working with children and families. (DfE, 2011b: 13)

There is a world of difference between these two images of social work and this chapter will look at ways in which you might develop your skills in a work environment that can help deliver the second vision and consign Jones' (2001) vision of social work to history.

WHAT DO ORGANISATIONS WANT FROM THEIR SOCIAL WORKERS?

Social work organisations want a committed and passionate workforce whose commitment is to a set of values about empowering, enabling and protecting vulnerable children and their families. Organisations seek workers with knowledge and principles who will be creative and innovative and able to work with individuals on a one-to-one basis as well as with partner agencies who may sometimes have different thresholds, backgrounds and perhaps a different focus from social workers themselves.

Contemporary social work organisations seek workers who have a grasp of the financial realities of everyday practice and who recognise that the public purse is not a bottomless one. Effective social workers are those who are able to advocate that children and families get as good a possible resourcing deal as they can from limited resources. Such an advocatory role may sometimes involve advising children and families that they should seek the services of a third party, a good social worker having contacts for advocacy services. Increasingly, social workers are expected to be IT competent as well as able to produce convincing and succinct reports for conferences and legal settings, which are clear in their argument and make recommendations that accordingly serve the best interests of children and families.

In order to be effective within modernised social work, you will need to work with the system, rather than against the system. Although rules are there to be worked around and challenged, they are to be respected as part of the system of welfare that has been developed since the post-war years. Bureaucratic requirements may at times seem overwhelming but there is usually a way around these.

A good professional and a good manager will recognise when workload stress is becoming unacceptable. Although a social worker should expect to be doing a demanding and difficult job, there is an unfortunate prevalence of a rather 'macho' culture in some social work teams whereby being seen as 'getting the job done' means being incredibly busy and working constantly unsociable hours. Such cultures should be challenged and it may be that unreasonable requests regarding workload should be referred on to professional associations or unions for advice and guidance. There is a clear managerial and political system that should ensure that social work does not become an unmanageable and highly stressful organisation in which workers burn out after only a few years' practice.

SHARING OUR KNOWLEDGE AND WORKLOAD

We believe that there are ways in which colleagues could help each other in sharing practice wisdom, expertise and techniques for being compliant with targets and systems while at the same time not spending too much time in trying to be perfect. A preoccupation with achieving procedural perfection or an approach that only values face to face contact and ignores procedural obligations will not make an effective social worker. Both the public and the *Munro Report* (DfE, 2011b) do not want social workers to be spending all their time behind their desks at computers but to be out there within our communities working face to face with people and their problems.

Reflective point

Think about colleagues in your workplace and the amount of time they spend recording or doing a court report.

While all families and their needs are different, is there perhaps room within your team for an agreed core rule about how many hours might be appropriately spent on say a court report or preparing a conference report?

The ability to create meaningful personal relationships still lies at the heart of contemporary social work and a good social worker is a professional who is able to live with reasoned and defendable risk which reflects the realities of family life within many of our communities. Reflective practice is not supposed to be an abstract concept but a practical way of ordering one's thoughts, taking on a range of perspectives and being able to act in the different ways the next time you meet a similar situation. Looking after yourself can be seen as a cliché in organisations which tend to promote a 'work, work, work' culture, and it is the responsibility of all us to ensure that that the much-wanted work–life balance is a reality rather than an aspiration. In these days of rapid technological advances (if that is always the right word) social workers can be contactable via handheld devices 24 hours a day and indeed some of you may like the flexibility that mobile/home-based ways of working can bring. The isolation that such modernised ways of working can sometimes bring with them is not always healthy, however, particularly for NQSWs or workers who need at hand the close support of colleagues and managers.

THE RESPONSIBILITIES OF MANAGEMENT

Effective management should be welcomed by any social worker as a way of helping them through the stresses and complexities of the job, and management has to share responsibility for the state of health and well-being among the workforce. The potential for first-line managers to provide support and 'resistance' against managerialism has been articulated by Evans (2010), and a therapeutic alliance is one that should be sought with your immediate manager. Evans (2010) talks about a culture of 'resistance' between social workers and first-line managers, whereby they are able to identify with issues at street level and to find ways on many occasions to get around the strictures and protocols that the bureaucracy surrounding much of social work demands. However, if staff are involved in cases for short time periods only, on interim contracts or indeed agency contracts, there is little opportunity for such trusting relationships to be built up. Also, if teams are inherently transient, the opportunity to build capacity with your local community in terms of the families and children with whom you work as well as the professionals with whom you have to work is severely hampered. Management also need to be appropriately directive at times and the days of professionals in social work or related professions setting their own goals and priorities as autonomous individuals are long gone, although the argument that discretion still exists in significant ways in social work is made by Evans and Harris (2004).

There is an obligation on the elected members of a local authority and indeed central government to ensure that the health and safety of their workforce is guaranteed. Social work is a particularly stressful profession, and given the fact that at the time of writing it does not command high respect or standing among the general public, social workers will often come in for criticism and even abuse about their role. You will need to develop strategies to deal with this, and although you will reasonably be expected to take certain levels of criticism, there will be other levels of criticism or abuse that would not be acceptable. You need the reassurance of a manager and an organisation that you will be supported in working in an environment that is both safe and healthy.

Some things to bear in mind are that you should not constantly work overtime, you should have a second person accompany you on visits which carry a degree of risk and your membership of professional associations and unions should be encouraged rather than discouraged.

FITTING INTO THE TEAM

Most local authorities and sizeable independent sector organisations will have their own specific support systems for NQSWs. When starting a new job you should always insist on a structured induction programme that covers not only the health and safety issues of the workplace but one which also enables you to meet key people in and outside the organisation. The Social Work Reform Board (2010) was concerned that many social workers did not seem to have induction periods when they started new jobs and has produced clear sets of guidelines that stipulate that structured programmes must be introduced on all occasions. In terms of the support you might need in a new job, you may find special interest groups on certain topics within your wider organisation. Also, your local university might be interested in facilitating such groups and encouraging you to continue on your lifelong learning path.

Some organisations have successfully introduced groups for NQSWs, who have been able to use this to learn as well as to develop new networks. Under current policy, the AYSE for NQSWs has to contain a specifically identified training and development programme so you will be able to meet colleagues in a similar situation within your organisation. Every opportunity should be made to make the most of these situations rather than such opportunities being seen as a distraction from 'getting on with the job'. All social work teams are busy, and always have been so. Good social work teams, however, do not overload their staff and do not permit a culture whereby burn out and high levels of stress and sickness are the characteristics of that team.

Fitting into a new team can be a difficult experience and even social work teams, despite their ethical base of being non-judgemental and inclusive, can have their own cliques and power struggles. Feeling your way into a team is often a tricky business, but be true to your values from day one and do not allow yourself to be dragged into any collusive games. Try to rise above any office politics that may be present. We all need allies at work and you will need to find kindred spirits who can help you establish yourself as a fulfilled and effective worker. Many teams these days do not seem to have a social side, and even office parties seem to have disappeared in contemporary office culture. While many of us do not want to necessarily socialise with our workmates, it is in our view a positive thing to have a social element to a social work team and it may be there are people within your office who have been around for some time and are happy to help you establish some kind of social side to your work.

Unfortunately, the rapid turnover of many social workers and the use of agency social workers as stop gaps have meant that some social work teams themselves do not know each other and the children, families and communities with whom they are working. Some type of social activity can help better bond such teams and some effort should be made to try to lighten the workplace by considering the possibility of certain social activities.

Reflective point

Consider the following account by Shelagh, a NQSW who is writing about her first paid job:

'I joined an established team of three established workers. They have their "own" room and along with three other new workers, one of whom was also newly qualified, we were placed in another office. The older workers seem to distance themselves from the new entrants to the team and now almost a year on, we do not have a good working relationship – the reasons for this I do not know. There seems [to be] hostility towards new workers – perhaps this is not managed well by our Team Manager, as there appears [to be] hostility towards him also.

In terms of the multiculturalism/politics of our team, I am a minority on my team in terms of my ethnicity. I have experienced some oppression in terms of other workers being told not to speak to me and engage with me because of my skin colour. I have learnt from this, and understand how it may feel to experience, in some part, racism. Clearly, this is not racism in terms of the whole of society, as I am part of the majority in terms of my white skin colour but I can now understand how it feels to be treated differently because of something you can't change and because of others' prejudice.

In many other ways, I benefit from the diversity of our team, I have a background that is distinctly non-diverse and I will be able to use this to inform my social work practice in the future. It has made me realise by looking at this experience at how individuals from ethnic minorities may feel and it has made me reflect upon how there are barriers in place within society which can inhibit Black and Minority Ethnic (BME) individuals succeeding at times in comparison to their white counterparts.'

- If you were faced with a team dynamic such as that faced by Shelagh, would you take such a philosophical view or might you take alternative action?
- What factors ought you to consider before taking any action?

DRESS CODES – DOES APPEARANCE MATTER?

The question of what to wear as a social worker is more than a light-hearted issue. Some professions have a uniform or established dress code but social work has neither, partly because it has recently evolved as a profession and partly because its roles are so varied, sometimes taking place in formal settings such as courts and at other times getting involved in play activities at a children's centre. Social work is distinct from other professions in several ways – its championing of the individual, its commitment to social justice, its politicisation and its use of self. Effective and appropriate use of self does not mean hiding behind status and distance but finding a balance that is somewhere between approachable and formal. 'Casual smart' (which has a range of interpretations!) is perhaps a good guideline for you to adopt in any social work situation; court settings are very formal and you must dress accordingly. To appear dressed in an 'anti-establishment way' in court is unlikely to help the children and families whom you might be supporting. There are stories of men in social work teams sharing the 'court tie', which is an amusing way of looking at this whole issue around how you need to present to best give out the right message to children and families and the other professionals with whom you work. Jeans and trainers might be quite appropriate in some settings, such as those of children's centres.

Your appearance and the car that you drive give out messages to the children and families with whom you work. To dress too ostentatiously and expensively or to drive a 'flashy' car may create an unnecessary barrier. Families may not be frank and open with you, as they may see such trappings of success as indicators that you are a person who is far removed from an understanding of what life might be for them in their sometimes desperate and often poverty-stricken environment.

Reflective point

- Do you agree or not agree with the above statement about 'flashy' cars and being expensively dressed?
- Think about the dress code and general professional demeanour in your organisation. Do you think that every member of your team is appropriate in their professional demeanour?
- Do you think that the general way in which your team works is professional?
- If not, how might things change and what might be your role in achieving any such change?

The sticky question (pun intended) arises regarding the messages you give out when undertaking a home visit. Do you sit down/accept a drink/any food from families whose hygiene levels may be questionable or have you always 'just had' a cup of tea at your last visit? These again, are not light-hearted issues, many families have little that they feel they can reciprocate, and you accepting their cup of tea may help them feel more respected and that the balance of power is perhaps not as weighted as they may have thought.

RULES OF PROFESSIONAL CONDUCT

Your organisation will have a range of policies on appropriate behaviour, and the Health Professions Council also has national criteria governing such issues. You should know your organisation's policy on the acceptance of gifts, which probably states that some token gifts might be acceptable whereas others may not. A painting done by a child, for example, would be perhaps a positive gift to accept, whereas other gifts of greater monetary value might turn the relationship into being a collusive one. A social worker generally needs to toe that fine line between being 'friendly' but not 'friends' with the children and families with whom they work.

Inappropriate friendships can be dangerous, given the nature of your work and your organisation should have clear guidelines/disciplinary proceedings for dealing with failures within the social work profession. Find out what your organisation's disciplinary and grievance procedures are before you ever need to use them. Grievance procedures are taken out by workers whereas disciplinary proceedings are instigated by organisations when professional standards are believed to have fallen to an unacceptable level. It is always best to try to resolve matters informally with colleagues or with management because grievance and disciplinary proceedings are very time consuming and not always productive experiences.

Your organisation is also likely to have a 'whistleblowing' policy, whereby a worker should be able to bring attention to any matters of illegality or unethical behaviours without fear of redress. Again, find out your organisation's policy on whistleblowing. Joining a union is essential for social workers and membership of the College of Social Work will also provide some independent support to social workers who find themselves in compromised positions at work. Social workers with less than 12 months in a job and social workers in the private sector in particular are more vulnerable in terms of employment security.

Consider the following reflections of Raj, who found himself in a difficult situation in his first independent sector fostering job after qualifying:

> Once I had taken up the post I hit the ground running with a high and complicated case load. The support from the team manager turned out to be minimal. The ethos of the agency was to secure placements, placements and more placements.
>
> I started to question some practices which seemed to me to be entirely profit driven rather than child-centred, with matches being made that did not seem to be within our foster carers' capabilities. I particularly objected to one placement being made as I believed that both child and foster carer were being set up to fail. Following this I was called into the Operational Manager's office and informed that my contract had been terminated. I was asked to leave the building immediately.
>
> I sought advice from my union, who were fantastic in supporting me to secure a fair and just reference that reflected the work and skills I had undertaken during the course of my work. The process was long and drawn out and led to my feeling depressed and questioning my own judgement and even my version of events. Until finding myself in this position, I had never considered my lack of employment rights due to having less than 12 months employment and never dreamed that a social care agency could act in such a way.
>
> My experience as an adult with this agency made me reflect on just how powerless children in their care, and foster carers, must feel whenever they want to speak out. I had a union to support me – they don't.

It is not only independent sector agencies that can work in ways such as those detailed above and the message is that, as well as personal resilience and support, you also need appropriate professional support and representation if you are to have a long, healthy and effective career.

RESILIENCE

Looking at the resilience required to be an effective social worker requires a lifestyle in which positive aspects of your life outside work (and make sure you have one!) can be used to balance/counteract some of the stresses and strains of working day in and day out with highly emotive issues. Social work with children and families is a very stressful job and you need the necessary resilience to ensure that you are strong enough both mentally and physically to be able to make difficult decisions on a day-to-day basis. Being sufficiently resilient means having coping mechanisms either within your family, friends or outside activities that give you a healthy perspective of the work that you carry out. We would like to think that you would be part of a new culture in social work that will be characterised by social workers staying in the job for many years, experiencing reduced levels of sickness and helping raise the overall profile and status of the profession.

Social work is an emotional job and we should have moved a long way from a model of professionalism in which we kept our emotions hidden. There is a time and a place, however, to let out your emotions. It is probably not a good idea to burst into tears too often when working with a family in dire straits but probably a healthy thing to have a good cry in the car on your way back from a visit or to show such emotion appropriately in the presence of colleagues or friends whom you can trust.

You will not always feel an expert in the face of all the challenges presented to you. Our definition of an expert is somebody who holds their hands up and says 'I do not know the answer' to a certain issue. Such an expert will use their intelligence and seek out help rather than pretend that they know the answers and go on to act in what might be possibly an ineffective and possibly even dangerous way. It is clearly more difficult to ask for help if you are not working in a setting that has a traditional office base but as a professional you must find ways of getting help and you must not act in situations where you are not confident about your ground, particularly when dealing with the lives of vulnerable children.

Reflective point

- How would you describe the level of comradeship in your team?
- How difficult is it to get a second opinion on an issue about which you are concerned?

(Continued)

(Continued)

- If you are not happy with the availability of face to face discussion and advice about your workload what might you be able to do to bring about a more effective way of working?
- How often do you have team meetings and how often are these meetings only dominated by 'business' concerns or do the humanistic support and development issues also get appropriate time on the agenda?
- What might you be able to do to bring about any change in the nature of your team meetings?

FAMILY-FRIENDLY WORKING

It is ironic that so many social work employers boast of being **family friendly**, equal opportunity and caring types of organisation, whereas the reality of the social work environment in general belies such claims. Stress among social workers is an issue that should be taken seriously, not only because of the effect this has in human terms but because a workforce that is not healthy will not be an efficient workforce. Stanley et al. (2007) demonstrated that stress levels could be alleviated when more flexible ways of working were introduced and by the ways in which organisations offered part-time work. However, the numbers of social workers who are offered any of these options were very small indeed, and this has also been cited (Unwin, 2009) as one of the reasons for social workers moving into agency employment. There is no doubt that some children and families and colleagues find part-time availability of social workers difficult. There is also no doubt that the number of meetings/administrative tasks that social workers currently have to attend does tend to give them a reputation for being unavailable when the needs of children and families are present seven days a week.

Asthana (2008) reported that one in five social workers are signed off work for more than 20 days per year because of issues of stress and anxiety. The cost of such absences is massive and managerial strategies should be brought into play to try to address the structural nature of such loss and expense. Smith (2010) found that high workloads were a particular problem for social workers and several respondents commented that their home life suffered in terms of their own ability to be a good parent because of the effort they expended around the parenting issues of others in their social work job. The additional media pressures from the recent child protection tragedies have further added to this stress identified by social workers. Pile (2009) states that social workers on average work an extra 25 days a year which means that they also had a problem in taking holidays. McGregor (2009) also identified social workers banking up huge amounts of time off in lieu and not taking their holidays, the analysis being that social workers are not only overworked but afraid to have a break from work due to worries of getting behind or showing other colleagues and their managers that they are not managing their workload. Morris (2009) reported that on average social workers take almost 12 days off during the year due to sickness, with one in ten calling in sick at least 20 times. This is clearly not a healthy culture, particularly for NQSWs to be entering into, and employers, managers, unions and indeed yourself have responsibility for ensuring that you do not become one of these statistics and end up leaving social work in an unhealthy state after years of unacceptable stress. The importance of good support and supervision has been recognised for many years in social work and is one of the claims that social work traditionally made to be a supportive and quality working environment.

Reflective point

- How might you ensure that you and your team take your time off in lieu/holidays?
- What other strategies might you employ to look after yourself at work?

Lombard (2011) suggests that because of the nature of much children and families social work, social workers should set aside half an hour each week for what he calls personal healing – allowing staff such time and space to reflect on their practice should be perhaps an implicit requirement for enabling professionalism and models the type of reflection we expect them to undertake with the children and families in their care.

There is a very unfortunate culture that has crept into social work of late regarding teams working very long hours (McNabb, 2010). The reality of burn-out rates in social work might suggest that this is a foolhardy culture to promote. There is also a view that if you cannot get your job done within standard working hours, you are not working effectively. Particularly if you have the support of a union, you should never be asked to work unreasonable hours and you should use your assertive skills appropriately, as well as workload management techniques such as blocking out days to do administrative work or booking your holidays well in advance so that you know those dates are protected.

THE ROLE OF SUPERVISION

In the past supervision in social work has been seen as poor quality, patchy and in some extreme cases completely non-existent. A survey of social workers' workloads, published by the Social Work Task Force in (2010), found that a quarter of children's social workers were not receiving monthly supervision. Hunter (2009) illustrates how the focus of contemporary supervision has become more managerialist, moving from reflection, support and looking at personal development to a dominance of targets, case discussion and action plans.

Professional issues of concern or celebration should be raised in supervision, supervision being a traditional quality hallmark of social work. Case discussions and action plans certainly need to make up part of supervision, but appropriate supervision should enable you to raise issues of concern and of development in regard to your professional career, including skill development, abilities and understanding. A further function of supervision is offering a restorative/supportive environment in which workers can reflect on their reactions to work (Wilson et al., 2008). Munro (DfE, 2011b) has also identified the need for good supervision and sees it as the opportunity to provide space for critical reflection and professional reasoning, thus facilitating better assessments and decision making.

You should be offered a guaranteed level of supervision and you should not accept cancellation of supervision meetings or appraisals when the day-to-day pressures of the office mean that your supervisor is unable to prioritise supervision. Your organisation will always be busy and things never settle down in a job such as social work to a situation whereby you will be coasting along without a care in the world. Legislation, policies, procedures, expectations and technology are ever-changing.

Social workers who receive more therapeutic styles of supervision have said that it contributed to their own well-being and ability to cope with stress (Social Work Taskforce, 2010). Group and peer supervision are also ways to look at the promotion of good practice and sharing of ideas and indeed sharing of concerns and worries. The mobile and flexible working arrangements that some social workers now find themselves in, makes it particularly difficult to be able to have regular informal discussions about the core concerns in your work.

Reflective point

In what ways might you promote regular informal discussion about work in your placement or work situation?

The Standards for Employers and Supervision Framework for supervision promoted by the Social Work Reform Board (2010) states that employers should ensure supervision sessions last for at least 90 minutes of uninterrupted time and that this should be weekly for the first six weeks that a NQSW is in employment. Then the supervision should be done fortnightly for the next six months and be at least monthly thereafter. A stipulation was also made that all practitioners should be supervised by a registered social worker. There have been some interesting moves in some local authorities such as Hackney (Cross et al., 2010), whereby consultant social workers have been identified as being senior practitioners with a wealth of practice wisdom and who can act in a supportive, developmental way with social workers and not be primarily concerned with managerial issues. This type of initiative received considerable support in the *Munro Report* (DfE, 2011b).

Such innovations are in their early days of being evaluated but it may well be that this consultant social worker role is a positive step forward that might separate managerial and workload issues from issues of personal development and the quality of social work. Wonnacott (2011) explains that supervisors need to take time to establish rapport with their supervisee so that a relationship of trust can be built up. This suggests that quality of work life and work environment has a relationship with the stability and retention of staff, particularly those in a supervisory capacity.

THE ROLE OF LEARNING AND DEVELOPMENT

A good social worker will be effective when they are open to learning and keen to develop new skills year on year and to use reflective practice. However, despite a range of initiatives in recent years to promote a learning culture within social work, the Social Work Reform Board states:

> CPD [continuous professional development] is not yet properly valued and supported in all places and organisations. We have heard that the framework as a whole is not sufficiently coherent, effective or widely understood, with weaknesses in choice, flexibility and relevance. Take up has varied across the country and has been disappointing overall. There are considerable barriers in many parts of the country to social workers undertaking courses, including lack of employer support and, particularly, a lack of time due to heavy workloads.

> Social work lacks shared understanding of the overall direction, shape and content of its programme of professional development. The current position is a recipe for inconsistency, confusion and poor practice. It is bad for retaining people in social work and for the status of the profession. We need more employing organisations ready to support ongoing training and learning (as well as initial training), in support of a profession with a much clearer sense of what career long development should mean. (2010: 38; emphasis added)

Some organisations still see training and development as an excuse to get out of 'real' work. This short-sighted view has led to a situation whereby many social workers only fulfil the minimum PRTL requirements. Opportunities for formal post qualifying training have only been poorly supported to date and a change in culture is essential if social work effectiveness is to be improved. There is an imperative for management and employers to ensure that such activities as supervision and training and development are seen as essential, rather than additional extras which cannot be afforded when times are tough.

Part of a professional culture should be to bring on the next generation, and social work organisations are currently struggling to find enough practice educators to train students. It is our contention that all social workers of more than two or three years standing should be expected to take on such mentoring roles as a necessary part of changing the landscape within the profession.

CHAPTER SUMMARY

Social work has in recent years been an unhealthy profession, characterised by high rates of sickness and absenteeism. Management and the top-down proliferation of procedural ways of working must take the major responsibility for this parlous state of affairs. Social work is not a business; it is a moral and political activity that needs an energised and supported workforce to help it reconcile its many tensions, stresses and challenges. You can also have some control over your career trajectory and stress levels by ensuring that you get appropriate support and reflective/relaxation time to ensure that you are in the right state of mind and body to carry out effective social work. The recommendations of recent government-backed reviews (DfE, 2011b; Social Work Reform Board, 2010) contain core themes around the need to establish a new supportive and learning culture around social work, in contrast to the experiences of recent years.

FURTHER RESOURCES AND READING

Barefoot Social Worker. This website challenges some of the more traditional perspectives of social work addressing radical solutions towards more contemporary social work (www.radical.org.uk/barefoot/).

British Association of Social Work (BASW, The College of Social Work). This website provides a rich source of literature, publications, journals, media releases and government updates (www.basw.co.uk/).

Communitycare.co.uk. This website has informative, up-to-date articles covering many aspects of social work (www.communitycare.co.uk/Home/).

Coulshed, V., Mullender, A., Jones, D.N. and Thompson, N. (2006) *Management in Social Work*, 3rd edn. Basingstoke: Palgrave Macmillan.

Joseph Rowntree Foundation. Very useful site concerned with the root causes of social problems and how best to solve them (www.jrf.org.uk).

Lawler, J. and Bilson, A. (2010) *Social Work Management and Leadership*. Abingdon: Routledge.

Social Worker Retention Project (2011) (www.westmidlandsiep.gov.uk/download.php?did=1960).

CONCLUSION

Social work with children and families is an exciting and complex profession. Rather than in any way being a lesser profession, it is a profession of the highest order that demands a range of practical, ethical, legal and emotional skills, all needing to be combined with effective use of self. Nobody needs to apologise for being a children and families social worker – safeguarding and promoting the welfare of children should be seen as the most important job in our society.

Somehow, however, the image of social work is the very opposite to the image that it should have. Its challenges should attract the best people, people who not only want to make a difference, but who do make a difference, because they are able to achieve the blend of skills discussed in this book in ways that are truly child-centred. We want you to be a social worker who is committed to lifelong learning and development, aware of your strengths and weaknesses, and able to work in genuine partnership with children and families, communities and key professionals. Many of the sad messages that have come up time and time again in enquiries and serious case reviews are the same sad messages – messages of lack of knowledge, poor recording, poor communication, poor leadership, poor knowledge base about diversity and child development and, critically, practice scenarios where the voice of the child is not heard.

The messages in this book about use of self, communication, analysis, looking after yourself and effective working in organisations are messages that seem to have often been forgotten in an increasingly pressured working environment that has become characterised by business mentality, performance indicators and an over-riding emphasis on resources rather than children. Time is a precious commodity and we are all busy professionals, but time is what we all have most of – we have far more time than we do other resources. Making best use of this time is at the core of effective social work and to question whether your time is most effectively being used is a reflective practice that should be at the heart of your everyday working life. The social work world is not short of codes of practice, guidelines, protocols, case reviews, case law and position statements, but it is you as an individual who will make such policies and values real at street level. It is at street level where we hope that you will spend the major proportion of your working life and we hope that you will be part of a new culture that turns around the percentage of time spent administering and accounting for your actions. We want your actions to speak louder than IT systems and your practice to make a real difference to the lives of children and families.

As we stated at the beginning of Chapter 1, social work is not a 'win-win' situation; tragedy and harm will befall our children and families again in the future but never again should this be because we do not have the knowledge and skills to intervene effectively with children and families who come to our attention. Knowledge about how to intervene and how to manage is developing all the time but the key knowledge and research base is already out there – we now need to use it for the best interests of children, families and ourselves.

To end on an optimistic note, the subtitle of the Social Work Reform Board's (2010) final report was *Building a Safe and Confident Future*. That aspiration should relate both to the lives of children and families who come into contact with social workers as well as to the working lives and conditions of social workers themselves. You have a personal, as well as a shared, responsibility to ensure that social work moves forward in this safe and confident way and you can play an effective part in this mission, particularly if you are prepared to promote best practice and challenge poor practice at every turn.

We wish you well.

APPENDIX 1

From: Social Work Reform Board (2011) *Building a Safe and Confident Future: One Year On*, pp. 6–7.

2.2 The proposed capabilities are:

PROFESSIONALISM – IDENTIFY AND BEHAVE AS A PROFESSIONAL SOCIAL WORKER, COMMITTED TO PROFESSIONAL DEVELOPMENT

Social workers are members of an internationally recognised profession, a title protected in UK law. Social workers demonstrate professional commitment by taking responsibility for their conduct, practice and learning, with support through supervision. As representatives of the social work profession they safeguard its reputation and are accountable to the professional regulator.

VALUES AND ETHICS – APPLY SOCIAL WORK ETHICAL PRINCIPLES AND VALUES TO GUIDE PROFESSIONAL PRACTICE

Social workers have an obligation to conduct themselves ethically and to engage in ethical decision making, including through partnership with people who use their services. Social workers are knowledgeable about the value base of their profession, its ethical standards and relevant law.

DIVERSITY – RECOGNISE DIVERSITY AND APPLY ANTI-DISCRIMINATORY AND ANTI-OPPRESSIVE PRINCIPLES IN PRACTICE

Social workers understand that diversity characterises and shapes human experience and is critical to the formation of identity. Diversity is multi-dimensional and includes race, disability, class, economic status, age, sexuality, gender and transgender, faith and belief. Social workers appreciate that, as a consequence of difference, a person's life experience may include oppression, marginalisation and alienation as well as privilege, power and acclaim, and are able to challenge appropriately.

RIGHTS, JUSTICE AND ECONOMIC WELL-BEING – ADVANCE HUMAN RIGHTS AND PROMOTE SOCIAL JUSTICE AND ECONOMIC WELL-BEING

Social workers recognise the fundamental principles of human rights and equality, and that these are protected in national and international law, conventions and policies. They ensure these principles underpin their practice. Social workers understand the importance of using and contributing to case law and applying these rights in their own practice. They understand the effects of oppression, discrimination and poverty.

KNOWLEDGE – APPLY KNOWLEDGE OF SOCIAL SCIENCES, LAW AND SOCIAL WORK PRACTICE THEORY

Social workers understand psychological, social, cultural, spiritual and physical influences on people; human development throughout the life span and the legal framework for practice. They apply this knowledge in their work with individuals, families and communities. They know and use theories and methods of social work practice.

CRITICAL REFLECTION AND ANALYSIS – APPLY CRITICAL REFLECTION AND ANALYSIS TO INFORM AND PROVIDE A RATIONALE FOR PROFESSIONAL DECISION MAKING

Social workers are knowledgeable about and apply the principles of critical thinking and reasoned discernment. They identify, distinguish, evaluate and integrate multiple sources of knowledge and evidence. These include practice evidence, their own practice experience, service user and carer experience together with research-based, organisational, policy and legal knowledge. They use critical thinking augmented by creativity and curiosity.

INTERVENTION AND SKILLS – USE JUDGEMENT AND AUTHORITY TO INTERVENE WITH INDIVIDUALS, FAMILIES AND COMMUNITIES TO PROMOTE INDEPENDENCE, PROVIDE SUPPORT AND PREVENT HARM, NEGLECT AND ABUSE

Social workers engage with individuals, families, groups and communities, working alongside people to assess and intervene. They enable effective relationships and are effective communicators, using appropriate skills. Using their professional judgement, they employ a range of interventions: promoting independence, providing support and protection, taking preventative action and ensuring safety whilst balancing rights and risks. They understand and take account of differentials in power, and are able to use authority appropriately. They evaluate their own practice and the outcomes for those they work with.

CONTEXTS AND ORGANISATIONS – ENGAGE WITH, INFORM, AND ADAPT TO CHANGING CONTEXTS THAT SHAPE PRACTICE. OPERATE EFFECTIVELY WITHIN OWN ORGANISATIONAL FRAMEWORKS AND CONTRIBUTE TO THE DEVELOPMENT OF SERVICES AND ORGANISATIONS. OPERATE EFFECTIVELY WITHIN MULTIAGENCY AND INTER-PROFESSIONAL SETTINGS

Social workers are informed about and pro-actively responsive to the challenges and opportunities that come with changing social contexts and constructs. They fulfil this responsibility in accordance with their professional values and ethics, both as individual professionals and as members of the organisation in which they work. They collaborate, inform and are informed by their work with others, inter-professionally and with communities.

PROFESSIONAL LEADERSHIP – TAKE RESPONSIBILITY FOR THE PROFESSIONAL LEARNING AND DEVELOPMENT OF OTHERS THROUGH SUPERVISION, MENTORING, ASSESSING, RESEARCH, TEACHING, LEADERSHIP AND MANAGEMENT

The social work profession evolves through the contribution of its members in activities such as practice research, supervision, assessment of practice, teaching and management. An individual's contribution will gain influence when undertaken as part of a learning, practice-focused organisation. Learning may be facilitated with a wide range of people including social work colleagues, service users and carers, volunteers, foster carers and other professionals.

4. DRAFT STANDARDS OF PROFICIENCY FOR SOCIAL WORKERS IN ENGLAND

Standards in bold are the overarching draft generic standards of proficiency, which we consulted on during 2011. The order of the standards may be changed in the light of further consultation.
Registered social workers must:

1 **Be able to practise safely and effectively within their scope of practice**

    1.1 know the limits of their practice and when to seek advice or refer to another professional
    1.2 recognise the need to manage their own workload and resources and be able to practise accordingly
    1.3 be able to undertake risk assessments of risk, need and capacity and respond appropriately
    1.4 be able to recognise and respond appropriately to unexpected situations and manage uncertainty

2 **Be able to practise within the legal and ethical boundaries of their profession**

    2.1 understand current legislation applicable to the work of their profession
    2.2 understand the need to promote the best interests of service users at all times
    2.3 understand the need to protect and safeguard children, young people and vulnerable adults
    2.4 be able to manage potentially competing or conflicting interests
    2.5 be able to exercise authority as a social worker within the appropriate legal and ethical frameworks and boundaries
    2.6 understand the need to respect and so far as possible uphold, the rights, dignity, values and autonomy of every service user
    2.7 recognise that relationships with service users should be based on respect and openness
    2.8 understand what is required of them by the Health and Care Professions Council

3 **Be able to maintain fitness to practise**

    3.1 understand the need to maintain high standards of personal and professional conduct
    3.2 understand the importance of maintaining their own health and well-being
    3.3 understand both the need to keep skills and knowledge up-to-date and the importance of career-long learning
    3.4 be able to establish and maintain personal and professional boundaries
    3.5 be able to manage the physical and emotional impact of their practice

4 **Be able to practise as an autonomous professional, exercising their own professional judgement**

    4.1 be able to assess a situation, determine its nature and severity and call upon the required knowledge and experience to deal with it

4.2 be able to initiate resolution of issues and be able to exercise personal initiative

4.3 recognise where they are personally responsible for, and must be able to justify, their decisions

4.4 be able to make informed judgements on complex issues in the absence of complete information available

4.5 be able to make and receive referrals appropriately

5 Be aware of the impact of culture, equality and diversity on practice

5.1 be able to reflect on and take account of the impact of inequality, disadvantage and discrimination on those who use social work services and their communities

5.2 understand the need to adapt practice to respond appropriately to different groups and individuals

6 Be able to practise in a non-discriminatory manner

6.1 be able to work with others to promote social justice

6.2 be able to use practice to challenge and address the impact of discrimination and disadvantage

7 Be able to maintain confidentiality

7.1 be able to understand and explain the limits of confidentiality

7.2 be able to recognise and respond appropriately to situations where it is necessary to share information to safeguard service users or the wider public

8 Be able to communicate effectively

8.1 be able to use interpersonal skills appropriate forms of verbal and non-verbal communication with service users and others

8.2 be able to demonstrate effective and appropriate skills in communicating advice, instruction and professional opinion to colleagues and service users

8.3 understand the need to provide service users (or people acting on their behalf) with the information necessary to enable them to make informed decisions or to understand the decisions made

8.4 understand how communication skills affect the assessment of and engagement with service users and how the means of communication should be modified to address and take account of factors such as age, capacity, physical ability and learning ability

8.5 be aware of the characteristics and consequences of verbal and non-verbal communication and how this can be affected by disability, culture, age, ethnicity, gender, religious beliefs and socio-economic status

8.6 understand the need to draw upon available resources and services to support service users' communication, wherever possible

8.7 be able to communicate in English to the standard equivalent to level 7 of the international English Language Testing System, with no element below 6.5

8.8 be able to engage in inter-agency communication and communication across professional and organisational boundaries

8.9 be able to prepare and present formal reports in line with applicable protocols and guidelines

9   Be able to work appropriately with others

9.1   understand the need to build and sustain professional relationships with service users and colleagues as both an autonomous practitioner and collaboratively with others

9.2   be able to work with service users to enable them to assess and make informed decisions about their needs, circumstances, risks, preferred options and resources

9.3   be able to work with service users to promote individual growth, development and independence

9.4   be able to support the development of networks, groups and communities to meet needs and outcomes

9.5   be able to work in partnership with others, including those working in other agencies and roles

9.6   be able to contribute effectively to work undertaken as part of a multi-disciplinary team

9.7   be able to support the learning and development of others

10   Be able to maintain records appropriately

10.1   be able to keep accurate, comprehensible records in accordance with applicable legislation, protocols and guidelines

10.2   recognise the need to manage records and all other information in accordance with applicable legislation, protocols and guidelines

11   Be able to reflect on and review practice

11.1   understand the value of critical reflection on practice and the need to record the outcome of such reflection appropriately

11.2   recognise the value of supervision, case reviews and other methods of reflection and review

12   Be able to assure the quality of their practice

12.1   be able to use supervision to support and enhance the quality of their social work practice

12.2   be able to contribute to processes designed to evaluate service and individual outcomes

12.3   be able to engage in evidence-informed practice, evaluate practice systematically and participate in audit procedures

13   Understand the key concepts of the knowledge base which are relevant to their profession

13.1   recognise the roles of other professions, practitioners and organisations

13.2   be aware of the different social contexts within which social work operates

13.3   be aware of changes in demography and culture and their impact on social work

13.4   understand in relation to social work practice:

- social work theory
- social work models and interventions
- the development and application of relevant law and social policy
- the development of social work and social work values
- human growth and development across the lifespan

- the impact of injustice, social inequalities, policies and other issues which impact on the demand for social work services
- the relevance of psychological, environmental and physiological perspectives to understanding personal and social development and functioning
- concepts of empowerment
- the relevance of sociological perspectives to understanding societal and structural influences on human behaviour.

14 **Be able to draw on appropriate knowledge and skills to inform practice**

14.1 be able to gather, analyse and critically evaluate and use information and knowledge to make recommendations or modify their viewpoint

14.2 be able to select and use appropriate assessment tools

14.3 be able to prepare, implement, review, evaluate and revise plans to meet needs and circumstances

14.4 be able to use social work methods and models to achieve change and development and improve life opportunities

14.5 be aware of a range of research methodologies

14.6 recognise the value of research and analysis and be able to evaluate such evidence to inform their own practice

14.7 be able to demonstrate a level of skill in the use of information technology appropriate to their practice

14.8 be able to change their practice as needed to take account of new developments or changing contexts

15 **Be able to establish and maintain a safe practice environment**

15.1 understand the need to maintain the safety of both service users and those involved in their care

15.2 be aware of applicable health and safety legislation and any relevant safety policies and procedures in force at the workplace, such as incident reporting, and be able to act in accordance with these

15.3 be able to work safely in challenging environments including being able to take appropriate actions to manage risk

15.4 be able to address behaviour which presents a risk to or from service users, the public or themselves

Source: Health Professions Council (2011) *Standards of Proficiency for Social Workers (England) Professional Liaison Group (PLG)*. London: Health Professions Council.

APPENDIX 3 – EXAMPLE OF A GENOGRAM

Ben Harris is a young person you are working with and the following is a pictorial representation of his family tree or genogram. His grandmother, Eileen is still alive; His father, Paul and mother, Cheryl are married and Ben is their only son. Ben's uncle is John (married to Tracey who has a child, Wayne, six years old, from a previous relationship with Mick Brown). Ben also has an Aunt, Maddy, who is married to Ian Kerr, Ian being divorced from Sharon Kerr with whom he had a child, Shane.

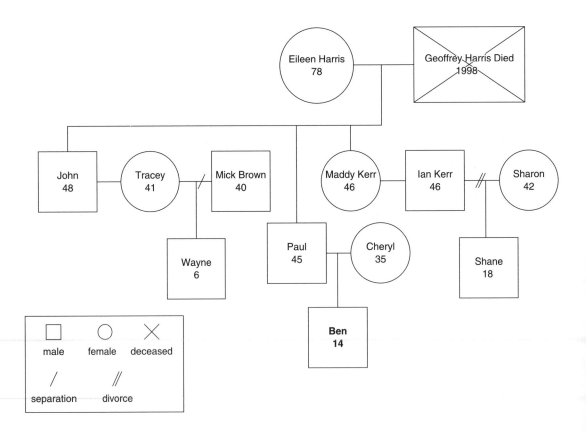

APPENDIX 4 – EXAMPLE OF AN ECO MAP FOR BEN HARRIS

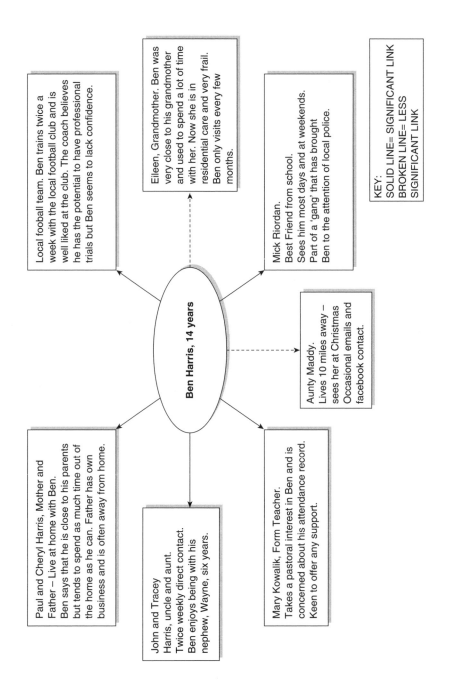

Local fooball team. Ben trains twice a week with the local football club and is well liked at the club. The coach believes he has the potential to have professional trials but Ben seems to lack confidence.

Eileen, Grandmother. Ben was very close to his grandmother and used to spend a lot of time with her. Now she is in residential care and very frail. Ben only visits every few months.

Mick Riordan. Best Friend from school. Sees him most days and at weekends. Part of a 'gang' that has brought Ben to the attention of local police.

KEY:
SOLID LINE= SIGNIFICANT LINK
BROKEN LINE= LESS SIGNIFICANT LINK

Ben Harris, 14 years

Aunty Maddy. Lives 10 miles away – sees her at Christmas Occasional emails and facebook contact.

Paul and Cheryl Harris, Mother and Father – Live at home with Ben. Ben says that he is close to his parents but tends to spend as much time out of the home as he can. Father has own business and is often away from home.

John and Tracey Harris, uncle and aunt. Twice weekly direct contact. Ben enjoys being with his nephew, Wayne, six years.

Mary Kowallik, Form Teacher. Takes a pastoral interest in Ben and is concerned about his attendance record. Keen to offer any support.

GLOSSARY

Accommodated – children received into voluntary care under section 20, Children Act 1989.

Adoption – a legal status which transfers parental responsibility to a new carer or carers. Legally the rights of an adopter are the same as those that would be held by a birth parent. A small number of adopted children will have ongoing contact with their birth parents.

Assessed and Supported Year in Employment (ASYE) – a mandatory requirement that newly qualified social workers receive structured support and supervision in their first year of employment.

Attachment theory – the theory that the first year in life in particular is a critical period when children need consistency in nurturing and parenting if they are to develop in emotionally healthy ways.

Authoritative practice – being confident, informed and appropriately assertive in the way in which social work is carried out.

Centiles – comparative measurements of a child's growth and development and weight with the normal, expected measurements in similar-age children.

Child abuse – physical abuse, sexual abuse, emotional abuse and neglect. Professional judgements need to be made about the context and seriousness of any suspected abuse.

Child and Adolescent Mental Health Services (CAMHS) – CAMHS are part of the National Health Service, specialising in the provision of help and treatment for children and young people with emotional, behavioural and mental health difficulties.

Child protection – the formal and legal systems that come into play once a child is deemed to have crossed the threshold of 'significant harm'.

Child Protection Plan – multiagency plan that concentrates on the actions needed to make the child safe. Child Protection Plans replaced the Child Protection Register, partly because the Child Protection Register was seen to have failed to protect children.

Children's centres – created as part of the *Every Child Matters* policy, these multidisciplinary centres deliver a range of services to the children and families in their localities, aimed at improving the life chances of children.

Children's Services – more properly known as Integrated Children's Services (ICS). Established by the Children Act 2004, to better ensure that key children's services such as education and social care work together effectively. There have been many bureaucratic difficulties in this way of working.

Children's Social Care – a wide range of services that embraces children's centres, foster care, residential care and social work with children and families.

Chronology – a systematic list of the developmental and social milestones and events in a child or adult's life.

College of Social Work – a government-sponsored college that is not a physical college but an association formed of professionals and service users to represent social work interests, excellence and endeavours.

Community psychiatric nurse (CPN) – a trained nurse who specialises in psychiatric disorders and works in the community alongside professionals such as social workers.

Continuous professional development (CPD) – the opportunities for social workers to take up or participate in a life-long learning culture to constantly update skills and interests.

Discrimination – any action that is unfair or illegal because it is based on a person's characteristics or background, such as their race, religion, culture, gender, sexuality, age or disability.

Domestic violence – verbal, physical or sexual actions that are forced on partners. Witnessing domestic violence is now recognised as being extremely detrimental to children's health and development.

Draft Standards of Proficiency for Social Workers in England – draft standards drawn up by the Health Professions Council (HPC) concerned with registration and regulatory powers of conduct and behaviour.

Ecomap – a wider visual representation of a child or adult's family, friends and wider support systems.

Emotional intelligence – your ability to know yourself and to be sensitive to the likely feelings of other people across a variety of situations.

Ethics – agreed sets of values or moral judgements.

Every Child Matters – a social policy initiative announced in 2003 that sought to bring about better interdisciplinary working by encouraging agencies to concentrate on five outcomes for all – being healthy, safe, enjoying and achieving, making a positive contribution and being economically active.

Evidence-based practice – practice that is guided by the findings of established research.

Flexible and family friendly working – systems of work within organisations that enable workers to balance family responsibilities with the demands of the workplace.

Fostering – voluntary or compulsory arrangements that lead to children being cared for, over short or longer periods by foster carers. Most foster children have ongoing contact with their birth families, who retain parental responsibility.

Framework for the Assessment of Children and their Families (Assessment Framework/Triangle) – an ecological approach to children that takes account of parenting capacity, wider support systems and the economic environment, and the child's own development.

Gastronomy feeding tube – a tube placed directly into the stomach to enable the administration of fluids, food and medication.

Genogram – a visual representation of a child or adult's family tree, using standardised shapes and symbols.

Guardian ad litem – Court-appointed professional with a social work background, whose role it is to represent the best interests of a child in legal proceedings.

Hot desking – the practice of sharing desk and office space on a 'first come, first served basis'.

In care – catch-all phrase to describe the status of children who are looked after either voluntarily under section 20, Children Act 1989, or as a result of a legal Care Order.

In-house – a service that is already part of an organisation.

Independent sector – non-statutory services that are either in the private or voluntary sector.

Integrated Children's Services (ICS) – established by the Children Act 2004, to better ensure that key children's services such as education and social care work together effectively. There have been many bureaucratic difficulties in this way of working.

Interdisciplinary working – very similar to multidisciplinary/multiagency working. 'Multi' tends to suggest a more compartmentalised approach whereas 'inter' suggests a more reciprocal way of working.

Kinetic – movement that is volatile, heated, ever-changing.

Legislation – sets of laws and regulations that cover all aspects of children's welfare.

Life (story) book – the joint process by which a child and social worker/or foster carers compile pictures, artefacts and memories, so that the child has some understanding of their background and history.

Local authorities – elected bodies such as county, city or borough councils with a wide range of duties and powers; these bodies are responsible for the commissioning or delivery of a range of public services from refuse collection to social work.

Local Safeguarding Children Board (LSCB) – a multidisciplinary body set up by the Children Act 2004 in order to promote and oversee the safeguarding systems within a specified locality.

Looked after – children who are 'looked after' by the local authority, or in care. The phrase 'looked after' reflects the philosophy that children in such situations often return to their parents.

Management – the layer of staff within organisations that is accountable for the overall performance of teams and budgets.

Managerialism – top-down processes and procedures that can stifle the opportunities of frontline staff to be innovative and creative.

Matching – the process by which the needs of a child are matched with the caring capabilities of a foster or adoptive carer.

Mobile and Flexible working – ways of working that rely on telecommunications and IT, much of this work taking place in employees' own homes.

Mores – Mores are the values and norms which make up the accepted moral codes accepted within a society.

Multidisciplinary/Multiagency working – when different professional disciplines/agencies, for example, police, health and children's social care all make contributions to planned interventions in the lives of children and families.

Munro Report – the product of a review board (2011) led by Professor Eileen Munro, which made recommendations about the future safeguarding of children in the UK.

Nature/nurture debate – the debate concerning whether children's outcomes are primarily shaped by their genetics or the environments in which they grow up.

Newly qualified social worker (NQSW) – social workers who have qualified as a result of passing a BA or MA in social work and who have gone on to achieve registration. NQSWs are expected to have a protected case load and additional levels of support and supervision in their first year of employment.

Oppression – the degrading or patronising treatment of an individual or group brought about by others' discrimination.

Outcomes – the effects that any intervention has on the life experiences of children, particularly in terms of their being healthy and safe.

Parallel planning – sometimes known as 'twin tracking', this refers to a system whereby parents, carers and extended family are being assessed for their ability to care for a child while at the same time a care plan is being developed that might lead to an outcome such as adoption.

Paramountcy principle – a key principle of the Children Act 1989 that places the welfare of the child above all other considerations.

Performance indicator – a measurement of a target or standard that is carried out in a quantitative rather than a qualitative manner.

Personalisation – a system of social care that gives more power to individuals in helping them shape the nature of the services they receive.

Peter Connelly – Peter Connelly was on the Child Protection Register when he was killed by his carers in 2007. The subsequent public outcry condemned social workers and other professionals, particularly as the mistakes that had been made in the Victoria Climbié tragedy had reoccurred in the same London borough of Haringey.

Political correctness – language, policies and behaviours that can lead to a failure to challenge appropriately within children's social care for fear of saying the 'wrong' thing in terms of gender, sexual orientation, race, culture and religion.

Post-registration teaching and learning (PRTL) – a requirement that a certain number of training and development days are undertaken by social workers to remain able to practise as a registered social worker.

Practice wisdom – wisdom amassed through working with people over years of practice, wherein knowledge and experience of localities are combined with traditional knowledge of research, legislation and procedures.

Proposed Professional Capabilities Framework for Social Workers in England – the Social Work Reform Board's framework against which social worker capabilities should be gauged throughout career development.

Reflective practice – reflecting on your professional activities and using this reflection to continually improve your personal and professional effectiveness.

Relationship-based practice – a belief that effective social work can only take place if it is based on a mutual relationship of trust and respect.

Residential care – largely consisting of small, specialist children's homes in the statutory and independent sector that care for children who are not suited to foster care by reason of their special needs.

Resilience – the ability of children and adults to access coping mechanisms within self or wider family and friends that enable them to keep healthy and safe, even when faced with very challenging circumstances.

Resistant families – families who may be overly compliant or aggressive/avoidant of intervention.

Respectful uncertainty – not taking at face value any explanations that may be offered by a child or family member without checking out the likelihood of its truth.

Safeguarding – a preventative approach to keeping children safe in all aspects of their everyday life that covers a wide spectrum from healthy eating campaigns, safe play areas and telephone helplines to formal child protection procedures.

Serious case reviews – independently chaired multidisciplinary panels that review cases when children have died or been seriously harmed as a result of failures in safeguarding. Their purpose is to learn lessons, rather than apportion blame.

Significant harm – any form of harm that would seriously impair a child's ability to achieve the developmental progress expected of a child of similar age.

Social Care Institute for Excellence (SCIE) – government-backed institute created as a forerunner to the College of Social Work that was charged with promoting best practice across the social care sector.

Social services – predecessor of children's social care, social services delivered both children and adult services. After a series of failures in both children and adult services, social services became rebadged as separate 'children's social care' and 'adult social care' following the institution of the Children Act 2004. 'Social services' is still the term used by lay people, sometimes shortened to 'the social'.

Social Work Reform Board – the body formed in 2011 to deliver the recommendations of the social work taskforce.

Social Work Task Force – government backed interdisciplinary review group that reported in 2009 on the state of generic social work in England.

Specialist services – services that are particularly focused on children with high levels of need or children in need of protection.

Statutory social work – derived from the word 'state', this term usually applies to social work carried out within local authorities. Organisations such as independent sector foster agencies also have to conform to statutory requirements in order to operate legally.

Strengths-based – practice that looks for the strengths in children and families on which to base interventions and plans.

Supervision – regular and structured opportunities for a supervisor to offer protected time to social workers so that their professional and personal development needs are addressed alongside issues of workload.

Sure Start centres – Children's centres with targeted funding.

Synapse – a junction in the body which passes nerve impulses between cells.

Systems theory – a theory that effective social work can only take place when the systems surrounding individuals and their problems are addressed.

Targeted services – services that focus on particular groups who have specific needs. Children's centres, for example, might run services for parents who needed help with their childcare and budgeting skills.

Team around the child (TAC) – A TAC is a multidisciplinary team of practitioners established on a case-by-case basis to support a child, young person or family.

Technicist ways of working – ways of working that give priority to forms, targets, protocols and procedures, for example, a 'tick-box' approach.

Thresholds of eligibility – advisory guidelines regarding the levels at which universal services, targeted services and specialist services such as social work should become involved with children and families.

Toxic trio – the combined presence of mental illness, substance abuse and domestic violence in families. This combination is 'toxic' to the health and development of children.

Trans-disciplinary working – ways of working that involve teams consisting of members with different professional backgrounds.

Transition – a significant period of change.

Universal services – services such as schooling and health care that are available to all children in the UK.

Use of self – Your insight into who you are; how you present and how your skills, experience and values can be used to best effect with children and families.

Values – sets of beliefs about the world.

Victoria Climbié – An eight-year-old African child who was killed at the hands of her carers in 2000. The harrowing details of this case caused a public outcry.

Whistleblowing – when an employee speaks out about illegal or unethical activities within an organisation. Legal safeguards exist to protect the person who is the whistleblower.

Work–life balance – the concept that social workers need to balance the stresses and strains of their job with areas of fulfilment in their home or social life.

REFERENCES

Adoption Act 1976. London: HMSO.

Adoption and Children Act 2002. London: HMSO.

Asthana, A. (2008) 'Social workers buckling under stress burden', *The Observer*, 15 June, (www.guardian.co.uk/society/2008/jun/15/socialcare, accessed 2 January 2011).

Atkinson, M., Jones, M. and Lamont, E. (2007) 'Multi-agency working and its implications for practice: a review of the literature' (www.nfer.ac.uk/nfer/publications/MAD01/MAD01.pdf, accessed 9 January 2011).

Banks, S. (2006) *Ethics and Values in Social Work*, 3rd edn. Basingstoke: Palgrave Macmillan.

Barlow, J. and Scott, J. (2010) *Safeguarding in the 21st Century – Where to Now.* Dartington: Research in Practice.

Barnardo's (2010) *Justice Select Committee Inquiry into the Working of the Family Courts* (www.barnardos.org.uk, accessed 10 February 2011).

Barter, C. (2003) *Abuse of Children in Residential Care.* London: NSPCC (www.nspcc.org.uk/Inform/research/Briefings/abuseofchildreninrestidentialcare, accessed 1 February 2010).

Beckett, C. (2007) *Essential Theory for Social Work Practice.* London: Sage.

Beckett, C., McKeigue, B. and Taylor, H. (2007) 'Coming to conclusions: social workers' perceptions of the decision-making process in care proceedings', *Child and Family Social Work*, 12: 54–63.

Belbin, R.M. (2010) *Team Roles at Work.* Oxford: Elsevier.

Bentovim, A., Cox, A., Bingley Miller, L. and Pizzey, S. (2009) *Safeguarding Children Living with Trauma and Family Violence: Evidence-based Assessment, Analysis and Planning Interventions.* London: Jessica Kingsley Publishers.

Beresford, P. (2007) 'The role of service user research in generating knowledge-based health and social care: from conflict to contribution', *Evidence and Policy*, 3 (3): 329–41.

Birmingham Safeguarding Children Board (2006) *Serious Case Review Under Chapter VIII 'Working Together to Safeguard Children' In respect of the death of Case Reference*: BSCB/2005-6/1 (www.lscbbirmingham.org.uk/images/stories/downloads/executive-summaries/BSCB+2005-6+1+SCR.pdf, accessed 02 September 2011).

Birmingham Safeguarding Children Board (2007) *Serious Case Review Under Chapter VIII 'Working Together to Safeguard Children In respect of the death of Case Reference*: BSCB/2006-7/1 (www.lscbbirmingham.org.uk/images/stories/downloads/executive-summaries/BSCB+2006-7+1+SCR.pdf, accessed 02 September 2011).

Birmingham Safeguarding Children Board (2009) *Serious Case Review Under Chapter VIII 'Working Together to Safeguard Children', In respect of the death of Case Reference*: BSCB/2007-8/3 (www.lscbbirmingham.org.uk/images/stories/downloads/executive-summaries/BSCB+2007-8+3+SCR.pdf).

Birmingham Safeguarding Children Board (2010) *Serious Case Review Under Chapter VIII 'Working Together to Safeguard Children' In respect of the Death of a Child Reference* BSCB/2008-9/2 (www.lscbbirmingham.org.uk/images/stories/downloads/executive-summaries/BSCB+2008-9+2+SCR.pdf, accessed 12 September 2011).

Blackburn with Darwen Local Safeguarding Children Board (2010) *Serious Case Review Executive Summary In Respect of Baby Z.* Blackburn with Darwen Local Safeguarding Children Board (www.lscb.org.uk/assets/files/Baby%20Z.pdf, accessed 11 February 2011).

Bowlby, J. (1980) *Attachment and Loss, Volume III: Loss, Sadness and Depression.* London: Hogarth Press.

Brammer, A. (2010) *Social Work Law,* 3rd edn. Harlow: Pearson Education Limited.

Brandon, M., Schofield, G. and Trinder, L. (with Stone, N.) (1998) *Social Work with Children.* Basingstoke: Macmillan.

British Association of Social Work (BASW) (2011) (www.basw.co.uk/about/code-of-ethics/, accessed 2 January 2011).

Butler, I. and Williamson, H. (1994*) Children Speak: Children, Trauma and Social Work.* London: Longman/NSPCC.

Butler-Sloss, Rt. Hon. (1988) *Report of the Inquiry into Child Abuse in Cleveland (1987).* Rt. Hon. Lord Justice Butler-Sloss. London: HMSO.

CAFCASS (2011) (www.cafcass.gov.uk, accessed 14 May 2011).

Cairns, K. (2002) *Attachment, Trauma and Resilience: Therapeutic Caring for Children.* London: BAAF.

Cameron, C., Bennert, K., Simon, A. and Wigfall, V. (2007) *Using Health, Education, Housing and Other Services: A Study of Care Leavers and Young People in Difficulty.* Thomas Coram Research Unit, Institute of Education, University of London.

Children Act 1989. London: HMSO.

Children Act 2004. London: The Stationery Office.

Children and Young Persons Act 2008. London: The Stationery Office.

Cleaver, H., Unell, I. and Aldgate, J. (1999) *Children's Needs – Parenting Capacity: The Impact of Parental Mental Illness, Problem Alcohol and Drug Use and Domestic Violence on Children's Development.* London: The Stationery Office.

Cocker, C. and Allain, L. (2008) *Social Work with Looked After Children.* Exeter: Learning Matters.

Collins, S. (2008) 'Statutory social workers: stress, job satisfaction, coping, social support and individual differences', *British Journal of Social Work*, 38 (6): 1173–93.

Coleman, N. and Harris, J. (2008) 'Calling social work', *British Journal of Social Work*, 38 (3): 580–99.

Cottrell, S. (2005) *Critical Thinking Skills: Developing Effective Analysis and Argument.* Basingstoke: Palgrave Macmillan.

Coulshed, V. and Orme, J. (2006) *Social Work Practice*, 4th edn. Basingstoke: Palgrave Macmillan.

Coulshed, V., Mullender, A., Jones, D.N. and Thompson, N. (2006) *Management in Social Work,* 3rd edn. Basingstoke: Palgrave Macmillan.

Crawford, K. and Walker, J. (2003) *Social Work and Human Development.* Exeter: Learning Matters Ltd.

Cree, V. and Myers, S. (2008) *Social Work. Making a Difference.* Bristol: The Policy Press.

Crime and Disorder Act 1998. London: HMSO.

Cross, S., Hubbard, A. and Munro, E. (2010) *Reclaiming Social Work. London Borough of Hackney Children and Young People's Services.* London: London School of Economics/ Human Reliability Associates.

Cummings, E.M. and Davies, P.T. (2010) *Marital Conflict and Children, an Emotional Security Perspective.* New York: The Guildford Press.

Curtis, L., Moriarty, J. and Netten, A. (2010) 'The expected working life of a social worker', *British Journal of Social Work*, 40 (5): 1628–43.

Data Protection Act 1998. London: The Stationery Office.

Davies, D. (2011) *Child Development: A Practitioners Guide (Social Work Practice with Children and Families).* New York: The Guildford Press.

Davis, L. (2009) *The Social Worker's Guide to Children and Families Law*. London: Jessica Kingsley Publishers.

de Boer, C. and Coady, N. (2007) 'Good helping relationships in child welfare: learning from stories of success', *Child and Family Social Work*, 12: 32–42.

Department for Children, Schools and Families (2008a) *Integrated Children's System – Enhancing Social Work and Inter-Agency Practice*. London: The Stationery Office.

Department for Children, Schools and Families (2008b) *Information Sharing: Guidance for Practitioners and Managers*. London: The Stationery Office.

Department for Children, Schools and Families (2009) *The Protection of Children in England: A Progress Report*. London: The Stationery Office.

Department for Children, Schools and Families (2010) *Working Together to Safeguard Children, A Guide to Interagency Working to Safeguard and Promote the Welfare of Children*. London: The Stationery Office.

Department for Education (2009) *Early Identification, Assessment of Needs and Intervention – The Common Assessment Framework for Children and Young People: A Guide for Practitioners*. Leeds: Children's Workforce Development Council (https://www.education.gov.uk/publications/eOrderingDownload/CAF-Practitioner-Guide.pdf, accessed 15 May 2010).

Department for Education (2010) *Haringey Local Safeguarding Board, Serious Case Review, Child 'A' March 2009*. London: The Stationery Office (http://media.education.gov.uk/assets/files/pdf/s/second%20serious%20case%20overview%20report%20relating%20to%20peter%20connelly%20dated%20march%202009.pdf, accessed 13 February 2011).

Department for Education (2011a) *Adoption Guidance, Adoption and Children Act 2002, First Revision: February 2011*. London: The Stationery Office.

Department for Education (2011b) *The Munro Review of Child Protection. Final Report. A Child Centred System*. London: The Stationery Office (www.education.gov.uk/munroreview/downloads/8875_DfE_Munro_Report_TAGGED.pdf, accessed 12 July 2011).

Department for Education (2011c) *Independent Review into Child Protection Says: Free Professionals from Central Government Control to Let Them Do Their Jobs Properly* (www.education.gov.uk, accessed 30 August 2011).

Department for Education and Skills (2003) *Every Child Matters*. CM 5860. London: HMSO.

Department for Education and Skills (2004) *Common Assessment Framework*. London: HMSO.

Department for Education and Skills (2006) *Information Sharing: Practitioners' Guide: Integrated Working to Improve Outcomes for Children and Young People* (www.londonscb.gov.uk/files/library/caf_practitioners_guide.pdf).

Department of Health (1997) *The New NHS: Modern, Dependable*. CM 3807. London: HMSO.

Department of Health (1998) *Someone Else's Children*. London: HMSO.

Department of Health (2000a) *Assessing Children in Need and their Families: Practice Guidance*. London: The Stationery Office.

Department of Health (2000b) *Framework for the Assessment of Children in Need and their Families*. London: The Stationery Office (www.dh.gov.uk/en/Publications andstatistics/Publications/PublicationsPolicyAndGuidance/DH_4003256, accessed 10 January 2011).

Doel, M. (2006) *Using Groupwork (The Social Work Skills Series)*. London: Routledge Taylor & Francis Group.

Dominelli, L. (2004) *Social Work, Theory and Practice for a Changing Profession*. Cambridge: Polity Press.

Donnelly, L. (2009) 'The children failed by social services', *The Telegraph*, 10 January 2009.

Doran, G.T. (1981) 'There's a S.M.A.R.T way to write management's goals and objectives', *Management Review*, 70 (11) (AMA Forum): 35–6.

Easton, C., Gee, G., Durbin, B. and Teeman, D. (2011) *Early Intervention, Using the CAF Process, and its Cost Effectiveness Findings from LARC3*. Slough: NFER.

Evans, T. (2010) *Professional Discretion in Welfare Services. Beyond Street Level Bureaucracy*. Farnham: Ashgate.

Evans, T. and Harris, J. (2004) 'Street-level bureaucracy, social work and the (exaggerated) death of discretion', *British Journal of Social Work*, 34 (6): 871–95.

Fahlberg, V. (2008) *A Child's Journey Through Placement*, UK edn. London: British Association for Adoption and Fostering.

Foley, P., Roche, J. and Tucker, S. (2001) *Children in Society: Contemporary Theory, Policy and Practice*. Basingstoke: Palgrave.

Fonagy, P., Steele, M., Steele, H., Higgitt, A. and Target, M. (1994) 'The Emmanuel Miller memorial lecture 1992. The theory and practice of resilience', *Journal of Child Psychology and Psychiatry and Allied Disciplines*, 35: 231–57.

Fostering Network (2010) *Recruiting the Foster Care Workforce of the Future: A Guide for Fostering Services*. London: Fostering Network.

Gardner, A. (2011) *Personalisation in Social Work*. Exeter: Learning Matters Ltd.

General Social Care Council (GSCC) (2002) *Codes of Practice for Social Care Workers*. London: GSCC.

Gillick, A.P. (Respondent) v. West Norfolk and Wisbech Area Health Authority and the Department of Health and Social Security (Appellants) (1985), United Kingdom House of Lords.

Gilligan, P. and Manby, M. (2008) 'The Common Assessment Framework: does the reality match the rhetoric?' *Child and Family Social Work*, 13 (2): 177–87.

Golding, K. (2007) *Nurturing Attachment: Supporting Children Who are Fostered or Adopted*. London: Jessica Kingsley Publishers.

Goleman, D. (1995) *Emotional Intelligence: Why it Can Matter More Than IQ*. New York: Bantam.

Green, R. and Willis, S. (2011) *Protecting Children from the Hidden Harm of Drug and Alcohol Misuse*. Safeguarding Children Conference, 2011, Richmond upon Thames, Local Safeguarding Children Board.

Habermas, J. (2004) *The Theory of Communicative Action. Reason and the Rationalization of Society*. Cambridge: Polity Press.

Haringey Local Safeguarding Children Board (2009) *Serious Case Review. Baby Peter*. London: Haringey Local Safeguarding Children Board (www.haringeylscb.org/executive_summary_peter_final.pdf, accessed 20 May 2010).

Harris, J. and Unwin, P. (2009) 'Performance management', in J. Harris and V. White (eds). *Modernising Social Work: Critical Considerations*. Bristol: Policy Press.

Harris, J. and White, V. (2009) *Modernising Social Work: Critical Considerations*. Bristol: Policy Press.

Harwin, J., Ryan, M., and Tunnard, J. with Pokhrel, S., Alrouh, B., Matias, C. and Momenian-Schneider, S. (2011) *The Family Drug and Alcohol Court (FDAC) Evaluation Project Final Report*. London: Brunel University.

Health Professions Council (2011) *Standards of Proficiency for Social Workers (England) Professional Liaison Group (PLG)*. London: Health Professions Council.

Healy, K. (2005) *Social Work Theories in Context: Creating Frameworks for Practice*. Basingstoke: Palgrave Macmillan.

Healy, K. and Mulholland, J. (2008) *Writing Skills for Social Workers*. London: Sage.

Herefordshire Safeguarding Children Board (2009a) *Serious Case Review Relating To Baby HA*. Hereford Safeguarding Children Board (www.herefordshire.gov.uk/hscb/docs/executive_summary_scr_ha_.pdf, accessed 11 January 2011).

Herefordshire Safeguarding Children Board (2009b) *Serious Case Review Relating to HB a Child Who Died Age 7 Years*. Herefordshire Safeguarding Children Board (www.herefordshire.gov.uk/hscb/docs/hb_-_executive_summary.pdf, accessed 15 January 2011).

Herefordshire Safeguarding Children Board (2010) *The Executive Summary of the Overview Report in to the Serious Case Review of the Circumstances Concerning Child HC*. Hereford Safeguarding Children Board (www.herefordshire.gov.uk/hscb/docs/Executive_Summary_HC_Final%281%29.pdf, accessed 12 January 2011).

Hester, M. and Radford, L. (2006) *Mothering Through Domestic Violence*. London: Jessica Kingsley Publishers.

Higgins, M. and Swain, J. (2009) *Disability and Child Sexual Abuse: Lessons from Survivors Narratives for Effective Protection, Prevention and Treatment*. London: Jessica Kingsley Publishers.

Holmes, L., McDermid, S., Jones, A. and Ward, S. (2009) *An Analysis of the Key Issues that Impact on Practice Pre- and Post Implementation of the Integrated Children's System*. London: Department for Children, Schools and Families.

Hollis, F. (1964) *Casework: A Psychosocial Therapy*. New York: Random House.

Horwath, J. (ed.) (2010) *The Child's World: Assessing Children in Need*. London: Jessica Kingsley Publishers.

House of Commons (2009) *Memorandum Submitted by the Children's Society*. London: TSO.

Howe, D. (2009) *A Brief Introduction to Social Work Theory*. Basingstoke: Palgrave Macmillan.

Howe, D., Brandon, M., Hinings, D. and Schofield, G. (1999) *Attachment Theory, Child Maltreatment and Family Support: A Practice and Assessment Model*. Basingstoke: Macmillan.

Human Rights Act 1998. London: The Stationery Office.

Humphreys, C. and Stanley, M. (2006) *Domestic Violence and Child Protection, Directions for Good Practice*. London: Jessica Kingsley Publishers.

Hunter, M. (2009) *Poor Supervision Continues to Hinder Child Protection Practice* (www.communitycare.co.uk/Articles/2009/04/22/111327/Poor-supervision-continues-to-hinder-child-protection.htm).

Ince, D. and Griffiths, A. (2011) 'A chronicling system for children's social work: learning from the ICS failure', *British Journal of Social Work* (http://bjsw.oxfordjournals.org, accessed 12 June 2011).

Iwaniec, D. (2006) *The Emotionally Abused and Neglected Child Identification, Assessment and Intervention, A Practice Handbook*, 2nd edn. Chichester: John Wiley and Sons.

Jackson, G. and Unwin, P. (2010) 'Sons and daughters of foster carers: invisible, vulnerable or valued?', in L. O'Dell and S. Leverett (2010) *Working with Children and Young People. Co-constructing Practice*. Basingstoke: Palgrave Macmillan.

Jones, C. (2001) 'Voices from the front line: state social workers and new labour', *British Journal of Social Work*, 31 (4): 550–1.

Jones, J. and Gallop, L. (2003) 'No time to think: protecting the reflective space in children's services', *Child Abuse Review*, 12: 101–6.

Jones, R. (2006) 'Social work must brace itself', *Community Care*, 18 (24): 32–3.

Jordan, B. (2004) 'Emancipatory social work: opportunity or oxymoron?', *British Journal of Social Work*, 34 (1): 5–19.

Klaus, M.H., Kennell, J.H. and Klaus, P. (1996) *Bonding: Building the Foundations of Secure Attachment and Independence*. New York: Perseus Books.

Koprowska, J. (2010) *Communication and Interpersonal Skills in Social Work*. Exeter: Learning Matters.

Laming, H. (2003) *The Victoria Climbié Inquiry Report*. CM 5730. London: The Stationery Office (www.victoria-climbie-inquiry.org.uk, accessed 20 October 2010).

Laming, H. (2009) *The Protection of Children in England: A Progress Report*. London: The Stationery Office.

Lawler, J. and Bilson, A. (2010) *Social Work Management and Leadership*. Abingdon: Routledge.

Lombard, D. (2011) *What Makes a Professional?* (www.communitycare.co.uk/Articles/2011/02/02/116192/what-makes-a-professional.htm, accessed 15 May 2010).

McGregor, K. (2009) *Social Workers Stretched and Overburdened (*www.community care.co.uk/Articles/2009/10/21/112926/social-workers-stretched-and-overburdened.htm, accessed 12 June 2010).

McLeod, A. (2010) 'A friend and an equal': do young people in care seek the impossible from their social workers?', *British Journal of Social Work*, 40 (3): 772–88.

McNabb, M. (2010) *Social Worker Caseload Pressure is Unsustainable* (www.communitycare.co.uk/blogs/community-care-editorial-comment/2010/09/social-worker-caseload-pressure-is-unsustainable.html, accessed 3 September 2010).

Merthyr Tydfil Local Safeguarding Children Board (2010) *Serious Case Review Executive Summary Child 'A'* (www.merthyr.gov.uk/NR/rdonlyres/DD0FFB06-B3FD-482D-98E3-38779C5C29E1/0/ExecutiveSummaryPublished140710PDF.pdf, accessed 22 June 2011).

Mid Staffordshire NHS Foundation Trust Inquiry (2010) *Independent Inquiry into Care Provided by Mid Staffordshire NHS Foundation Trust January 2005 – March 2009, Volume I*. London: The Stationery Office.

Ministry of Justice (2011) *Achieving Best Evidence in Criminal Proceedings Guidance on Interviewing Victims and Witnesses, and Guidance on Using Special Measures*. CPS, Department of Education and Department of Health.

Morris, N. (2009) '"Shocking" sickness rates in social work', *The Independent*, 16 September 2009 (www.independent.co.uk/news/uk/home-news/shocking-sickness-rates-in-social-work-1787970.html, accessed 12 February 2011).

Mullender, A., Kelly, L., Hague, G., Malos, E. and Iman, U. (2002) *Children's Perspectives on Domestic Violence*. London: Routledge.

Munro, E. (2009) *Guide to Analytic and Intuitive Reasoning*. Community Care Inform (www.ccinform.co.uk/Articles/2009/08/20/3390/Guide+to+analytic+and+intuitive+reasoning.html, accessed 15 June 2011).

National Children's Bureau (2006) *Communicating with Children: A Two-Way Process Resource Pack*. London: The National Children's Bureau.

Neate, P. and Philpot, T. (1997) *The Media and The Message – A Guide to Using the Media for Everyone in Social Care (Community* Care). Sutton: Reed Business Information.

Netten, A. and Knight, J. (1999) 'Annuitizing the human capital investment cost of health service professionals', *Health Economics*, 8 (3): 245–55.

North Tyneside Local Safeguarding Children Board (2010) *Serious Case Review RE: Child F*. North Tyneside Local Safeguarding Children Board.

O'Dell, L. and Leverett, S. (2010) *Working with Children and Young People. Co-constructing Practice*. Basingstoke: Palgrave Macmillan.

Oliver, C. and Mooney, A. with Statham, J., Thomas Coram Research Unit, Institute of Education, University of London. (2010) *Integrated Working: A Review of the Evidence*. Children's Workforce Development Council.

Parsloe, P. (1999) *Risk Assessment in Social Care and Social Work*. London: Jessica Kingsley Publishers.

Payne, M. (2005) *Modern Social Work Theory*, 3rd edn. Basingstoke: Palgrave Macmillan.

Perry, B.D., Pollard, R.A., Blakley, T.L., Baker, W.L. and Vigilante, D. (1995) 'Childhood trauma, the neurobiology of adaption, and "use-dependent" development of the brain: how "states" become "traits"', *Infant Mental Health Journal*, 16 (4): 271–91.

Pile, H. (2009) *Social Work Sickness Rates – UNISON Response* (www.unison.org.uk/asp-presspack/pressrelease_view.asp?id=1574, accessed 2 January 2010).

Public Law Outline (2008) *Guide to Case Management in Public Law Proceedings*. Judiciary of England and Wales, Ministry of Justice.

Ruch, G. (2010) *Relationship-Based Practice: Getting to the Heart of Practice*. London: Jessica Kingsley Publishers.

Saleebey, D. (1996) '"The strengths perspective" in social work practice: extensions and cautions', *Social Work*, 41: 296–305.

Schön, D.A. (1991) *The Reflective Practitioner*. Aldershot: Arena.

Sheridan, M.D., Sharma, A. and Cockerill, H. (2007) *From Birth to Five Years, Children's Developmental Progress*. London: Routledge Taylor and Francis Group.

Silverman, J. and Bancroft, L. (2002) *The Batterer as Parent: Addressing the Impact of Domestic Violence on Family Dynamics*. London: Sage.

Smith, R. (2010) *High Caseloads: Stress Takes Toll on Social Workers' Health* (www.communitycare.co.uk/Articles/2010/09/08/115260/high-caseloads-stress-takes-toll-on-social-workers-health.htm, accessed 8 February 2011).

Social Work Reform Board (2010) *Building a Safe and Confident Future: One Year On. Progress Report from the Social Work Reform Board. December 2010*. Crown Copyright (www.education.gov.uk/swrb).

Social Work Task Force (2009) *Facing Up to the Task. The Interim Report of the Social Work Task Force July 2009*. Crown Copyright (https://www.education.gov.uk/publications/standard/publicationdetail/page1/DCSF-00752-2009).

Social Work Task Force (2010) *Social Workers' Workload Survey. Messages from the Frontline. Findings from the 2009 Survey and Interviews with Senior Managers*. Crown Copyright.

Social Worker Retention Project (2011) (www.westmidlandsiep.gov.uk/download.php?did=1960, accessed 8 August 2011).

Stanley, N., Manthorpe, J. and White, M. (2007) 'Depression in the profession: social workers' experiences and perceptions', *British Journal of Social Work*, 37 (3): 281–98.

Torbay Safeguarding Children Board (2009) *Serious Case Review C18*. Torbay Safeguarding Children Board (www.torbay.gov.uk/c18-execsumm.pdf, accessed 28 January 2011).

Trevithick, P. (2000) *Social Work Skills. A Practice Handbook*. Buckingham: Open University Press.

Tuckman, B.W. (1965) 'Developmental sequence in small groups', *Psychological Bulletin*, 63: 384–99. The article was reprinted in *Group Facilitation: A Research and Applications Journal* – Number 3, Spring 2001, and is available as a Word document (http://dennis-learningcenter.osu.edu/references/GROUP%20DEV%20ARTICLE.doc).

Turnell, A. and Edwards, S. (1999) *Signs of Safety. A Solution Oriented Approach to Child Protection Casework*. London: W.W. Norton.

Turney, D (2009) *Analysis and Critical Thinking in Assessment: Change Project Literature Review*. Dartington: Research in Practice.

UNISON (2008) *Memorandum to Lord Laming: Progress Report on Safeguarding Submitted to the Baby P Inquiry* (www.unison.org.uk/, accessed 7 December 2010).

United Nations General Assembly (1989) *UN Convention on the Rights of the Child*. New York: United Nations.

Unwin, P. (2009) 'Modernisation and the role of agency social work' in J. Harris and V. White (eds), *Modernising Social Work – Critical Considerations*. Bristol: Policy Press.

Unwin, P. (2011a) *The Kinetic Pie of Social Work, NQSWs: Learning Development and Assessment*. Paper presented at Skills for Care/University of Worcester Workshop, YCMA, Worcester, 16 February. University of Worcester.

Unwin, P. (2011b) *A Slice of the Kinetic Pie, NQSWs: Learning Development and Assessment*. Paper presented at Skills for Care/University of Worcester Workshop, YCMA, Worcester, 16 February. University of Worcester.

Vygotsky, L.S. (1978) *Mind in Society. The Development of Higher Psychological Processes*. Cambridge, MA: Harvard University Press.

Wilson, K., Ruch, G., Lymbery, M. and Cooper, A. with Becker, S., Brammer, A., Clawson, R., Littlechild, B., Paylor, I. and Smith, R. (2008) *Social Work: An Introduction to Contemporary Practice*. Harlow: Pearson Education.

Wonnacott, J. (2011) *How to Deliver Effective Supervision* (www.communitycare.co.uk/Articles/2011/02/14/116283/how-to-deliver-effective-supervision.htm, accessed 29 June 2011).

Worcestershire Safeguarding Children's Board and Worcestershire Children's Trust Board (2011) *Thresholds Guidance for Practitioners: Responding to the Needs of Children and Young People in Worcestershire* (https://www.edulink.networcs.net/, accessed 7 July 2011).

INDEX